THE GREAT NIXON TURN- AROUND

THE GREAT NIXON

N TURN-
AROUND

**America's New Foreign Policy in the Post-Liberal Era
(How a Cold Warrior Climbed Clean Out of His Skin)**

Essays and articles, with an introductory statement
by Lloyd C. Gardner, Rutgers University

NEW VIEWPOINTS | A DIVISION OF FRANKLIN WATTS, INC.
NEW YORK 1973

Library of Congress Cataloging in Publication Data

Gardner, Lloyd C   1934–   comp.
The great Nixon turnaround.

CONTENTS: The Cold Warrior transformed: Address by
Richard M. Nixon to the Commonwealth Club of California,
April 2, 1965. Nixon, R. M.   Khrushchev's hidden weak-
ness. Address by Richard M. Nixon at the Herbert
Hoover 91st Birthdate Commemorative Program, West Branch,
Iowa, August 10, 1965. Nixon, R. M.   Asia after
Vietnam.—The Liberal, perplexed: Von Hoffman, N.
Psyching Nixon. [etc.]
    1. United States—Foreign relations—1945–
—Addresses, essays, lectures.   2. Nixon, Richard
Milhous, 1913–   I. Title.

E840.G34   327.73   73-1478
ISBN 0-531-05551-5 (pbk.)

Design by Batten, Friedman, Kreloff
Photos by Jeannie Friedman
Cover design by Nicholas Krenitsky

ALSO BY LLOYD C. GARDNER

Economic Aspects of New Deal Diplomacy
Architects of Illusion
The Creation of the American Empire
  (with Thomas McCormick and
  Walter LaFeber)

ACKNOWLEDGMENTS

"Address by Richard M. Nixon to the Commonwealth Club of California, April 2, 1965," *Congressional Record,* April 19, 1965.

"Khrushchev's Hidden Weakness," by Richard M. Nixon. Copyright © 1963 by the *Saturday Evening Post.* By permission of the President.

"Address by Richard M. Nixon at the Herbert Hoover 91st Birthdate Commemorative Program, West Branch, Iowa, August 10, 1965," *Congressional Record,* August 11, 1965.

"Asia After Vietnam," by Richard M. Nixon. Reprinted by permission from *Foreign Affairs* (October 1967). Copyright © 1967 by the Council on Foreign Relations, Inc., New York.

"Psyching Nixon," by Nicholas von Hoffman. Copyright © 1971 by *The Washington Post.*

"The New China Policy," by Richard M. Nixon, *Department of State Bulletin,* March 13, 1972.

"Making History in Peking," by Hugh Sidey, *Life* Magazine, © 1972, Time Inc.

"Ten Points of Note: Asia and the Nixon Doctrine," by John Dower. Copyright © 1970 by *Bulletin of Concerned Asian Scholars;* Bay Area Institute.

"The Nixon Doctrine and Our Asian Commitments," by Earl C. Ravenal. Reprinted by permission from *Foreign Affairs* (January 1971). Copyright © 1971 by the Council on Foreign Relations, Inc., New York.

"Anybody See *Patton?*" by Hugh Sidey, *Life* Magazine, © 1970, Time Inc.

"President Nixon Discusses Foreign Policy During Texas Visit: April 30, 1972," *Department of State Bulletin,* May 22, 1972.

"Asia's Emerging Industrial Revolution." Copyright © 1969 by *Business Week.*

"A Strong Economy and a Strong National Defense: Address by President Nixon to the Veterans of Foreign Wars, Dallas, Texas, August 19, 1971," *Department of State Bulletin,* September 13, 1971.

"Richard de Nixon, Gaullist?" by James Burnham. Copyright © 1969 by *National Review,* 150 East 35 Street, New York, N.Y. 10016.

"The Moscow Summit," by William Safire. Copyright © 1972 by The New York Times Company. Reprinted by permission.

"U.S.–Soviet Grain Deal: Case History of a Gamble," by Murrey Marder and Marilyn Berger. Copyright © 1971 by *The Washington Post.*

"In Support of Nixonomics," by Pierre A. Rinfret. Copyright © 1972 by The New York Times Company. Reprinted by permission.

"The Five-Power World of Richard Nixon," by James Chace. Copyright © 1972 by The New York Times Company. Reprinted by permission.

"Weighing the Balance of Power," by Stanley Hoffmann. Reprinted by permission from *Foreign Affairs* (July 1972). Copyright © 1972 by the Council on Foreign Relations, Inc., New York.

The Vice-President of the United States is forty-two years old, robust, intelligent, conscientious, ruthless, affable, articulate, competitive, telegenic, and breathtakingly adaptable. He comes from a large state, leads an apparently blameless personal life, has an attractive family, has never been called a security risk, and is blessed with many friends and admirers—some of whom, as we learned from the campaign of 1952, have been willing to invest solid cash in his career. Those people showed good investor judgment. The actuarial tables and the laws of chance favor the Vice-President greatly. If he takes the elementary precautions with his health and does not squander the formidable political assets that are now his, he has ahead of him a full quarter-century of service to the Republic and to the good name of Richard Milhous Nixon.

What does this quarter-century hold? It would be rash to say that there is anything it does *not* hold.

But if Nixon misses in 1956, he will be conspicuously available in 1960. Indeed, almost as far as one can see down the corridors of time—1956, 1960, 1964, 1968, 1972, 1976, 1980, and even 1984—Nixon will be available. With giant strides being taken in the field of geriatrics, it is even conceivable that Nixon will be a hard man to count out in the Republican convention of 2000 —held, perhaps, at some pleasant American resort on Mars. Whether or not the prospect pleases, it imposes. And if, for some now obscure reason, Nixon never does capture the grand prize, we may be fairly assured that he will somehow or other be part of our lives—an influence, a force to reckon with in the affairs of the country for some time to come.

——Richard Rovere, *The Eisenhower Years*
"The Vice-President: September 1955"

CONTENTS

SECTION 3

SECTION 4

THE GREAT NIXON TURN- AROUND

BEHOLD THE KISSINBUNDY.

THE KISSINBUNDY IS AN ADVISOR TO PRESIDENTS IN THE FIELD OF FOREIGN POLICY.

THE FIRST THING A PRESIDENT DOES IN OFFICE...

IS CALL IN THE KISSINBUNDY.

WHO, BASED ON INTELLIGENCE REPORTS AND YEARS OF EXPERTISE...

ADVISES THE PRESIDENT OF HIS OPTIONS.

AFTER EVERYTHING GOES WRONG...

THE PRESIDENT GOES OUT OF OFFICE.

THE FIRST THING THE NEXT PRESIDENT DOES IN OFFICE...

IS CALL IN THE KISSINBUNDY.

THIS NOVEMBER YOU WILL VOTE TO SEE WHICH OF TWO CANDIDATES...

WILL BE ADVISED OF HIS OPTIONS BY THE KISSINBUNDY.

PRESIDENTS CHANGE, BUT KISSINBUNDY..

IS FOREVER..

INTRODUCTION

PEKING, FEBRUARY 21, 1972

A disenchanted conservative journalist with the official party was appalled at the scene in the Great Banquet Hall: "He would toast Alger Hiss tonight, if he could find him." For a few disappointed purists, liberal as well as conservative, there was nothing to see on this trip to China but the irony. Most Americans, however, had forgotten about Alger Hiss. The famous case of the ex-State Department official, convicted of perjury for denying he had committed espionage by handing over secret documents to a Communist agent in the years just before World War II, belonged to a different era, a different place, and, it seemed, even to a different Richard M. Nixon.

Representative Nixon's leading role in exposing Hiss, presumed to be a key figure in the Communist conspiracy that had operated deep within the government during the New Deal, had catapulted the young California congressman into the vice-presidential nomination in 1952. His assignment during that campaign, and thereafter in the Eisenhower administration, was simple: Keep it up! Keep the pressure on. Remind the people that the Democrats had allowed Red agents to infiltrate the executive branch; warn them that it could happen again unless Republicans are re-elected. In 1960 Nixon ran on his own against John F. Kennedy in a contest of Cold Warriors. Kennedy promised vigorous action against Fidel Castro in Cuba, and looked healthier than Nixon on television. He won the election by a razor-thin margin.

Two years later the former Vice-President promised California voters that if they elected him governor he would give the state "the best Communist control of any state in the United States." He lost again, this time by a big margin.

Since Republicans had made domestic anti-Communism a partisan issue, and since "Tricky Dick" had used it so effectively against them, the Democrats were happy to have done with him. Nixon had even obliged them with his own political obituary, telling a group of reporters early on the morning after the election, "you won't have Nixon to kick around anymore. . . ." Then things started to happen to the Democrats. John Kennedy was assassinated. The Vietnam War appeared out of nowhere—or so it seemed at the time—and got bigger and bigger. "I can't get out," Lyndon Johnson confessed to his wife. "I can't finish it with what I have got. So what the hell can I do?"

Whether they wanted him to win the war or simply to bring the boys home, the voters were fed up with Lyndon Johnson. They were so fed up that Richard Nixon was able to go through the entire campaign without once having to explain how he would end the war. "If the war is still going on next January," Nixon declared in 1968, "it can best be ended by a new administration . . . neither defending old errors nor bound by the old record." What did that mean? No one knew except the Republican candidate himself; and he had a perfectly good reason for not telling. Hubert Humphrey, his opponent, had called upon Nixon not to jeopardize the effort to get peace negotiations started by offering a detailed plan to end the war.

The simple truth was that Humphrey had no plan to offer the voters either and had hoped to neutralize the issue by declaring Vietnam off-limits for the campaign. In effect, however, the strategy gave Nixon a free ride all the way to the White House. The war went on. But Nixon managed the politics of the situation by calling upon the "silent majority" for support. More important, he brought the boys home (all but 30,000 of them in his first term), and American casualties fell off to "acceptable" levels.

Something else was happening. The new President had proclaimed the beginning of an era of negotiations in his inaugural address. And now here he was in Peking, toasting Premier Chou En-lai:

There is no reason for us to be enemies. Neither of us seeks the territory of the other; neither of us seeks domination over the other; neither of us seeks to stretch out our hands and rule the world.

Premier Chou had reaffirmed his government's desire to have a "frank exchange of views between our two sides to gain a clearer notion of our differences and make efforts to find common ground," but the President had gone much further in his remarks. He had all but declared the Cold War over, at least so far as Sino-American relations were concerned.

Even after Soviet-American relations had begun to thaw somewhat in the mid-1960's, it had been considered improper if not immoral to talk about normalizing relations with the People's Republic of China. Both Democrats and Republicans asserted that Peking was lurking behind Hanoi's effort to conquer South Vietnam—the first step in a plan to conquer all of Southeast Asia through guerrilla wars. No one had prosecuted the "free world's case" against Communist China more effectively or persistently than Richard Nixon. It *was* astounding, then, to hear his toast and then to see him strolling along the top of the Great Wall of China surrounded by smiling Chinese officials and American reporters.

One thing was certain: he was not looking for Alger Hiss anymore. The dialogue on the Great Wall went like this:

The President: So, all in all, I would say, finally, we have come a long way to be here today, 16,000 miles. Many things that have occurred on this trip have made me realize that it was worth coming, but I would say, as I look at the wall, it is worth coming 16,000 miles just to stand here and see the wall. Do you agree, Mr. Secretary?

Secretary Rogers: I certainly do, Mr. President. It is really a tremendous privilege we have had.

The President: We will not climb to the top today. We are already meeting at the summit in Peking.

Let me ask the members of the press, Do you think it was worth coming?

Reporters: Yes, Mr. President.

It was badly written, but the drama was there, complete with a chorus of reporters to supply the necessary highlighting and accompaniment.

From atop the Great Wall, the historical process seemed to speed up; even the wrenching and searing experience of Vietnam, while not lessened, now took its place in the past. The far-off past, on the other hand, seemed closer to present reality. Several times before, going back to the 1780's when European nations and empires refused to open their ports to the new nation's foreign trade, Americans had sought out China. Again in the 1890's, Americans looked to China as a "new frontier." There are parallels between the visits of American sailing ships and the petitions of railroad builders then, and Nixon's new quest to re-open the door to China. In each instance, also, a bloc of nations in Europe pursued policies that limited American options and were at odds with its future aspirations. Always before when Americans approached China, however, it was a China defined by us. The China of 1972 defined its own image.

President Nixon found himself in this new China not by chance, a traveler wandering aimlessly through the world, but on a mission mandated by a post—Cold War consensus in the United States among policy elites. Once the available man for the 1950's, Nixon had emerged, partly through his own efforts and partly by fate, as the appropriate man to undertake this assignment.

NOT QUITE MAKING IT

Richard Nixon arrived in Washington in 1947 having defeated the Democratic incumbent, Jerry Voorhis, for the right to represent the people of California's Twelfth Congressional District. He was one of seven Republicans to defeat incumbent Democrats in California, and one of fifty-five Republicans across the country who would occupy formerly Democratic seats in the Eightieth Congress. The Republican campaign slogan for 1946 was simple and effective: "Had Enough?" The Nixon-Voorhis contest, moreover, resembled several other races that year that matched political old-timers of both parties against returning "war heroes." Democrat John F. Kennedy, like Nixon a Navy veteran, used his war record against a spate of rivals in his party's primary, and came out the sure-bet winner in Massachusetts' Eleventh Congressional District.

Cracked and damaged by years of hard usage, the New Deal alliance that had dominated American politics for so long had lost much of its appeal and strength. Harry Truman's Fair Deal program never stirred up any great enthusiasm as such, though Truman did succeed in getting bits and pieces of it through Congress. It was the Cold War that excited Congress and the public. For a variety of reasons, the Republicans were in a better position to profit from Cold War "issues." In Dick Nixon's case, as he recalled in *Six Crises,* an issue popped up one "hot, sultry Washington morning—Tuesday, August 3, 1948," when Whittaker Chambers appeared before the House Un-American Activities Committee to testify concerning a supposed Soviet spy ring that had operated inside the federal government in the 1930's. This investigation was one of several "leads" congressional Republicans were pursuing in the postwar years in search of evidence to convict the New Deal for adopting "socialist" measures at home and "selling out" national interests and faithful allies at wartime conferences with the Russians.

At first Chambers made little impression on the members of the committee; Congressman Nixon, for example, had considered skipping the public session altogether in order to catch up on his mail. Nixon did stay, however, and was impressed by Chambers' story and his way of telling it. Still, he offered very little new information, and, at this point, no spy tales. In fact, the witness specifically excluded espionage as the purpose of the underground group he named in his original testimony. Their purpose, said Chambers, was simply "infiltration." And all but two of the names, Alger and Donald Hiss, were familiar to the committee. Nixon's interest rose when Chambers added that he had come forward in 1939 with this information, but had been ignored by higher ups.

Alger Hiss had enjoyed a long and successful career in public service, and was now president of the Carnegie Endowment for Peace. Chambers was an admitted ex-Communist, a man who by his own testimony had lived a double life, with little regard for veracity or honor, until he broke with the party some time in 1937. The contrast between the two men could not have been greater, all the more so when Hiss appeared before the committee to deny the charge and to deny that he had ever known anyone named Whittaker Chambers. His manner, Nixon wrote, "was coldly courteous and, at times, almost condescending."

It was his manner that put Nixon on the scent, however, when the other members of the committee were all for dropping the matter. Nixon described the scene in great detail:

When Robert Stripling, the Committee's chief investigator, handed him a photograph of Chambers, he looked at it with an elaborate air of concentration and said, "If this is a picture of Mr. Chambers, he is not particularly unusual looking." He paused and then, looking up at Congressman Karl Mundt, the acting Chairman of the Committee, added: "He looks like a lot of people, I might even mistake him for the Chairman of this Committee."

Hiss's friends from the State Department, other government agencies, and the Washington social community sitting in the front rows of the spectator section broke into a titter of delighted laughter. Hiss acknowledged this reaction to his sally by turning his back on the Committee, tilting his head in a courtly bow, and smiling graciously at his supporters.

That "sally and the gestures accompanying it planted the first doubts in Nixon's mind, but the other members of HUAC were embarrassed by charges that they had allowed Hiss to take the stand without checking into Chambers' story to verify any part of it. The mood in the committee room was gloomy. Everyone but the freshman congressman from California favored turning over the testimony to the Department of Justice. Nixon held out for making an attempt to verify or discredit Chambers' testimony. To do anything else, he argued, would amount to a public confession that the committee was incompetent and reckless in its procedures. It was an election year. All the committee members had a stake in this case. This was the big one—either way.

Chairman Mundt realized the stakes full well and appointed Nixon to head a subcommittee to question Chambers in executive session. If anything went wrong, Nixon would have to take the rap. Every effort was made to keep this session from becoming known until the results had been evaluated. A second meeting with Alger Hiss was also kept secret, although leaks to the press did occur in both instances. The committee was unsure enough of its position to reject Hiss' suggestion of a public confrontation in favor of a private one in a New York hotel room.

Nixon's gamble paid off—bigger than anyone, even he, could have expected. He had decided to attack Hiss' rebuttal at its weakest point: the latter's failure to rule out the possibility that he might have known Chambers under some other name. He did not expect to be able to prove the charge that Hiss had been a member of the Communist Party, for that would be one man's word against another. However, if he could demonstrate that Hiss was "lying" about never having known Chambers, he could show that he "might also be lying about whether or not he was a Communist." That alone would be enough to exonerate the committee in the public mind.

When Hiss finally identified Chambers under pressure as a man who once called himself George Crosley, and went into the details of their relationship in the mid-1930's, Nixon was ready for a public confrontation. The atmosphere at this hearing was far different from that on the first occasion, when Hiss had made his denials. This time it was Nixon who made the sallies, and Hiss who was chagrined by audience reaction. At the private session Hiss had explained that the man he called Crosley had very bad teeth. He had not been able to identify Chambers as that man until he had satisfied himself that Chambers had had major repair work done on his mouth. Hiss' insistence upon examining Chambers' mouth close up led to this exchange at the public hearing:

Mr. Hiss: My strongest recollection is of the bad teeth. When I saw him for the first time after these hearings began, I asked, as the record will show, if he would please open his mouth so I could look at his teeth.

Mr. Nixon: Mr. Hiss, on that point there is considerable in the record which will be released today in which you did request Mr. Crosley to open his mouth and in which you even asked the name of his dentist and wanted to consult with his dentist before you made the identification positive.

My question may sound facetious, but I am just wondering: Didn't you ever see Mr. Crosley with his mouth closed? [Laughter]

I am serious. . . .

Mr. Hiss: The striking thing in my recollection about Crosley was not when he had his mouth shut, but when he had his mouth open.

Mr. Nixon: As far as you are concerned, the only way you can identify a person is when he has his mouth open? Is that correct?

"Had millions of Americans seen Hiss on the stand that day," Nixon later wrote in *Six Crises,* "there would not have been the lingering doubts over the Hiss case which have continued for so many years." The Hiss case entered a second stage when Chambers produced documents that he claimed to have received from Alger Hiss while the latter was serving in the State Department. Two trials were held in an effort to determine whether Hiss had committed perjury either by denying that he had obtained the secret documents for Chambers, or by denying that he had not seen Chambers after January 1, 1937. The first ended with a hung jury, but the second jury convicted Hiss on both counts on January 21, 1950.

The events surrounding the Hiss case, from the beginning to the end, have been explored in great depth by several authors. Both Chambers and Hiss wrote their own accounts; a psychiatrist tried to find an explanation for the unexplainable in the workings of their subconscious minds. An English writer suggested that what really happened was that a nation put a generation on trial. There was something in that idea: Hiss often did, as Nixon complained, wrap himself in a New Deal cloak; and Nixon did, as Hiss suspected, see the case as an indictment of New Deal foreign and domestic policies.

There were other aspects of the case, however, which offer insight into Nixon and his times, and even provide a few clues into the future President's ability to adapt to a post—Cold War consensus. In the first place, Nixon's reaction to Hiss as an "establishment" figure in Washington, the mixture of envy and dislike that shows up so clearly in his writing about the episode, had strong sectional and class roots. The divisions within the country over New Deal policies and American entrance into World War II were only partly submerged in the bipartisan alliance called into being by the Axis challenge, and then again by the Soviet challenge. Prevented from making a frontal assault, at least until the Korean War, Republicans went over the record of the New Deal again and again. Here they were on safe ground because many conservative Democrats were more than ready to believe that Franklin Roosevelt had misjudged Stalin, or had been led into error by "fuzzy-minded" liberals.

Second, and related to the first point, Nixon's attacks on subversives in government reflected a larger concern in conservative circles about the possibility of a postwar super New Deal that would take the country all the way over to socialism. His 1946 campaign against Jerry Voorhis was constructed largely around an attack on the CIO's Political Action Committee. Nixon's campaign managers wanted him to get the idea across that Congressman Voorhis was the candidate of radical labor groups and of those sympathetic to Henry Wallace. "It should be a matter of great concern to the voters of the Twelfth District," the Republican challenger declared, "that the National Citizens Political Action Committee which so loudly applauded Wallace's proposal that Russia be given a free hand, is the same radical organization that has endorsed my opponent." Voorhis actually opposed Wallace's positions on foreign policy, but Nixon made the point he had wanted to make: Voorhis was supported by a nascent "Labor Party" that had an identifiable foreign and domestic policy.Further, the two were linked, whether an individual subscribed to Wallace's particular views or not.

In the Hiss case, as we have just seen, Nixon hoped to establish that the former government official had lied about knowing Chambers, a confessed Communist. If so, he "might" have lied about being a Communist himself. Espionage *was not* an issue in the original hearings. It is interesting also that Congressman Nixon seldom took part in the floor debates on the great foreign policy issues of the early Cold War: the Truman Doctrine, the Marshall Plan, NATO. In fact he seldom spoke at length on any issue, with the single exception of anti-subversive legislation. This is all the more remarkable when one finds Nixon saying in later years that he had always felt the country could almost run itself without a president; the man in the White House should concentrate on foreign affairs. What was remarkable, of course, was that he was not speaking abstractly, but about himself.

The men around Eisenhower were never very enthusiastic about the vice-presidential nominee. He was there for one purpose. Ike himself instructed his running mate on that purpose: whenever possible he, Eisenhower, would stress the moral issues, the positive side of the Republican crusade, while Nixon was to go after the Democratic presidential candidate, Adlai Stevenson. Nixon was, in the words of one of his biographers, to represent a "Republican meld of Paul Revere and Billy Sunday." The essential point about Paul Revere and Billy Sunday, one recalls, was that however useful the former became to the leaders of the American Revolution or however the latter stood out as a spokesman for law and order in the 1920's, neither was ever admitted to the inner circle. Nixon's awareness of the situation, of being defined by others, of not quite making it, was acute.

The men who advised Eisenhower, after all, were not so different from the members of the Washington establishment in the later years of the New Deal and World War II. Who had hired Hiss at the Carnegie Endowment? John Foster Dulles, of course, Eisenhower's Secretary of State designate. Who had sought Ike for the Republican nomination? Tom Dewey and Henry Cabot Lodge, representatives of that Eastern wing of the party which had sidled up to the New Deal. Nixon was a giveaway to the Midwestern and Far Western contingents in the party. Ever since 1860, to go back to the beginning, the Republican Party had been a marriage of convenience between divergent geographical and interest group factions, which eyed one another with suspicion and distrust except when Democrats were around. Nixon's choice had all the aspects of a traditional power play within the party. But things don't always turn out the way they're planned, and the future Vice-President had already been underestimated once by opponents and colleagues alike. His opportunities and perils were balanced about evenly.

So even if the Eisenhower-Nixon ticket swept the nation, as it seemed sure to do, Nixon's image would have been set before the voters in a negative framework. On the other hand, second place in the Eisenhower administration offered a better chance to escape that image than second place in California. It was a gamble. What he soon realized was that his political future was unimportant to the Eastern Establishment, which had selected Eisenhower to head off Senator Robert A. Taft, the Ohio "isolationist," who represented a double threat. Taft could not be elected, according to the moguls of Eastern Republicanism, but if he could, that would be worse yet. Once Ike was elected, the future would take care of itself.

Any remaining doubts Nixon may have had about his standing with the Eisenhower entourage vanished when the "Nixon Fund" story broke in September as the 1952 campaign got under way. The fund had been established so that supporters of Congressman and then Senator Nixon could contribute and solicit contributions on an ongoing basis instead of just at election time. Nixon responded to the attacks on the fund from the Democratic press, but no word of support came from Eisenhower or his top aides. Then someone asked him if he had heard about the editorials in *The Washington Post* and the *New York Herald Tribune*. "What editorials?" he replied. The papers both planned to run editorials stating that Nixon should offer his resignation. *The Post* editorial could be dismissed as another partisan blast, but the *Herald Tribune* was the most influential Republican newspaper in the East.

Nixon recalled what went through his mind at that moment:

I . . . knew that the publishers and other top officials of the *Tribune* had very close relations with Eisenhower and with some of his most influential supporters. I assumed that the *Tribune* would not have taken this position editorially unless it also represented the thinking of the people around Eisenhower. And, as I thought more about it, it occurred to me that this might well be the view of Eisenhower himself, for I had not heard from him since the trouble began, two days before.

Although Nixon carefully separated Eisenhower from the people around him when he discussed the episode in *Six Crises,* there came a moment of truth for both men when Nixon bluntly demanded a decision from the

General. His famous "Checkers Speech" on television had been a great *political* success. What more did Eisenhower—or his people—want from him before deciding about his place on the ticket? Ike's somewhat belated assurance that Nixon had indeed vindicated himself subtly changed the relationship between them: Nixon had shown independence, but by doing so had only confirmed what others said about him to Eisenhower, that he was an ambitious and clever politician—a type Ike detested—but certainly nothing more.

Commenting on the Hiss case and the slush-fund speech, Nixon noted that both had been cited by others as reasons for his defeat in 1960. Perhaps so, he would remind them, but if it had not been for those incidents he would never have been the candidate in that year. It was, without meaning to be, his most perceptive reflection on the agony of not quite making it. Those who really made it in America in the days when Richard Nixon was growing up not only had to achieve independent wealth and independence, but had to do it without picking up invisible encumbrances along the way. That was the code. Nixon, again without knowing it himself, belonged to a later age when the certainties and verities of a simpler time no longer applied. The straightforward hero and villain gave way to the ambiguous and tortured protagonists of the postwar era. Put it another way: whether hero or villain, FDR was an outsize man to others; Nixon was, by those standards, undersize. But that would not always be a disadvantage.

When William Howard Taft was elected President in 1912, to take another example, his brother supplied him with additional financial resources so that he could be his own man, as Teddy Roosevelt had been, in dealing with the corporate leaders of America. When Richard Milhous Nixon became Vice-President, he was more than ever dependent on others, not in a financial sense (although that was true, too) but in other ways less obvious. But again, that would not always be disadvantageous.

Nixon had summed up the 1952 campaign at his first post-nomination press conference: "Communism at home and abroad." His characterization of Secretary of State Dean Acheson demonstrated how he would knot these together with the Hiss case: "Dean Acheson has a form of color blindness—a form of pinkeye—toward the Communist threat in the United States." To be sure, Nixon sounded all the usual Republican themes on foreign policy, especially the Democrats' responsibility for the "loss" of China. But his specialty remained domestic subversion.

With midterm elections close at hand in 1954, Eisenhower ordered his Vice-President to step up the pace. Governor Tom Dewey of New York exhorted Nixon to "hit harder . . . people like a fighter." The explicit comparison with a prizefighter was an accurate way of describing Nixon, right down to the men who owned pieces of his contract. In speech after speech he slugged away at the Democrats with remarks like, "thousands of Communists, fellow travelers and security risks have been thrown out" of government jobs by the Republicans, and, "when the Eisenhower administration came to Washington . . . it found in the files a blueprint for socializing America." These statements did him and the Republican candidates little good. They were wildly inaccurate and, even for campaign rhetoric, deliberately misleading. It turned out, for example, that 41.2 percent of those dismissed for security reasons had been hired by the Eisenhower administration, and that the supposedly secret blueprints for socializing America consisted of legislative proposals for enacting a welfare program.

The elections saw the Democrats regain control of both the House and the Senate. Nixon was naturally disappointed; he had a right to be. Those who had been urging him to "hit harder" were nowhere around when the votes were counted. Everyone, including the President, assured him that he was doing well and "constantly becoming better and more favorably known to the American public." "This is all to the good," Eisenhower wrote. But Nixon had been there, and it wasn't good at all. No one else in the administration had helped. And the caliber of the candidates put forward by the organization was, as Nixon knew full well, too low to produce any other result.

Eisenhower, after he finally decided not to dump Nixon in 1956 in yet another demonstration of the Vice-President's expendability, advised his running mate that he should start making more statesmanlike speeches, though, of course, he would still be responsible for carrying the attack to the opposition. Once the 1956 election was over, a new speculation arose: Who would Eisenhower support as his successor? All Nixon really hoped for at this point was neutrality. The most likely Establishment candidate for the nomination was Governor Nelson Rockefeller of New York, who had bucked the national trend by winning in 1958. Rockefeller's chances looked better on paper than they really were, however; first, because he was regarded as a *parvenu* within the Establishment, and second, because he had made no secret of his intention to side with critics of the Eisenhower administration's defense and economic policies.

Eisenhower may not have wanted to be neutral about Richard Nixon as a possible successor, but he had left himself no other option. Who was there besides Nixon? Ike had refused to use the White House to rebuild the party in his (or anybody else's) image, with the result that by 1960 there were only 35 Republicans out of 100 senators, and just 135 Republicans left in the 437-member House of Representatives. His lack of support for Nixon's efforts, and his failure to offer the Vice-President better guidance, had created a situation filled with irony for both. The President had sent Nixon into the political arena while he remained aloof; imagine how Nixon must have felt at their first meeting after the 1960 Republican convention. Eisenhower assured him that he wanted to do everything he could for a Republican victory, but he felt it essential that the nominee establish his "own identity as the new leader of the party." If he were to take an active part in the campaign from the outset, it would tend to over-shadow Nixon's appearances. Then came this blockbus-ter: "He also expressed the conviction that his great influ-ence with the American people was due in substantial part to his image of being President of all the people, and not just a partisan as Truman had been."

Just a partisan like Truman! Was that what the General meant to imply? Perhaps not, but was he suggesting that Nixon should attempt to make himself over during the election campaign? Nixon staff men began to worry that Ike might do the candidate more harm than good before the election was over. Their fears seemed to be confirmed when Eisenhower gave this reply to a question about the decisions for which Nixon had been responsible in his ad-ministration: "If you give me a week, I might think of one. I don't remember."

Nixon had made a list of his opponent's strengths: Jack Kennedy had "high intelligence, great energy, and a par-ticularly effective television personality." He also en-joyed unlimited financial backing and was unencum-bered by ties to an administration suddenly grown old and stodgy. The Soviet Union had rushed past the United States in putting a satellite into orbit. The contrast in space achievement seemed all the greater because of the sluggish performance of the American economy during the last three years of the Eisenhower tenure. Given a choice, Nixon might easily have decided to trade places with Kennedy.

The Democrats looked forward eagerly to the television debates between Kennedy and Nixon. Republican strategists would have liked to have avoided this spectacular, but Nixon himself overruled suggestions that his managers set impossible conditions. In *Six Crises* he wrote that "from a purely political standpoint," Kennedy had much more to gain from their joint appearances. Observers of Richard Nixon's political style point out that in his case things are seldom what they seem at first glance. He would never have agreed to the debates, it is argued, if he had had any doubts about coming out of the encounters worse off than when he went into the TV studios. He expected to win.

There is another point about this decision that deserves consideration. Nixon's ambiguous relationship to the General in the White House may have been a powerful factor operating just at or below the level of consciousness. To refuse the challenge would have been too partisan for a man running on the Eisenhower record. Throughout the debates Nixon tried to take the high road, to become the statesmanlike figure Ike wanted to succeed him in the nation's highest office.

Kennedy offered him a chance to strike this pose on the Cuban issue by advocating direct aid to exile groups seeking to overthrow Fidel Castro. He also put Nixon in a real bind. The Vice-President had spoken out in administration councils in favor of stronger action against Castro; he knew, and was informed that Kennedy also knew, about the Central Intelligence Agency's secret training bases for Cuban exiles with "the eventual purpose of supporting an invasion of Cuba itself"; finally, Nixon was sure that the American people favored a strong anti-Castro policy.

He could not say that Kennedy's policy had already been adopted without jeopardizing the operation. The only thing to do, he reasoned, was to "go to the other extreme" by attacking the Kennedy proposal as wrong and irresponsible, a violation of American treaty commitments. In the fourth and final TV debate Nixon presented an eloquent brief against intervention, citing American obligations and the charter of the United Nations. He added some practical reasons as well:

If we were to follow that recommendation, . . . we would lose all of our friends in Latin America, we would probably be condemned in the United Nations, and we would not accomplish our objective. I know something else. It would be an open invitation for Mr. Khrushchev to come in, to come into Latin America and to engage us in what would be a civil war, and possibly even worse than that.

We have Nixon's own word for it that he did not believe a thing he was saying; he even tells us that he was providing a cover story, at great political cost to himself, so that the operation would succeed no matter who became president. Kennedy should have reread the transcript of this debate before launching the ill-fated Bay of Pigs invasion six months later, in April, 1961. Whether from cynicism or patriotic instincts, Nixon had made an airtight case against the plan.

But the Democratic President's decision to go ahead with the Bay of Pigs involved him in an even greater display of national disregard for "the opinions of mankind." He allowed the authors of the Bay of Pigs to lie to his ambassador to the United Nations, Adlai Stevenson, so that he would lie to the world organization about American involvement. Even so, Kennedy's reputation remained virtually untarnished, while, after the 1962 California election, Nixon's sank to its lowest point.

Kennedy's justification for engaging in such a deception was the supposed Soviet offensive in the "Third World" of underdeveloped nations. The Communists were known to be (in J. Edgar Hoover's phrase) "masters of deceit." To survive an encounter, or a Cold

War, one had to be willing to use every weapon they did, only more efficiently. Kennedy and Nixon both believed that. So did a whole host of "realist" policymakers who walked the halls of the State Department and Pentagon in those years. This kind of thinking reached its logical end in the Vietnam War.

Nixon had gone to Russia in 1959 to open a United States exhibition in Moscow's Sokolniki Park. It was there that the famous "kitchen debate" with Soviet Premier Khrushchev took place, with the Russian leader and the Vice-President trading barbs on all subjects from washing machines to missiles. They also held a private conference at Khrushchev's summer *dacha* on the Moscow River that lasted for more than five hours and produced more serious exchanges. Nixon delivered the message the State Department wanted to convey: the Soviets were playing a dangerous game by stirring up revolutions in places like Cuba and Vietnam. Khrushchev responded as expected: the Russian government could not be blamed for policy mistakes by the capitalists that had produced this hatred for the United States.

Nothing surprising in that, nothing at all. What is interesting is that Kennedy and Khrushchev had almost exactly the same conversation two years later in Vienna. Over and over again JFK kept returning to the subject of Soviet responsibility for revolutionary trouble spots around the world, while the Premier simply repeated what he had told Nixon in Moscow. The question is: What difference did the election of 1960 actually make? So long as the Cold War consensus in the United States posited Russian responsibility for the world's difficulties, or, better put, America's difficulties with the rest of the world, what was there left to discuss except tactics and style? Admittedly an oversimplification; but one might—as an intellectual exercise—argue the proposition that Nixon's election would have made the Bay of Pigs less likely. It was Kennedy, after all, who had publicly demanded vigorous action against Castro and military aid for the Cuban exiles. The Vice-President had denounced military intervention, listing his reasons during a national television debate. Regardless of whether he believed his own arguments, could he have managed to reverse himself so soon? If that seems far-fetched, remember that in 1960 the public still took statements by government officials and public leaders seriously. The years of the "credibility gap" were still to come.

To argue the alternative proposition, that events would have transpired in much the same way, may be more satisfying on one level and perhaps less far-fetched, but the implications of that line of reasoning still lead back to the question: What difference did the election of 1960 make? And then to the answer: No difference whatsoever. If Nixon had been elected and had gone ahead with the Bay of Pigs, moreover, that would have meant that the American people had elected a man who deliberately misinformed them of his foreign policy views. Turn the argument around any way you will, substitute other issues for the Bay of Pigs, the conclusion remains unchanged: the Cold War concensus reduced the differences between a Kennedy and a Nixon to matters of style and tactics.

"You know, Dick," Republican campaign manager Leonard Hall quipped several weeks after the election, "a switch of only 14,000 votes and we would have been the heroes and they would have been the bums." Hall's comment makes the point beautifully: where there is no serious debate, no fundamental issues drawn, 14,000 votes really do decide whether a man is a hero or a bum. From 1946 through 1962, Dick Nixon had handled the messy things for the party. No one had forced him to do it. After his defeat for the governorship of California, he realized that there would have to be a "new" Nixon. This Nixon would have to make himself independent and prove he could operate within a different circle.

He would never have become "new" enough to be elected President, however transformed his image, without a series of improbable events that added up to a political miracle. Equally incredible, the miracle put him in a position not simply to carry out the mandate of a post–Cold War consensus, but to pull it along at a much faster pace than his critics believed possible or his old friends sometimes desired.

ROOM AT THE TOP

Nixon's defeat in the California race sent him east in search of fortune, and something else. Fame he had. There were plenty of offers that would ensure financial security—which he still needed. But as an aide put it later, "There was no foreign policy angle in California. It had to be the East. He had to have his cake (money) and eat it too (his interest in foreign policy)." [1] Eisenhower had stimulated his interest in foreign policy questions by example and by advice. The California election had demonstrated, moreover, that the internal "Communist menace" was no longer a viable domestic issue. In the aftermath of the Cuban missile crisis, on the other hand, it was still possible to strike a statesmanlike pose with a few stalwart anti-Communist phrases.

Another reason for going east was his determination to make it among the very people who, he believed, were responsible for his defeats at the polls. With the encourage-

---

[1] Jules Witcover, *The Resurrection of Richard Nixon* (New York: Putnam, 1970), p. 41.

ment of several old friends and some new acquaintances, Nixon joined the New York law firm of Mudge, Stern, Baldwin and Todd. He brought with him the Pepsi-Cola account, a lucrative entrance fee for any new partner.

The New York "crowd" still was not much impressed, however. Nixon's Cold War views were regarded by sophisticates as very definitely "middlebrow," like his life style. Surrounded by new associates, the former began to change. Lawyer Nixon made his specialty international trade, an area where his Washington contacts proved particularly useful to the firm's new clients. He lunched twice a week at The Recess, an appropriately named club where the table talk was all about multinational corporations. For the first time since law school days he found time for reading, mostly current events, but also some American history. He studied the careers of Theodore Roosevelt and Woodrow Wilson, men who had combined thought and action in making the United States a responsible world power.

In the mid-1960's the former Vice-President's Cold War views, as expressed in a series of speeches and articles in the *Readers Digest*, actually became harsher, in accordance with what he apparently thought a Republican party leader should say and the nation would want to hear. If the Democrats had flayed the Eisenhower administration for allowing Cuba to fall to Castro, Nixon would repay in kind by denouncing the " 'liberal' members of the White House staff" around Kennedy for ignoring Republican warnings of the Soviet missile emplacements on the island. And while the Democrats celebrated Kennedy's "finest hour" in the Cuban missile crisis, Nixon could not resist pointing out that by JFK's own announced standards—Communism in the Western Hemisphere was not negotiable—the outcome of the crisis had actually strengthened Castro's position because he had gained a no-invasion pledge from the United States. Fair's fair, and on this point Nixon was absolutely right, if one agreed with America's basic Cold War premises.

"The Cold War isn't thawing;" he wrote in one article, "it is burning with a deadly heat. Communism isn't changing; it isn't sleeping; it isn't relaxing; it is, as always, plotting, scheming, working, fighting." What was needed in Vietnam, he said in 1964, was only the will to win. The blackest moment in the story of that war, he went on, was the murder of President Ngo Dinh Diem, which he interpreted to mean that "the United States will use a friend until he no longer serves our purposes and then let him be liquidated." There again, the criticism of the Democrats was fair and within the parameters of Cold War sensibility. If Kennedy and then Johnson felt that Vietnam was vital to the strategic position of America in the final outcome of the Cold War, such criticism had a proper place in American politics.

Even as he wrote, the premises of the Cold War were weakening, not least of all within Nixon's mind, where a new vision of Wilson's old dream began to take shape. "It is a time when a man who knows the world will be able to forge a whole new set of alliances," he told an interviewer, "with America taking the lead in solving the big problems. We are now in a position to give the world all the good things that Britain offered in her Empire without any of the disadvantages of nineteenth-century colonialism." [2] The vision was not Nixon's alone. It was in the air. "We are not without cunning," declared an expert on economic affairs. "We shall not make Britain's mistake. Too wise to govern the world, we shall merely own it." [3]

---

[2] Garry Wills, *Nixon Agonistes: The Crisis of the Self-Made Man* (Boston: Houghton Mifflin, 1970), p. 20.

[3] Quoted in Charles Levinson, *Capital, Inflation and the Multinationals* (London: Allen & Unwin, 1971), pp. 73–74.

The reality that supported this vision was the growth of the multinational corporations. Old alliances became less important in the 1960's, in part because of diminished Cold War tensions (especially in Europe), but to an even greater extent because of the growth of interlocking corporate power on the world scene. By the end of the decade the multinationals had become formidable rivals to nation-states. On the basis of output alone, fifty-four out of the first one hundred economic powers in the world were not countries but enterprises. General Motors, for example, with a total of $24,000,000,000 in 1969 stood fifteenth on the list, behind Spain, Sweden, and Holland, but ahead of Belgium, Argentina, and Switzerland.

The multinationals seemed to offer a solution to a variety of older problems. One was the old issue of how to reconcile rivalries between industrial nations for markets and raw materials. The nineteenth-century solution, a loose open-door alliance among metropolitan powers in the colonial areas, had never had a chance. It was first tried in the 1880's at the Berlin Conference on the Congo, when each of the major European nations agreed to respect the principle of equal treatment for all economic enterprise in the Congo basin regardless of nationality. The United States pushed the same idea in the following decade as an answer to the threat of China's dismemberment and partition. Woodrow Wilson's determined effort to found a League of Nations based on Fourteen Points of enlightened liberal capitalism climaxed nearly fifty years of searching for the means to overcome nationalism and war. But World War II came anyway. The multinationals, it was hoped, would make nationalism, at least that kind of exaggerated nationalism that led to war, obsolete.

Second, the multinationals might stand a better chance of resolving tensions between industrial nations and underdeveloped countries. By bringing in partners from other capital-exporting nations, an individual American firm interested in investing in some Latin American country could get around local laws by making the proposed enterprise into a joint venture. This strategy would also spread whatever political and economic risks were present in the situation among several nations, and effectively increase the protection for all. If this were handled in a sophisticated manner, it would be difficult for political leaders in the host countries to charge that such enterprises were manifestations of British neo-colonialism or Yankee imperialism.

Third, corporate leaders in America began to see the multinationals as the answer to reintegrating Russia, and even China, into the world economy. American economic policymakers lagged behind their European counterparts in this respect but, once convinced of the soundness of the idea, went at it with growing enthusiasm. Judd Polk, an economist with the U.S. Council of the International Chamber of Commerce, testified before the Joint Economic Committee of Congress in 1970 that broad "interproducing arrangements" between the United States and "the Eastern world" had not been achieved, but that Russian interest in such arrangements with Fiat, an Italian-based firm, and the Ford Motor Company indicated what could develop in the future, politics permitting. At the conclusion of the hearings, Illinois Senator Charles Percy, formerly chairman of the board of Bell and Howell, which had an interproducing arrangement with Japanese camera lens manufacturers, declared:

I have always said that European countries look on us as suckers when they see restrictions by the U.S. Government on our doing business with Eastern European countries when goods are freely available in France, Germany, Great Britain, and other countries. They are amazed that we have such blinders on. In our ideological battle, what we forget is that what we lack is gold, and what we need is trade. We need to improve the balance of payments, and we are restricting artificially our doing business abroad and opening these markets to European countries.

The Vietnam War, paradoxically, speeded up the formation of a post–Cold War consensus. Despite Secretary of State Dean Rusk's insistence upon drawing analogies between the German threat in the 1930's and North Vietnam's "aggression" against the South Vietnamese, it was difficult for many to believe that "appeasement" was a real issue in this case. The more the administration harped on the point, the more recalcitrant congressional critics became.

None of America's old Cold War allies supplied material or moral aid, and some even took advantage of the situation to increase shipping to North Vietnam. Others began to feel, as Senator Percy said, that America was being taken for a sucker in Vietnam by a corrupt and venal regime that lacked popular support, and that survived only because of the presence of 500,000 American troops. The growing dissatisfaction with administration responses led Senator Stuart Symington, once a firm defender of Cold War orthodoxy, to pose this question to Secretary Rusk:

Senator Symington: At the end of the German war, European war, we split Germany and stayed over there with billions of dollars and hundreds of thousands of people. We have nearly a million people living in Europe today, counting dependents.

The next was China. Everybody else went home but we stayed around with billions of dollars and some people.

Then we agreed to split Korea, and just about everybody else went home and we stayed around, with billions of dollars and tens of thousands of people.

Now, it looks as if we may split a fourth country, and stick around with billions of dollars and hundreds of thousands of people.

How many more splits do you think this economy can take? Putting it another way, how long do you think the United States can be almost the only financier of freedom and at the same time the defender of freedom, as it is, if our balance-of-payments problems continue to worsen?

Rusk slid around the main issue by replying that the United States had not split the countries Symington had named. When the Senator pressed him, the Secretary of State would say only, "We have to do what is required." The limits of what was required and what was possible were reached in 1968, when, following the February Tet offensive by the Vietcong and the North Vietnamese, President Lyndon Johnson summoned a "Council of Wise Men" to the White House. Their advice was to find a way out, before this country's political and economic institutions were damaged even more seriously than they had been already.

Johnson's decision to step aside in favor of Vice-President Hubert Humphrey left room for Richard Nixon to move out ahead in the 1968 presidential campaign. Robert Kennedy's assassination eliminated the possibility, moreover, that the Democrats would repudiate their President and his war policies. The 1960 situation was, in effect, reversed in this election year. Now it was Humphrey who was not his own man, dependent upon the "old man" in the White House, and forced to defend policies he personally disliked. Nixon, on the other hand, had been set free. While Humphrey continued to warn about the danger of Communist China in Southeast Asia, Nixon was already calling for a reassessment of our China policy. "We simply cannot afford to leave China forever outside the family of nations," he wrote in the fall of 1967 in *Foreign Affairs*.

Humphrey was addressing the audience Nixon had hoped to reach in 1946, 1948, 1950, 1952, 1956, 1960, and 1962; Nixon was writing for the foreign policy elite. The article was designed to show that the "new" Nixon was adept at something more than old Cold War clichés. In addition, he gave a new twist to an old tale—the winning of the West—and made it sound attractive to corporate leaders in a postwar Asia. "In a sense it could be said that a new chapter is being written in the winning of the West: in this case, a winning of the promise of Western technology and Western organization by the nations of the East."

Nixon's selection of Harvard Professor Henry Kissinger as his chief foreign policy adviser further reassured those who remained doubtful that he would know how to run the shop he would inherit from Kennedy and Johnson. Kissinger's balance-of-power views blended perfectly with the Republican candidate's vision of the future. Nixon had already decided on the main lines of his foreign policy, however, beginning with an effort to reach an understanding with the nations of Western Europe. He wanted to explain the "real world" as it now appeared to American policy-makers and to offer the Europeans an insight into how his administration proposed to find the best way to live in it.

"The West does not today have the massive nuclear predominance that it once had," the President informed the April 10, 1969, NATO Council meeting, "and any sort of broad-based arms agreement with the Soviets would codify the present balance." It was a remarkable statement. For two decades American policy-makers had warned against negotiating with the Soviets except from a position of strength. The search for a perfect negotiating position was, of course, a way of avoiding serious disarmament discussions. Nixon spoke about the need for keeping up conventional strength to ensure a flexible military response in an emergency, but the emphasis clearly was on facing up to a permanent condition of nuclear parity. The remainder of his remarks were concerned with setting new goals for the alliance in order to achieve "a new sense of idealism and purpose in coping with an automating world.'' The automating world, it should be noted, was peopled with new citizens, the multinationals.

Nixon expanded on another element of his European policy in a background news conference with editors on October 12, 1970. The North Atlantic Treaty Organization had been set up in 1949 not alone to protect Western Europe from Soviet aggression, but for another very important reason as well—to find a home for the West Germans. Germany, he continued, was still the heart of the problem in Europe. For twenty years the United States had insisted that nothing be changed in the status of Berlin, the former German capital, located since the war deep within the Soviet occupation zone. Twice East-West tensions over Berlin had reached a crisis point—first in 1948–49 at the time of the Berlin blockade, and then again from 1959 to 1961 when Khrushchev threatened to impose a unilateral solution. Kennedy's special task force of advisers on Germany, headed by former Secretary of State Dean Acheson, had warned in the latter crisis against budging an inch. If necessary, Acheson said, the United States must appear ''irrational'' on the subject of Berlin. The Western sectors of the city were an outpost of freedom behind the Iron Curtain, and a promise that the United States would carry out its commitments.

On a visit to West Berlin in February, 1969, President Nixon called for an end to Cold War tensions in the city. Acheson was disturbed by this turn of events, and by the administration's encouragement of West German efforts to negotiate something like a permanent Berlin settlement. Nevertheless, a four-power pact was signed on September 3, 1971. In exchange for firm guarantees that civilian traffic between the city and the Federal Republic of Germany would not be impeded by Russian or East German actions, the Western powers promised that West Berlin would not be incorporated into the Federal Republic. Ten years earlier the United States would have rejected any offer to the Russians including such a pledge, and stood ready to fight if the Soviets had insisted upon "normalizing" the Berlin situation.

After touring Asia in the summer of 1969, the President announced his so-called "Nixon Doctrine" for lowering the risks of future Vietnams. From now on, he said, the United States would supply a nuclear shield for nations threatened by big-power aggression, but in the case of those threatened by "other types" of aggression, it would fall to the country itself to provide the manpower. Critics pointed out that it was an ambiguous statement, as indeed it was, but by June, 1971, more than 57,000 troops had been withdrawn from South Korea, Thailand, Japan, and the Philippines.

Vietnam remained the key foreign policy issue—and the key domestic political issue. The word was out that all Nixon wanted was a "decent interval" to allow him to withdraw American ground forces in an orderly manner without making it appear that Vietnam had been a military defeat. His speeches to the American public, on the other hand, did not indicate a willingness to settle for a chance to save face. On several occasions he admitted that the original decision to go into Vietnam could be debated, but the pressing question was how to get out safely, without suffering "a collapse of confidence in American leadership" that would not be limited to Asia.

Until the Cambodian "incursion" of May, 1970, Nixon managed to keep the anti-war protest off-balance by announcing small troop withdrawals. The "plan" he had talked about during the 1968 campaign turned out to be nothing more than a "hope" that the Soviets would help the United States to extricate itself by convincing the North Vietnamese to accept an offer of a political role for the Vietcong in a freely elected government in Saigon. When this hope disappeared, and when it became apparent that "Vietnamization" (the process of replacing American ground forces with a modernized Vietnamese army supported by an expanded American air role) was not working, he decided upon an invasion of "Communist sanctuaries" in nearby Cambodia. There were reports that both Secretary of Defense Melvin Laird and Secretary of State William Rogers had expressed doubts about the plan. But Nixon was determined to go ahead. "Nixon is facing his Rubicon," a high official in the State Department told reporters.

The operation may have gained him the time he felt had been running out in South Vietnam, but it widened the war in ways that would effectively reduce the President's later options. The color of the corpses was indeed changing, as the American ambassador in Saigon had once said in explaining Vietnamization, but the end of the war was nowhere in sight. The bombing campaign was resumed, at an even higher level than under Lyndon Johnson, with the same result. A second "incursion," into Laos, in the spring of 1971 proved to be a disaster. Far from demonstrating that the South Vietnamese could "go it alone," the only conclusion was that without overwhelming American naval and air support the Saigon regime was doomed.

The President had reached down to the bottom of the barrel and come up empty-handed. Then on July 15, 1971, the President made a surprise appearance on national television to announce that he had accepted an invitation to visit the People's Republic of China. He explained afterward that he had had Peking "very much in mind" in his inaugural address, announcing that, after a period of confrontation, "we are entering an era of negotiation." It was far better for the chances of a lasting peace in Asia, the President said in a lengthy report to Congress on February 9, 1972, "that the People's Republic of China play its appropriate role in shaping international arrangements that affect its concerns. Only then will that great nation have a stake in such arrangements; only then will they endure." The last President to talk about an "appropriate role" for China had been Franklin D. Roosevelt. The subject came up during a candid exchange between F.D.R. and Stalin at the 1943 Teheran Conference. At issue was the American insistence that China participate in the big-power directorate for the postwar world.

Marshal Stalin then stated he still was dubious about the question of Chinese participation.

The President replied that he had insisted on the participation of China in the Four-Power Declaration at Moscow not because he did not realize the weakness of China at present, but he was thinking farther into the future and that after all China was a nation of 400,000,000 people, and it was better to have them as friends rather than as a potential source of trouble.

Stalin's doubts were shared by his successors, right down to Alexei Kosygin and Leonid Brezhnev. Indeed, Nixon took into account those doubts and questions in calculating the positive results to be gained from reopening the door to China. Whatever else it accomplished, a Sino-American "connection" would give the Soviets pause and might encourage serious negotiations on a broad range of issues.

Roosevelt had hoped that a unified China might replace Japan as the principal stabilizer in postwar Asia. There was a similar concern in the background when President Nixon arrived in Peking. Chinese Premier Chou En-lai readily offered his interpretation of the new American policy to anyone, especially Americans, who was willing to listen. It was really quite simple, Chou told a *New York Times* editor: the United States was concerned about Japan. Referring to statements emanating from Washington about Japan's resurgence as a powerful competitor, Chou called special attention to Nixon's August 6, 1971, warning in Kansas City that, "four other powers [Russia, Western Europe, China, and Japan] have the ability to challenge us on every front."

Speaking to a group of American students, a delegation representing the Committee of Concerned Asian Scholars, Chou expanded on this theme:

The revival of Japanese militarism is being single-handedly by U.S. imperialism. President Nixon also admitted this point in his public statements saying that they are fostering their former enemies. But now Nixon is also saying that Japan is his competitor.

The Chinese Premier's cool analysis of the shift in U.S. policy was no doubt intended to cause consternation in Tokyo, and should be regarded in that light. But Nixon's sudden announcement of his trip to Peking caused even more consternation in Tokyo. The Japanese had not been consulted, or even informed, about the journey Nixon planned to Peking. To some Americans and Japanese there was a distinct feeling of *déjà-vu* in the way Washington was handling its supposedly new China policy. Memories of four decades of big-power rivalry and intrigue over China came back to the consciousness with a sudden rush of foreboding.

There was a key difference, however—China was no longer the object of the diplomatic game. It was one of the players. If the United States was to reduce its military presence in the Far East, moreover, at least a minimal Sino-American understanding was essential. Neither Peking nor Washington wanted Japan to move into the vacuum in Southeast Asia, either politically or militarily. Without some assurance of such an understanding, the unstable countries of Southeast Asia might look to Tokyo for support. And ambitious figures in Japan could use that situation to promote a serious revival of militarism. A few statements along these lines had already been overheard by Western reporters—remarks about the need for a naval force to protect trade routes, and so on.

What risk was there, on the other hand, that Nixon's China policy, or at least the method of handling that policy, might produce the very result it was intended to forestall? No one could predict the final outcome. Or what would happen if, as many still feared, those same countries started moving toward Peking? Again, no one had the answer. The first returns in Asia seemed encouraging. For more than twenty years the truce line in Korea had been a taut barrier between "Communism" and the "Free World." Several times it had almost snapped. But now it was lowered to allow a North Korean delegation to travel to Seoul for talks on the possible reunification of the divided country.

Exactly one month after announcing his acceptance of the invitation to visit China, President Nixon once again startled both his friends and his critics, this time with a declaration of his New Economic Policy. The United States, having aided the economies of the major industrial nations to recover from the war, would no longer compete "with one hand tied behind her back." New restrictions on imports and other measures would continue in effect until other nations agreed to cooperate in reducing barriers against American trade, and took steps to correct unfair exchange rates that gave them an advantage in the U.S. domestic market.

The Japanese called this statement "Nixon Shock." The President's NEP, coming on top of the China turnaround, seemed clearly directed at them. That was not entirely accurate, but economic relations with Japan were an example, probably the best, of a persistent condition government economists in the United States were saying would produce a greater-than-$2,000,000,000 trade deficit overall for 1971 and the first since 1893, a year of panic and depression. Japanese-American trade balances for that year just happened to reflect exactly the same deficit balance, $2,000,000,000. More important than those figures, which at $6,000,000,000, overall would be even worse in 1972, was the pattern of Japanese-American trade, which was increasingly asymmetrical. The bulk of Japan's imports from the United States were agricultural products and industrial raw materials; its exports to this country were increasingly concentrated in sophisticated technology-intensive products. When one looked at Japan's trade with other nations in the world, moreover, its surplus, largely because of these products, was $4,000,000,000 in 1970, $6,000,000,000 in 1971, and was projected to reach $11,000,000,000 by 1975.

Putting it all together, the Cold War world view that Richard Nixon had once helped to formulate was simply no longer capable of sustaining either American power or prosperity. Fifty years earlier, in 1921, Lenin had called off (at least for the time being) the world revolution and announced a New Economic Policy. Comparisons with the Nixon shift were obvious; the President had called off the world counterrevolution (at least for the time being) and announced a New Economic Policy.

The China visit enabled the United States to take maximum advantage of the Sino-Soviet split. In Vietnam, for instance, American policy-makers had for more than five years wanted to bomb Hanoi and mine Haiphong Harbor, but had always concluded that the risks were too great. The attacks might drive the Chinese and Russians back together and lead to a much wider war. When the North Vietnamese 1972 spring offensive threatened to divide South Vietnam in two along a line south of Hue, Nixon gambled that he could get away with both measures— and won. He was still a long way from "winning" the war, however, or even from securing a "decent interval" before the Saigon government collapsed.

In the first nine months of 1972 the bombs dropped in

Southeast Asia had exceeded the total of 1971. More than 800,000 tons of "air ammunition" had been used over North and South Vietnam, Cambodia, and Laos. Over a longer period, twenty-one months, Nixon had ordered 1,560,000 tons dropped on Vietnam, more than the total delivered against German targets between 1940 and 1945. Aggregate figures for the last seven and one-half years showed that the United States had launched 7,550,800 tons of explosives against targets in North and South Vietnam, roughly three and one-half times the tonnage of explosives used by the Allies in all theaters of war in World War II.

Nixon had scheduled a visit to the Soviet Union in May, 1972. The bombing campaign and the mining of Haiphong Harbor caused hardly more than a ripple in Soviet-American relations. Whether it was the China visit or something more, the Soviets behaved as if nothing unusual had happened in Vietnam when Nixon arrived in Moscow. A strategic arms limitation agreement was signed with great ceremony and handshaking all around. The Russians were even amenable to reopening negotiations on the settlement of their World War II Lend-Lease debt to the United States. No President had succeeded in convincing the Russians to pay up that obligation or even to talk about the question. More significant, no President since Harry S Truman *had wanted* the Russians to talk seriously about the matter of repayment. Truman and his successors, both Democratic and Republican, were happy enough with the situation, which they could cite as one more example of Soviet perfidy and general disregard for obligations. The United States had sent the Russians about $12,000,000,000 in Lend-Lease aid in World War II; Nixon's negotiators were thinking in terms of $750,000,000 or less, as a final settlement!

With a Lend-Lease settlement, the President could ask Congress for credit to expand Russian-American trade.

The Soviet Union and China offered potentially huge markets for technology-intensive exports, the very kind of manufactures that Japan and Western Europe were exporting to the world with great success, often at American expense. If the Great China Market was at last about to materialize, and if there was also to be a Great Russian Market, it was essential for the United States to get in early, and not come trailing after the other industrial powers. Once again the first results were highly encouraging: the Chinese agreed to purchase ten passenger aircraft from the United States in the summer of 1972, while Soviet purchases of American wheat totaled 25 percent of the crop for that year.

Liberals, many of whom had just shed hawks' feathers, harped on the theme that there was no "new" Nixon, only the same calculating, unprincipled exponent of the expedient. Ironically, those very "qualifications" made Nixon, in Garry Wills' phrase, the appropriate man in a "new" world setting. He could improvise and carry out policies liberal Democrats had advocated only in private, and not fear the public's response. He failed in Vietnam in his first term for precisely the same reason that John Kennedy and Lyndon Johnson failed there. Like them, Nixon believed that Vietnam was somehow a crucial test of American will and stamina. Even after he threw over the outdated Cold War world view and brought home more than half a million soldiers from Vietnam, he was still clinging to the belief that a "defeat" in Indochina would have worldwide implications. It was a fixation shared by at least three Presidents. "I am not going to lose Vietnam," Lyndon Johnson had said the weekend of John Kennedy's assassination. "I am not going to be the President who saw Southeast Asia go the way China went."

That seemed absurd in 1972, all the more so when juxtaposed with TV pictures of Richard Nixon quoting Mao Tse-tung: "So many deeds cry out to be done, and always urgently. The world rolls on. Time passes. Ten thousand years are too long. Seize the day, seize the hour."

BOMBING A PATH OUT OF VIETNAM

Nixon had promised that Vietnam would not be a campaign issue in 1972. His opponent, Senator George McGovern, had banked on the President's inability to keep that promise. When asked about the President's other achievements in foreign policy, McGovern replied tartly that it was a little like being told that your physical condition was all right, except for lung cancer. Less than two weeks before the election, on October 26, 1972, Henry Kissinger told a hastily convened press conference that "peace was at hand" in Vietnam. Only a few minor details remained to be worked out.

The Democrats had feared just such a ploy. In this instance, however, it appeared that the North Vietnamese had forced the issue by releasing details of a draft peace agreement. Perhaps Hanoi believed that it could forestall a possible Nixon repudiation of the draft by making it public just before Americans went to the polls. McGovern's chances of winning, and, therefore, of being able to end the war quickly as he promised, must already have seemed nil to the North Vietnamese and their Vietcong allies. They were ready to take Nixon's advice and come to terms before the election—but they were also anxious to make sure that the terms they signed before the election were those they would be asked to accept after the election. Given the mix-up after the 1954 Geneva Accord on Vietnam, which the United States had interpreted to mean the establishment of two Vietnams, who could blame them?

After listening to Kissinger's recital of the draft agreement, a newsman asked: "Do you feel that this program

could not have been achieved four years ago?" The negotiator replied that there had been no possibility of such an
agreement four years ago, because before the other side
had always insisted on linking military and political questions, on predetermining the political future of South Vietnam. Xuan Thuy, Hanoi's No. 2 negotiator, disagreed
flatly. He said on November 5, 1972: "If the U.S. had accepted those points [in the agreement] in 1969, we would
have accepted conditions like the present ones."

North Vietnam had not achieved all it wanted in the October draft agreement; it had not been able to force an immediate resignation of the Thieu government in Saigon.
On the other hand, the agreement, as read to the press in
Paris with explanations by Le Duc Tho, talked about "two
present administrations in South Vietnam," and required
them to "hold consultations" and to schedule general
elections. Americans had been fighting and dying in Vietnam for a decade to prevent recognition of the Vietcong
on an equal basis with the Republic of South Vietnam. The
most Nixon had been willing to grant was a political
share; the most the North Vietnamese had been demanding was a coalition government.

Other terms in the draft agreement raised doubts about
Kissinger's insistence that it marked a significant departure from previous North Vietnamese demands. There
was a provision, for example, permitting the North Vietnamese to retain what was estimated to be more than
100,000 troops in place in the south during the truce period. Previous elections in South Vietnam (and those in
the North, of course) had been determined by who occupied the territory in which the elections were held. If Thieu
could not control the territory with his own men, he could
not win the general election. That was axiomatic. Washington had not gotten Thieu's agreement to such terms,
nor could it in succeeding days. That was one of the
"minor details" yet to be worked out.

After consultations in Saigon, Kissinger had to go back to Paris and ask that the document be re-negotiated on what the North Vietnamese and Vietcong representatives complained were "the most principled, most important questions." Kissinger kept up a good face, stressing that "we have an agreement that is 99 percent completed." But he said later, "What remains on the agreement itself is a fundamental point." In reply, the North Vietnamese re-opened a few points of their own for further discussion.

By mid-December the two sides were almost back to the beginning. Nixon was infuriated. The other side was not negotiating seriously, he said; it was preparing to launch a new military offensive. Kissinger tried to make that argument stick, telling the press that the real reason for the breakdown was that the North Vietnamese had gone back on agreements concerning the size and duties of an international truce team. He admitted that at issue was still the question of Saigon's authority, or lack thereof, over areas where the North Vietnamese troops remained. He did not say what questions the United States had asked to have re-discussed.

What came next is still a matter of dispute, and will probably remain so for years to come. Unable to convince Thieu, or to budge the North Vietnamese, the President ordered a resumption of heavy bombing in the Hanoi-Haiphong area. The bombing would continue, warned White House aides, until the other side came back to the peace table prepared to negotiate in good faith. Heavy damage was done to North Vietnam as wave after wave of B-52's struck at targets in the heavily populated areas around the capital city. Aircraft losses were heavy, too, as North Vietnam's ground-to-air missiles (supplied by the Soviet Union) found their targets.

When talks resumed in January, both sides claimed credit for the achievement. A settlement was signed, which both sides promptly labeled victory, or, in President Nixon's favorite phrase, "peace with honor." The October document had as its first article: "The United States respects the independence, sovereignty, unity and territorial integrity of Vietnam as recognized by the 1954 Geneva agreements." The first article of the final agreement actually read: "The United States and all other countries respect the independence, sovereignty, unity and territorial integrity of Vietnam as recognized by the 1954 Geneva Agreements on Vietnam." The slight change here, and in other places in the two documents may have been worth the added pain and destruction. Diplomats have their reasons which are often not apparent to lesser mortals, yet the essential fact is that the United States had fully recognized the legitimacy of the original Geneva agreement, *and* the North Vietnamese contention that there was but one Vietnam.

Vice-President Spiro Agnew made a well-publicized tour through Asia after the peace-signing ceremonies were concluded, making sure that newsmen reported his repeated insistence at each stop along the way that the United States still recognized only the Saigon regime as the legitimate government of South Vietnam. Yet the document itself had the last word even on this point: There were only "two South Vietnamese parties" mentioned, no South Vietnamese government(s). These parties were obliged, as in the October draft, to organize "free and democratic general elections."

For years Republicans, often with Nixon as their spokesman, had demanded that the United States see it through this time, that there be no "elegant bug-out" in Southeast Asia. Nixon had insisted time and again that the future was too important to risk the consequences of not living up to national commitments. Indeed, the era of negotiations he talked about could not begin if America proved itself unworthy. With the nation's emotions ab-

sorbed in the drama of the returning POWs, few stopped
to think about the terms of the peace the United States
had in fact imposed on its ally in Saigon. But skeptics had
been saying even before the truce agreement that Nixon
was backing out of the saloon with his six-shooters blaz-
ing.
So what, said others. The Cold War was over, wasn't it?
The President had achieved peace with honor all along
the line, in Berlin, in Peking, and in Moscow. Kissinger
himself went to Hanoi in mid-February, 1973, to inaugu-
rate talks with the North Vietnamese on American economic aid for the postwar reconstruction of their country.
Ironically, the President faced a new alliance of former
"hawks" and "doves" in Congress against any plan to rebuild Vietnam. Among the opponents, Senator George
McGovern was perhaps the most surprising, and, to many
supporters, the most disappointing.

From Hanoi Kissinger went to Peking, a prelude to the
announcement that China and the United States were re-
suming something like formal diplomatic relations, and
on to Tokyo, where Kissinger talked with Japanese officials about cooperation in problems of Indochinese reconstruction. A few days later a truce was signed in Laos.
There was a strong likelihood that hostilities would end
soon in Cambodia as well, thus bringing to an end the war
which had begun against French colonialism, and which
had become America's longest war.

Whether or nor the North Vietnamese and the Vietcong
in 1969 would have accepted the terms they finally settled
for cannot yet be answered from available documents. It
does seem clear, however that question is answered, that
Nixon would not have accepted those terms then. Still, his
management of the Vietnam crisis, right down to the
agreement itself, was a study in Cold Warriormanship at
its best (or worst, depending on one's point of view).

Nixon's determination to prepare America for the new era in international relations was already apparent in economic measures announced in his 1973 budget message to Congress. Liberals complained that his dropping of many Great Society welfare programs reflected a basic conservative insensitivity to the plight of the poor and racial minorities. Perhaps. More likely they were underestimating their man once again. Even if he fails, it probably will not be for the reasons liberals attribute to Nixon and the men around him. To be sure, the President *is* "hung-up" on the protestant work ethic, but as *Business Week* magazine headlined its January 20, 1973, story on the President's new economic team for the second administration, he was seeking: "A structure to mesh domestic and international economic policymaking." The article continues: "Faced with a balance-of-payments deficit that has totaled $40-billion in the past two years, and the worst trade deficit in nearly a century, Administration bargainers [in international negotiations] must come up with something that works better for the U.S. than the old monetary system and trade rules did."

Something that works better, also, than the Cold War.

SECTION

THE COLD WARRIOR TRANSFORMED

RICHARD NIXON'S VIEWS ON THE COLD WAR AND ON LIBERAL FAILURES IN THAT STRUGGLE WITH "WORLD COMMUNISM" WERE ALWAYS CLEAR-CUT. THEY SEEMED TO GET STRONGER AS THE CRISIS IN VIETNAM DEEPENED. THEN, IN 1967, IN AN ARTICLE ADDRESSED TO AN ENTIRELY DIFFERENT AUDIENCE, NIXON TOOK THE "LONG VIEW" AND SUGGESTED WHAT AMERICAN POLICY SHOULD BE IN A POST-WAR ASIA.

ADDRESS BY RICHARD M. NIXON TO THE COMMONWEALTH CLUB OF CALIFORNIA APRIL 2, 1965

Today the most difficult decision facing President Johnson is South Vietnam, the most difficult decision he will make during his Presidency, I believe, at home or abroad. And it is the most important decision for the United States and the free world.

There are times when the loyal opposition should support an administration. Lyndon B. Johnson needs this support not only because of the validity of his policy but because there is a deep division in his own party.

Our greatest danger to the future of our policy on Vietnam is because the Democratic party is divided. Forty-five Democratic Senators have indicated opposition.

The interests of America, the free world and of South Vietnam are being served by the present policy.

Some claim the United States has no legal right in South Vietnam and that we are involved in a civil war. Some say the war will not be won because the Vietnamese are not willing to do what is necessary.

Others believe that, even if the war could be won, the risks are too great. Many suggest another way out—negotiation—neutralization.

Lyndon Johnson should answer each of these objections now. He might well have done this before now. Not enough people know why we should support the South Vietnamese.

First, who is responsible for the war? If it were not for support of the guerrillas by North Vietnam there would be no war; no war, at least, which would require our support.

49

If it were not for Chinese support for North Vietnam there would be no war requiring American support.

This is a confrontation—not fundamentally between Vietnam and the Vietcong or between the United States and the Vietcong—but between the United States and Communist China.

This must not be glossed over because if we gloss it over we underestimate the risks and do not understand the stakes.

Those who question our presence ignore certain facts. In 1954 a convention was signed in Geneva guaranteeing South Vietnam its independence. The North Vietnamese are there as lawbreakers. We are there as law enforcers, by invitation of the South Vietnamese Government.

What are the risks, the stakes? First, the fate of 15,000,000 Vietnamese. Two hundred thousand Vietnamese casualties in the fight against Communism over the years, prove they have the desire and will to keep their country free and independent.

In Vietnam today there is determination of the people to save their freedom—provided they have the conviction they will win.

These are fundamental reasons the stronger course of action will be more effective than may seem today.

Fifteen million people are worth saving but many argue that this is not enough to risk major confrontation and Chinese Communist intervention.

If South Vietnam fails, through U.S. withdrawal, political settlement, or neutralization (which is surrender on the installment plan), there is no doubt that Cambodia (already on the brink) will go; that Laos, practically gone now because of our gullibility, will go; that Thailand (which wants to be on our side but has held her independence by being on the winning side) will go; that Burma, an economic basket case; and that Indonesia will go.

Indonesia will follow Sukarno and Sukarno once said

that because of the American failure in Asia, the Communists were the wave of the future and he would be on the winning side.

Indonesia has half the world's tin; half the world's rubber. It is only 14 miles from the Philippines where guerrillas and Huk activity have begun again—guerrilla activity easily supported by Indonesian Communists.

In three or four years, then, we would have the necessity of saving the Philippines. Could we avoid a major war to save the Philippines?

Japan is the biggest prize in Asia, a miracle of economic recovery, the only possible economic counterpart to China. Strong neutralist forces are now growing in Japan. If Southeast Asia goes Communist, Japan will eventually be pulled irresistibly into the Red orbit.

If the United States gives up on Vietnam, Asia will give up on the United States and the Pacific will become a Red sea. These are the stakes. And this is the reason the Johnson administration has decided to win in Vietnam—no more, no less.

The possibilities of winning? How could it be possible that, where 300,000 Frenchmen on the ground failed, 25,000 Americans can expect success? But when the French were in Vietnam they were fighting to stay in— while the United States is fighting to get out.

The Vietnamese had very little interest in fighting to preserve French colonialism. The Vietnamese have a very great interest in fighting against Communist colonialism. That's why they fight with a will today.

Risks must always be weighed. There is a risk of Russian intervention. This risk is small due to the logistic problems involved, and because the Soviets are not particularly interested in seeing the Chinese Communists succeed in their foreign policy objectives for Asia.

A greater risk is Chinese Communist intervention. Some say this is inevitable, that the Chinese Communists would come in to save North Vietnam from defeat. That is subject to serious question.

Comparing the situation now with Korea in 1950, there are major differences. Now Russia and Communist China are opponents. Then they were allies.

China without Russia is a fourth-rate military power. And that is the situation China must confront if it decides to intervene. That is probably the reason Communist China is talking big but acting little without risking a confrontation with the United States, at this point, over Vietnam.

Adding it all, we must assume that Communist China might intervene. What should our decision be, weighing that risk and that possibility? It must be the same, because it is a choice not between that risk and no risk—but that risk and a greater risk.

In the event that Vietnam falls, and in the event that the balance of Southeast Asia falls, in four to five years, the United States would be confronted inevitably with a war to save the Philippines or in some other area in Asia and we would be confronting a China stronger than she is now. China today is diplomatically and militarily weaker than she will ever be in the future.

Today China has a minimal nuclear capability but that capability increases daily. It is a risk we must weigh. Do we stop Chinese Communist aggression in Vietnam now or wait until the odds and the risks are much greater?

The United States must make a decision as to what our goals are to be. Our goals are presently limited to winning the war, without unconditional surrender, without destroying North Vietnam, without destroying Communist China. It is a limited objective but one which must be achieved.

What are the alternatives? Many well-intentioned people have suggested, Why not negotiate? Negotiation is a good word. All wars are ended by negotiation. But to negotiate now would mean that the United States could negotiate only surrender, coalition government, a division of South Vietnam, or neutralization, which is surrender on the installment plan.

Negotiating with the Communists now would be like negotiating with Hitler when he had France practically occupied.

We must negotiate independence and freedom for Vietnam. We cannot do that now. Once we have gained the military advantage, once North Vietnam and Communist China are convinced they cannot take over South Vietnam, then we can negotiate the freedom and independence of South Vietnam. Until then, we cannot.

Neutralization? Neutralism, where Communists are concerned, means only three things: we get in, we get out; they stay in, and they take over. That is why we can't agree to a neutralization of South Vietnam. The choice we have is to get out completely or to stay in until we achieve freedom and independence for Vietnam.

The future is our main problem. The world has been given the impression that this is our war; that we are there unilaterally for our own selfish purposes. We are there for our purposes, true, but we are there because the freedom of all Asia, not just Vietnam, is involved.

Several suggestions can be made for future policy. Once the war is won in Vietnam, we must recognize that it will only be the winning of a single battle as far as the Communists are concerned.

It took Mao twenty years to conquer China. This is Mao Tse-tung's theory of a long war. He lost many battles, but he won the long war. If Vietnam is lost to Communist China, the long war will be stepped up in Indonesia or somewhere else.

There must be a counterforce, an alternative to Mao's long war. Let me make several suggestions. There is no question as to Communist China's purpose and plan.

They have one. And they are determined. But free Asia does not have a plan. It does not have a purpose. It is necessary to mobilize free Asia's economic and military resources so there will be the lasting alternative of peace under freedom as against the long war of Communism.

President Johnson started down this road when he suggested an Asian economic plan. Let's go further; we need a conference of free Asian nations, including South Vietnam, Cambodia, Laos, Thailand, Malaysia, Burma, Indonesia, Taiwan, the Philippines, Japan, South Korea, and possibly Australia and New Zealand.

Such a conference would have three major objectives: One, economic development—a Marshall plan for Asia; a Marshall plan involving industrial development, free trade areas, and all other aspects which mean economic development for the whole area.

The difficulty is in stopping there and that is all that is suggested by the administration. Economic strength alone is not enough to stop Communism, for in South Vietnam, economic conditions are much better than in the North.

Second, in Europe, the Marshall plan could not have succeeded economically unless it had the NATO military shield. There needs to be a military alliance of free Asian nations to stop any Communist aggression against freedom.

The third step is to meet the problem of indirect aggression. There should be something like the Caracas resolution of 1954 that in event of a revolution with Communist support from abroad (as in Vietnam), all nations involved would band together to resist conquest by indirect aggression.

Now that we've stepped up military activity in Vietnam, we need to step up our diplomatic offensive in all of Asia.

We need a charter for freedom for the Pacific—an alternative to the seeming inevitability, at least to many in Asia, of Chinese Communist domination.

Often overlooked today is the fact that the economic power of the nations cited is twice as great as that of Communist China today—if it can be mobilized, if it can be united, if the United States can support it.

There is no question but that this could be the great step forward which would stop Chinese Communist aggression and the inevitable takeover of the heartland and peripheral areas of Asia as well.

I spoke of the stakes—Southeast Asia, Japan, the Pacific—but they're much greater than that. A great debate is going on in the Communist world and what happens in Vietnam will determine its course. The debate is between the hardliners in Peiping and the so-called softliners in Moscow. The softliners (oversimplified), because of a risk of confrontation with the United States, are not supporting revolutions to the same extent that they did. The hardliners say, "We must step up our tactics and support of revolution all over the world."

In the event the hardliners succeed in Vietnam, that will be the green light for aggression in Africa, Latin America —all over the world. If they are stopped in Vietnam, that will be a lesson just as Korea was a lesson on the use of overt aggression.

It will be a lesson to the Communists attempting to take over a nation through indirect aggression that the United States and the free world have an answer to it.

So what is involved here is not just Asia, but a battle for the whole world and because that is so, risks must be taken—risks which, I believe, in the long run will bring peace and freedom. But the alternatives could be war and loss of freedom.

In 1938, immediately after Munich, Winston Churchill said: "The belief that you can gain security by throwing a small state to the wolves is a fatal delusion." He was right about Czechoslovakia in 1938. And today, with regard to Vietnam, the belief that we can gain security by throwing a small state to the wolves is a fatal delusion. In this year when we honor Churchill the man, we will do well to heed Churchill's principles.

KHRUSHCHEV'S HIDDEN WEAKNESS
BY RICHARD M. NIXON

Last July 24 I went into East Berlin escorted by five carloads of Communist agents and East German newsmen. The people I met were obviously afraid to show any signs of recognition or friendship. Those who did speak to me were immediately questioned by the police.

That evening I went back to East Berlin without advance notice. This time the secret police were not aware of my presence until I had been in the city for two hours. Now people came up to me eager to express their friendship for America and their hatred of the Communist government. As I was about to cross Checkpoint Charlie and return to freedom, a man walked up in the dark. "We are glad you came to East Berlin," he said. "The Americans are our only hope."

Last summer I also visited Budapest, where seven years ago—in October 1956—Khrushchev put down a revolution, while the request of the free Hungarian government for U.S. help went unanswered. For this reason I did not expect a friendly reception. Yet everywhere my wife and daughters and I went, we were swamped by people who wanted to shake hands, or say a word of greeting, or ask a question about America. It seemed that every other person I met had a relative who had fled to the United States after the revolution. One after another, even with policemen standing nearby, said, "I wish I had gone, too."

These experiences brought back memories of my arrival in Warsaw in 1959. Only three weeks before, Khrushchev had been given a cool reception in Poland, despite the Polish government's efforts to provide a "spontaneous" demonstration of affection. The people had even been given free flowers to throw at his car in a "typical

Polish welcome." But most of the Poles simply kept the flowers.

I was therefore amazed to find that, although the time of my arrival in Warsaw and my route through the city had not been announced, 100,000 cheering people lined the streets shouting, *"Niech zyje* America"—Long live America. So many hundreds of bouquets of flowers were showered on us that the driver had to keep stopping to clear the windshield. These personal incidents could be multiplied a thousandfold by the experiences of other Americans who had traveled in Communist-controlled Eastern Europe.

And this is why Khrushchev reacted so violently to the 1959 Captive Nations Resolution in which Congress called on free people to pray for the liberation of "enslaved peoples" behind the Iron Curtain. Khrushchev knows that he is sitting on a powder keg. He knows that the overwhelming majority of the people of East Germany, Hungary, Czechoslovakia, Poland, Bulgaria and Romania hate their Communist governments and would rise against them if they thought they had a chance to succeed. He knows that millions behind the Iron Curtain would leave their homes and go to Free Europe or the United States if they were allowed to do so by their governments. And he knows that the people of the captive nations consider America their main hope for ever obtaining freedom.

POTENTIAL SELLOUT

Today, Khrushchev hopes to keep the lid on this Pandora's box of troubles for his Communist empire by negotiating a nonaggression pact between the NATO nations and the Communist Warsaw Pact group. This would give him exactly what he wants—recognition by the West of the legality and permanence of his Eastern European Communist regimes. He knows that all he now has are squatter's rights in these countries, obtained through force, subversion or coup d'état. For him, a nonaggression pact would be a quit claim deed—a legal title from the West.

Yet there are strong pressures from within as well as from outside the Kennedy administration to make such a deal. I believe that only the mobilization of an aroused and informed American public opinion will prevent the sellout of the right of 97 million enslaved people in Eastern Europe to be free. More and more we hear talk about "accommodation," "disengagement," and other devices which add up to our approval of Soviet domination of Eastern Europe. A negative do-nothing policy can only destroy the morale of millions of anti-Communists in the Communist world.

I believe the time has come for a complete change of direction and emphasis in U.S. foreign policy toward that area. We must begin by doing some clear thinking about what is at stake for the Eastern Europeans, for the Communists, and for the free world.

THE ISSUE: FREEDOM OR SLAVERY

The Communist goal is to impose slavery on the free world. Our goal must be nothing less than to bring freedom to the Communist world. Our policy must be guided by one overriding principle: we stand for freedom—not only for ourselves but for *all* people. I believe that we can and must accomplish this objective without war.

Eastern Europe is Khrushchev's greatest potential weakness; it is the area of our greatest potential strength. What, then, can we do to help these people achieve their freedom?

We must first recognize that there are some things we cannot do. There should be no loose talk of starting revolutions in these countries in which thousands of Soviet troops are stationed, with millions more poised on the border. We need only recall the tragedy of the Hungarian Revolution. This was a true people's revolution. Thousands of workers and students succeeded in overthrowing the tyrannical Communist government. Then the Soviet army marched into the streets of Budapest. The freedom fighters asked for help; we gave them sympathy. What more could have been done short of risking world war is open to question.

I think the crime committed by Khrushchev and his Communist puppets in Hungary was so great, however, that more dramatic methods should have been used to bring it to the attention of the world. First, when Khrushchev refused to withdraw his troops from Budapest, we should have broken off diplomatic relations with the Soviet Union. Second, we should have permitted the organization of "volunteers" in free countries to help the freedom fighters. This is the action the Kremlin has taken in corresponding situations. Third, when the puppet Kadar government was set up in place of the free government, we should have recognized a government-in-exile. This would have been a symbolic rallying point not only for Hungarians but for people throughout Eastern Europe who admired their courage and shared their ideals of freedom.

Americans have always contended that if we are to retain freedom for ourselves, we must support the cause of freedom for others. It is ironical that in the United States those who pride themselves on being liberal are the most violent opponents of any move to launch a peaceful offensive for freedom for the Eastern European peoples. The only appropriate "liberal" point of view is to downplay the "freedom issue" in our discussions with Khrushchev so that we can make progress on the "peace issues." To inject talk of captive nations in East-West negotiations will "rock the boat." Yet these same voices are uncompromising in demanding freedom for Angola and for the black population of South Africa.

I believe that we must have a single standard for freedom. Its denial anywhere, in any place in the world, is surely intolerable. The ghetto, that grim relic of man's injustice to man, must go, wherever it exists. And this includes Eastern Europe, the most shocking ghetto of them all. We cannot write off 97 million people—people who now live in a place they are not allowed to leave, under a government they did not choose, and with no right to demonstrate, to vote, or otherwise to voice their opinions against the tyranny which has been imposed upon them. Let us continue to be against those few remaining outposts of the old colonialism imposed by whites on nonwhites. But let us be just as vigorous in our opposition to the new Communist colonialism imposed by whites on whites which we see in Eastern Europe.

ON THE FRONT BURNER

Let us take at face value the claim that Khrushchev will be irritated by our raising the issue of freedom for the captive peoples. Is this not the time to test his intentions? We have recently agreed with him to a nuclear test ban. The "new" Khrushchev is being pictured all over the world as the leader in the fight for peace and in reducing tensions between East and West. But what has he actually done to reduce tensions?

It is claimed that the danger of a war has been lessened by the signing of the test ban. But there is no doubt that if the danger of war has been decreased, the danger of defeat without war has been substantially increased. In

Western Europe, in the United States and in Latin America the Communist parties are stepping up their programs aimed at the overthrow of free governments. Communism has made its greatest gains through this kind of indirect aggression. All signs point to an inescapable conclusion: A great new Communist offensive is being launched against the free world, an offensive all the more dangerous because it is without resort to war, difficult to recognize and to meet effectively.

We cannot meet and defeat such an offensive by a static policy of defense. It is altogether right and necessary that the President of the United States has declared to the people of West Berlin that if they are attacked we will help defend them. But our goal must not be simply to keep freedom from shrinking; we must make it grow, too. Our goal must be a free Cuba, a free Eastern Europe, a free Russia, a free China. And every policy must be directed to reach that goal through peaceful means.

The great and vital issue of freedom for the oppressed is being kept on the back burner. It is high time for us to put it on the front burner, to make it a top-priority objective in every international negotiation.

OUR ALLIES BEHIND THE CURTAIN

What are some positive things the United States could do on behalf of freedom for the 97 million people of Eastern Europe?

We must above all keep the hope of freedom alive in their hearts. This means we must resist Khrushchev's every attempt to gain recognition of the legality and permanence of Communist domination of their countries.

We must treat each of the East European countries on an individual basis. Although their governments are Communist, they are no longer a bloc in the monolithic sense.

The people in each of these nations fear and distrust the Russians. They also have great national differences among themselves. Nationalism, which is growing in Eastern Europe, is a problem for Khrushchev. But it is our ally. Congress should give the administration the power to be flexible in its economic and diplomatic policies toward each country.

We should do nothing for any of the Communist governments unless its effect will be to help the people get relief from oppression. For example, we provided nearly $2,300,000,000 in military and economic assistance to Yugoslavia from mid-1945 through mid-1962. We gave most of this because Tito had split with the Kremlin, and we believed that by subsidizing Tito we could widen the split. Now Khrushchev and Tito have thrown their arms around each other, and it is apparent that the military equipment we provided for Tito would be on the Soviet side in the event of world conflict.

We should set these goals: (1) get the Soviet occupation forces out of the countries of Eastern Europe; (2) get the Communist governments to allow citizens to leave if they desire to; (3) get the Communist governments to adopt a let-live policy toward the countries' established churches and other institutions of freedom; (4) increase direct contact with the *people,* including visits from high-ranking U.S. officials to remind them that they are not forgotten; (5) increase the exchange of publications, broadcasts, and other instruments of communication, especially those designed to keep the young people in contact with the Western world. There is a real danger that a new generation will grow up with no knowledge of any other way of life, because of lack of contact with the free world.

We should agree only to those economic programs that will have the effect of serving the objectives I have listed. Programs of trade and aid are our biggest potential weapons; at the same time, they are the most difficult to use effectively. No U.S. trade should be approved if it strengthens a Communist government's stranglehold on the people.

In policy and pronouncements, we must always distinguish between the Kremlin and puppet governments on the one hand and the people on the other. The Kremlin's failure to win the voluntary allegiance of the peoples of Eastern Europe is one of the strongest deterrents to Soviet actions that might lead to war. We must never forget that the great majority of the people living under the Communist governments are our friends.

In the Budapest railroad station, as our train was about to leave for Vienna, a railroad worker came up to me. Speaking in halting English, he said, "My brother left in 1956 and is now living in Columbus, Ohio. If you should see him, will you tell him that he was right? I should have gone, too. And I hope to join him before it is too late."

The train started to move before he finished, but he kept running alongside. "The address," he shouted. "I forgot to tell you. It is on Euclid Avenue in Columbus. Tell him I hope to join him—tell him—tell him. . . ." The train had pulled away before I could get his name.

He was trying to send a message to his brother. But as far as I was concerned he was sending a poignant and unforgettable message through me to the heart of America: "Don't let us down. We want freedom, too."

October 12, 1963

ADDRESS BY RICHARD M. NIXON AT THE HERBERT HOOVER 91ST BIRTHDATE COMMEMORATIVE PROGRAM, WEST BRANCH, IOWA AUGUST 10, 1965

This distinguished gathering, honored by the presence of General Eisenhower, is, in itself, an eloquent tribute to one of America's greatest leaders. The honor which has been accorded me to add to that tribute provides a wide and rich choice of subjects.

For over fifty years Herbert Hoover walked as an equal among the giants of the earth. We could honor him for his service as President of the United States. We could honor him for his achievements as an engineer and as an author. We could honor him for his contribution to the cause of more efficient government through the reports of the Hoover Commissions on Government Reorganization. We could honor him for the selfless service which earned him worldwide recognition as the great humanitarian of the 20th century.

But, great as were his achievements, Eugene Lyons was probably correct in concluding that Herbert Hoover will be remembered more for what he was than what he did.

In terms of public esteem, never has one man fallen so low and risen so high. Thirty-three years ago he left the White House vilified by his enemies and forsaken even by some of his friends. Like Secretary Rusk, he had learned how viciously cruel so-called scholars can be in writing of their contemporaries.

In that dreary March of 1932, Herbert Hoover could well have been described as the "man nobody knows." This warm, kind, generous, shy, witty, and progressive humanitarian was painted as a cold, heartless, selfish, aloof, humorless reactionary.

But time has a way of healing the wounds inflicted by excessive partisanship. If the commentators of the decade were cruel, the historians of the century will be kinder. Before his death he became a living example of the truth of the words Sophocles wrote 2,000 years ago: "One must wait until the evening to see how splendid the day has been."

His legion of friends can be forever grateful that Herbert Hoover was one of those rare leaders who lived to hear the overwhelmingly favorable verdict of history on his public career.

No words can add luster to the special place he has earned in the hearts of his countrymen. But let it be noted that for generations to come his magnificence in adversity will be an everlasting example to those who would achieve greatness. A lesser man would have lashed back at his critics. But, Herbert Hoover was one of those unique individuals who was capable of great anger against corruption, brutality, and evil but never against people.

His serenity, in the face of the most brutal attacks, in the end made his detractors seem like pygmies and allowed his fellow Americans to see even more clearly the great character of the giant who walked among them.

To limit my remarks on this occasion to a discussion of his achievements would certainly be appropriate. But the highest tribute a nation can pay to one of its great men is to honor his principles in the adoption of national policy.

In that spirit, let us test our policy in Vietnam against the foreign policy principles of Herbert Hoover.

It would be presumptuous to say what position he would take on Vietnam if he were alive today. But the principles which would guide him in making that decision ring out true and clear from the record of his public statements.

Speaking at the Republican Convention in Chicago in 1944, he said:

"We want to live in peace.

"We want no territory.

"We want no domination over any nation.

"We want the freedom of nations from the domination of others.

"We want it both in the cause of freedom and because there can be no lasting peace if enslaved people must ceaselessly strive and fight for freedom."

There was no fuzzy-mindedness in his analysis of the cold war. To him the choice between communism and freedom was crystal clear. He said: "The world is divided by opposing concepts of life. One is good, the other is evil."

Yet, while he hated the Communist idea, the great humanitarian had no hatred for the Russian people. It was his leadership after World War I which helped feed and save the lives of millions of Russian children.

In summary, the principles which Herbert Hoover would apply in making a foreign policy decision could be summed up in one sentence. He wanted peace, freedom, nonintervention, self-determination, and progress for all peoples and all nations.

America's critics at home and abroad contend that our policy at Vietnam is diametrically opposed to every one of these principles.

They contend that America is intervening in a civil war.

They contend that we are fighting a losing battle to perpetuate white colonialism in Asia.

They contend that we are on the side of reaction, resisting the forces of change and progress.

They contend that we are increasing the danger of World War III.

Even among the majority of Americans who support our policy too many seem to believe that we had no business getting involved in Vietnam in the first place and that all we can hope or try to do is to make the best of a bad situation.

There is no reason for Americans to be defensive or apologetic about our role in Vietnam. We can hold our heads high in the knowledge that—as was the case in World War I, World War II, and Korea—we are fighting not just in the interests of South Vietnam or of the United States but for peace, freedom, and progress for all people.

This is not a case of American intervention in a civil war. We are helping South Vietnam resist Communist intervention.

We are not attempting to impose American colonialism in Vietnam. We are there to prevent Communist colonialism and to preserve the rights of self-determination without outside intervention for the people of South Vietnam.

We are fighting on the side of progress for the Vietnamese people; the Communists are fighting against progress. One of the reasons the South Vietnamese have been willing to fight so long and so bravely against the Communists is that they know that North Vietnam, under Communism, is an economic slum. The per capita income of South Vietnam under freedom is twice as high as that of North Vietnam.

The greatest fallacy is the contention that U.S. policy in Vietnam increases the danger of war. On the contrary, stopping Communist aggression will reduce the danger of war. Failing to stop it will increase the danger of war.

This is true because if the Communists gain from their aggression, they will be encouraged to try it again.

It is true because if aggression is rewarded those who advocate the hard line in Peiping and Moscow will have won the day over those who favor "peaceful coexistence" and we shall be confronted with other Vietnams in Asia, Africa, and Latin America.

It is true because if the Communists gain from their aggression in Vietnam all of Southeast Asia would come under Communist domination and we would have to fight a major war to save the Philippines.

A crucial issue is being decided in Vietnam: Does the free world have an answer to the Communist tactic of taking over a free country not by direct attack as in Korea, not by winning a free election, but by fomenting and supporting a revolution? If this tactic proves unsuccessful in Vietnam, the steady Communist march to world domination will be halted. If it succeeds, the Communists will have the green light for conquest by support of revolution all over the world and we will be helpless to stop it.

This is one of those critical turning points in history. Today, Russia and Red China are not allies. Red China without Russia is a fourth-rate military power with no significant nuclear capability. Five years from now the two Communist giants may have patched up their differences. Even if they have failed to do so, Red China will then have a dangerous nuclear capability.

Time, therefore, is not on our side. If the Communist aggressors are not stopped now the risk of stopping them later will be infinitely greater.

Too much of the discussion on Vietnam has been in the dreary terms of day-to-day tactics, of targets to be hit or excluded, of the cost involved.

It is time for all Americans to raise their eyes proudly to the great goals for which we are fighting in Vietnam.

We are fighting in Vietnam to prevent World War III.

We are fighting for the right of self-determination for all nations, large and small.

We are fighting to save free Asia from Communist domination.

We are fighting for the right of all people to enjoy progress through freedom.

We are fighting to prevent the Pacific from becoming a Red sea.

To achieve these goals, Americans must be united in their determination not to fail the cause of peace and freedom in this period of crisis.

The noisy minority which constantly talks of the need to make concessions to the Communist aggressors in order to gain peace are defeating the very purpose they claim to serve. This kind of talk discourages our friends, encourages our enemies, and prolongs the war.

The Communists do not have to be told that we are for peace; they have to be convinced that they cannot win the war.

We shall agree to any honorable peace but on one issue there can be no compromise: There can be no reward for aggression.

Forcing the South Vietnamese into a coalition government with the Communists would be a reward for aggression.

Neutralizing South Vietnam would be a reward for aggression.

Forcing the South Vietnamese to give up any territory to the Communist aggressors would be a reward for aggression.

History tells us that a coalition government would be only the first step toward a complete Communist take-over.

Neutralization, where the Communists are concerned, as we learned in Laos, would mean—we get out, they stay in, they take over.

Attempting to buy peace by turning over territory to the Communist aggressors would only whet their appetites for more.

We welcome the interest of the United Nations in seeking a settlement. But we must insist that where the security of the United States is directly threatened by international Communist aggression, the final policy decision must be made by the United States and not by the United Nations.

We respect the views of nations who choose to remain neutral in the struggle between Communism and freedom. But in evaluating those views let us remember that no nation in the world could afford the luxury of neutrality—if it were not for the power of the United States.

The struggle will be long. The cost will be great. But the reward will be victory over aggression and a world in which peace and freedom will have a better chance to survive.

Herbert Hoover's record gives us guidance also with regard to our future policy when peace finally comes in Vietnam.

The man who hated Communism helped save the lives of millions of Russian people living under Communism after World War I.

The man who hated dictatorship set up the Committee for Small Nations to aid the people forced to live under Hitler's dictatorship in World War II.

Herbert Hoover took a dim view of trade or aid programs which might strengthen the power of dictatorial governments over their people. That is why he insisted that American aid to the starving Russian people be administered not by the Communist Government but by the American Relief Administration which he headed.

We must continue to step up our air and sea attacks on North Vietnam until the Communist leaders stop their aggression against South Vietnam. But completely consistent with that policy would be the establishment now of an American Committee to Aid the People of North Vietnam.

What I am suggesting is not a government-to-government program which would simply strengthen the domination of the Communist Government of North Vietnam over the people of that unhappy country but a people-to-people program. The American people through contributions to such a committee would send to the people of North Vietnam food, medicine, clothing, and other materials which would help them recover from the devastating destruction of war.

If the Government of North Vietnam raised objections to allowing an American agency to administer the program, the distribution of supplies could be undertaken by an independent agency like the International Red Cross.

Certainly a program of this type would be in the great humanitarian tradition of Herbert Hoover.

As we consider the problems we face, let us not overlook one great factor which is working in our favor in Asia.

Twelve years ago, the Communist propaganda in Vietnam and in other free Asian nations was based on one major theme—choose communism and you will enjoy a better way of life.

Today that propaganda line no longer has any credibility. Those who join the Vietcong in Vietnam do so not because they like communism, but because they fear it.

In the past 12 years the only nations in Southeast Asia and the Pacific which have enjoyed sustained economic progress are those in which freedom has been given a chance—Japan, South Korea, Taiwan, the Philippines, Thailand, and Malaysia. The economic failures have been Communist China and Communist North Vietnam, and Burma and Indonesia—both of which chose the Socialist road to economic bankruptcy.

There is a lesson in this record for America. At a time when other nations are turning toward freedom, let us not turn away from it.

Herbert Hoover spoke eloquently on this subject at West Branch on his 75th birthday:

"A splendid storehouse of integrity and freedom has been bequeathed to us by our forefathers. Our duty is to see that that storehouse is not robbed of its contents.

"We dare not see the birthright of posterity to independence, initiative, and freedom of choice bartered for a mess of a collectivist system."

Again on his 80th birthday he returned to the same theme:

"It is dinned into us that this is the century of the common man. The whole idea is another cousin of the Soviet proletariat. The uncommon man is to be whittled down to size. It is the negation of individual dignity and a slogan of mediocrity and uniformity.

"The greatest strides of human progress have come from uncommon men and women.

"The humor of it is that when we get sick, we want an uncommon doctor. When we go to war, we yearn for an uncommon general. When we choose the president of a university, we want an uncommon educator.

"The imperative need of this Nation at all times is the leadership of the uncommon men or women."

And, just one year ago on his 90th birthday, he reminded his fellow countrymen again for the last time: "Freedom is the open window through which pours the sunlight of the human spirit and of human dignity."

We were privileged to have lived in the same century with this uncommon, extraordinary man. As we meet in this typically American town, in the heartland of our country, may we honor his principles as we pay tribute to his memory.

ASIA AFTER VIETNAM
BY RICHARD M. NIXON

The war in Vietnam has for so long dominated our field
of vision that it has distorted our picture of Asia. A small
country on the rim of the continent has filled the screen of
our minds; but it does not fill the map. Sometimes dramatically, but more often quietly, the rest of Asia has been undergoing a profound, an exciting, and on balance an ex-
traordinarily promising transformation. One key to this
transformation is the emergence of Asian regionalism;
another is the development of a number of the Asian
economies; another is gathering disaffection with all the
old isms that have so long imprisoned so many minds and
so many governments. By and large the non-Communist
Asian governments are looking for solutions that work,
rather than solutions that fit a preconceived set of doc-
trines and dogmas.

Most of them also recognize a common danger, and see
its source as Peking. Taken together, these developments present an extraordinary set of opportunities for a
U.S. policy which must begin to look beyond Vietnam. In
looking toward the future, however, we should not ignore
the vital role Vietnam has played in making these developments possible. Whatever one may think of the "domino" theory, it is beyond question that without the American commitment in Vietnam Asia would be a far different
place today.

The U.S. presence has provided tangible and highly
visible proof that Communism is not necessarily the wave
of Asia's future. This was a vital factor in the turnaround in
Indonesia, where a tendency toward fatalism is a national
characteristic. It provided a shield behind which the anti-
Communist forces found the courage and the capacity to
stage their counter-coup and, at the final moment, to rescue their country from the Chinese orbit. And, with its 100

million people, and its 3,000-mile arc of islands containing the region's richest hoard of natural resources, Indonesia constitutes by far the greatest prize in the Southeast Asian area.

Beyond this, Vietnam has diverted Peking from such other potential targets as India, Thailand, and Malaysia. It has bought vitally needed time for governments that were weak or unstable or leaning toward Peking as a hedge against the future—time which has allowed them to attempt to cope with their own insurrections while pressing ahead with their political, economic, and military development. From Japan to India, Asian leaders know why we are in Vietnam and, privately if not publicly, they urge us to see it through to a satisfactory conclusion.

II

Many argue that an Atlantic axis is natural and necessary, but maintain, in effect, that Kipling was right, and that the Asian peoples are so "different" that Asia itself is only peripherally an American concern. This represents a racial and cultural chauvinism that does little credit to American ideals, and it shows little appreciation either of the westward thrust of American interests or of the dynamics of world development.

During the final third of the twentieth century, Asia, not Europe or Latin America, will pose the greatest danger of a confrontation which could escalate into World War III. At the same time, the fact that the United States has now fought three Asian wars in the space of a generation is grimly but truly symbolic of the deepening involvement of the United States in what happens on the other side of the Pacific—which modern transportation and communications have brought closer to us today than Europe was in the years immediately preceding World War II.

The United States is a Pacific power. Europe has been withdrawing the remnants of empire, but the United States, with its coast reaching in an arc from Mexico to the Bering Straits, is one anchor of a vast Pacific community. Both our interests and our ideals propel us westward across the Pacific, not as conquerors but as partners, linked by the sea not only with those oriental nations on Asia's Pacific littoral but at the same time with occidental Australia and New Zealand, and with the island nations between.

Since World War II, a new Asia has been emerging with startling rapidity; indeed, Asia is changing more swiftly than any other part of the world. All around the rim of China nations are becoming Western without ceasing to be Asian.

The dominant development in Asia immediately after World War II was decolonization, with its admixture of intense nationalism. But the old nationalist slogans have less meaning for today's young than they had for their fathers. Having never known a "colonialist," they find colonialists unconvincing as scapegoats for the present ills of their societies. If dissatisfied with conditions as they see them, the young tend to blame those now in power.

As the sharp anticolonial focus blurs, the old nationalism is evolving into a more complex, multi-layered set of concepts and attitudes. On the one hand are a multitude of local and tribal identifications—the Montagnards in Vietnam, the Han tribes in Burma, the provincial and linguistic separatisms that constantly claw at the fabric of Indian unity. On the other hand, there is a reaching-out by the governing élites, and particularly the young, for something larger, more like an Asian regionalism.

The developing coherence of Asian regional thinking is reflected in a disposition to consider problems and loyalties in regional terms, and to evolve regional approaches to development needs and to the evolution of a new world order. This is not excessively chauvinistic, but rather in the nature of a coalescing confidence, a recognition that Asia can become a counterbalance to the West, and an increasing disposition to seek Asian solutions to Asian problems through cooperative action.

Along with the rising complex of national, subregional and regional identification and pride, there is also an acute sense of common danger—a factor which serves as catalyst to the others. The common danger from Communist China is now in the process of shifting the Asian governments' center of concern. During the colonial and immediately post-colonial eras, Asians stood opposed primarily to the West, which represented the intruding alien power. But now the West has abandoned its colonial role, and it no longer threatens the independence of the Asian nations. Red China, however, does, and its threat is clear, present, and repeatedly and insistently expressed. The message has not been lost on Asia's leaders. They recognize that the West, and particularly the United States, now represents not an oppressor but a protector. And they recognize their need for protection.

This does not mean that the old resentments and distrusts have vanished, or that new ones will not arise. It does, however, mean that there has been an important shift in the balance of their perceptions about the balance of danger, and this shift has important implications for the future.

One of the legacies of Vietnam almost certainly will be a deep reluctance on the part of the United States to become involved once again in a similar intervention on a similar basis. The war has imposed severe strains on the United States, not only militarily and economically but socially and politically as well. Bitter dissension has torn the fabric of American intellectual life, and whatever the outcome of the war the tear may be a long time mending. If another friendly country should be faced with an externally supported Communist insurrection—whether in Asia, or in Africa or even Latin America—there is serious question whether the American public or the American Congress would now support a unilateral American intervention, even at the request of the host government. This makes it vitally in their own interest that the nations in the path of China's ambitions move quickly to establish an indigenous Asian framework for their own future security.

In doing so, they need to fashion arrangements able to deal both with old-style wars and with new—with traditional wars, in which armies cross over national boundaries, and with the so-called "wars of national liberation," in which they burrow under national boundaries.

I am not arguing that the day is past when the United States would respond militarily to Communist threats in the less stable parts of the world, or that a unilateral response to a unilateral request for help is out of the question. But other nations must recognize that the role of the United States as world policeman is likely to be limited in the future. To ensure that a U.S. response will be forthcoming if needed, machinery must be created that is capable of meeting two conditions: (1) a collective effort by the nations of the region to contain the threat by themselves; and, if that effort fails, (2) a collective request to the United States for assistance. This is important not only from the respective national standpoints, but also from the standpoint of avoiding nuclear collision.

Nations not possessing great power can indulge in the luxury of criticism of others; those possessing it have the responsibility of decision. Faced with a clear challenge, the decision not to use one's power must be as deliberate as the decision to use it. The consequences can be fully as far-reaching and fully as irrevocable.

If another world war is to be prevented, every step possible must be taken to avert direct confrontations between the nuclear powers. To achieve this, it is essential to minimize the number of occasions on which the great powers have to decide whether or not to commit their forces. These choices cannot be eliminated, but they can be reduced by the development of regional defense pacts, in which nations undertake, among themselves, to attempt to contain aggression in their own areas.

If the initial response to a threatened aggression, of whichever type—whether across the border or under it —can be made by lesser powers in the immediate area and thus within the path of aggression, one of two things can be achieved: either they can in fact contain it by themselves, in which case the United States is spared involvement and thus the world is spared the consequences of great-power action; or, if they cannot, the ultimate choice can be presented to the United States in clear-cut terms, by nations which would automatically become allies in whatever response might prove necessary. To put it another way, the regional pact becomes a buffer separating the distant great power from the immediate threat. Only if the buffer proves insufficient does the great power become involved, and then in terms that make victory more attainable and the enterprise more palatable.

This is particularly important when the threat takes the form of an externally supported guerrilla action, as we have faced in Vietnam, as is even now being mounted in Thailand, and as could be launched in any of a half-dozen other spots in the Chinese shadow. Vietnam has shown how difficult it is to make clear the distinction between this and an ordinary factional civil war, and how subject the assisting power is to charges of having intervened in an internal matter. Vietnam's neighbors know that the war there is not internal, but our own allies in Europe have difficulty grasping the fact.

The fragmenting of the Communist world has lent credence to the frequently heard argument that a Communist advance by proxy, as we have seen attempted in Vietnam, is of only peripheral importance; that with the weakening of rigid central control of the Communist world, local fights between Communist and non-Communist factions are a local matter. This ignores, however, the fact that with the decentralization of Communist control has come an appropriately tailored shift in Communist tactics. National Communism poses a different kind of threat than did the old-style international Communism, but by being subtler it is in some ways more dangerous.

SEATO was useful and appropriate to its time, but it was Western in origin and drew its strength from the United States and Europe. It has weakened to the point at which it is little more than an institutional embodiment of an American commitment, and a somewhat anachronistic relic of the days when France and Britain were active members. Asia today needs its own security undertakings, reflecting the new realities of Asian independence and Asian needs.

Thus far, despite a pattern of rapidly increasing cooperation in cultural and economic affairs, the Asian nations have been unwilling to form a military grouping designed to forestall the Chinese threat, even though several have bilateral arrangements with the United States. But an appropriate foundation stone exists on which to build: the Asian and Pacific Council. ASPAC held its first ministerial-level meeting in Seoul in June, 1966, and its second in Bangkok in July, 1967. It has carefully limited itself to strengthening regional cooperation in economic, cultural, and social matters, and its members have voiced strong feelings that, as Japan's Foreign Minister Takeo Miki put it at the Bangkok meeting, it should not be made "a body to promote anticommunist campaigns."

Despite ASPAC's present cultural and economic orientation, however, the solidifying awareness of China's threat should make it possible—if the need for a regional alliance is put in sufficiently compelling terms—to develop it into an alliance actively dedicated to concerting whatever efforts might be necessary to maintain the security of the region. And ASPAC is peculiarly well situated to play such a role. Its members (South Korea, Japan, Taiwan, Thailand, Malaysia, South Vietnam, the Philippines, Australia, and New Zealand, with Laos as an observer) all are acutely conscious of the Chinese threat. All except Malaysia have military ties with the United States. It has the distinct advantage of including Australia and New Zealand, which share the danger and would be able to contribute substantially to its strength, without an unbalancing great-power presence.

I do not mean to minimize the difficulties of winning acceptance of such a concept. In Japan, public opinion still lags behind official awareness of military needs. The avowedly neutralist nations under China's cloud would be reluctant, at present, to join any such grouping. But looking further down the road we can project either an erosion of their neutralism or the formation of their own loose association or associations, which might be tied into a militarily oriented ASPAC on an interlocking or cooperative basis. One can hope that even India might finally be persuaded to give its support, having itself been the target of overt Chinese aggression, and still cherishing as it does a desire to play a substantial role beyond its own borders.

III

Military security has to rest, ultimately, on economic and political stability. One of the effects of the rapidity of change in the world today is that there can no longer be static stability; there can only be dynamic stability. A nation or society that fails to keep pace with change is in danger of flying apart. It is important that we recognize this, but equally important that in trying to maintain a dynamic stability we remember that the stability is as important as the dynamism.

If a given set of ends is deemed desirable, then from the standpoint of those dedicated to peace and an essential stability in world order the desideratum is to reach those ends by evolutionary rather than revolutionary means. Looking at the pattern of change in non-Communist Asia, we find that the professed aims of the revolutionaries are in fact being achieved by an evolutionary process. This offers a dramatic opportunity to draw the distinction between the fact of a revolutionary *result* and the *process* of revolutionary change. The Asian nations are showing that evolutionary change can be as exciting as revolutionary change. Having revolutionized the aims of their societies, they are showing what can be achieved within a framework of dynamic stability.

The "people," in the broadest sense, have become an entity to be served rather than used. In much of Asia, this change represents a revolution of no less magnitude than the revolution that created the industrial West, or that in the years following World War II transformed empires into new and struggling nations. It is precisely the promise of this reversal that has been at the heart of Communist rhetoric, and at the heart of the popular and intellectual appeal which that rhetoric achieved.

Not all the governments of non-Communist Asia fit the Western ideal of parliamentary democracy—far from it. But Americans must recognize that a highly sophisticated, highly advanced political system, which required many centuries to develop in the West, may not be best for other nations which have far different traditions and are still in an earlier stage of development. What matters is that these governments are consciously, deliberately and programmatically developing in the direction of greater liberty, greater abundance, broader choice, and increased popular involvement in the processes of government.

Poverty that was accepted for centuries as the norm is accepted no longer. In a sense it could be said that a new chapter is being written in the winning of the West: in this case, a winning of the promise of Western technology and Western organization by the nations of the East. The cultural clash has had its costs and produced its strains, but out of it is coming a modernization of ancient civilizations that promises to leap the centuries.

The process produces transitional anomalies—such as the Indian woman squatting in the mud, forming cow-dung patties with her hands and laying them out to dry, while a transistor radio in her lap plays music from a Delhi station. It takes a long time to bring visions of the future to the far villages—but time is needed to make those visions credible, and make them achievable. Too wide a gap between reality and expectation always produces an explosive situation, and the fact that what the leaders know is possible is unknown to the great mass of the peasantry helps buy time to make the possible achievable. But the important thing is that the leaders do know what is possible, and by and large they are determined to make it happen.

Whether that process is going to proceed at a pace fast enough to keep one step ahead of the pressure of rising expectations is one of the great questions and challenges of the years ahead. But there is solid ground for hope. The successful Asian nations have been writing extraordinary records. To call their performance an economic miracle would be something of a semantic imprecision; it would also be a disservice. Precisely because the origins and ingredients of that success are not miraculous, it offers hope to those which have not yet turned the corner.

India still is a staggering giant, Burma flirts with economic chaos, and the Philippines, caught in a conflict of cultures and in search of an identity, lives in a precarious economic and social balance. But the most exciting trends in economic development today are being recorded by those Asian nations that have accepted the keys of progress and used them. Japan, Hong Kong, Taiwan, Thailand, Korea, Singapore, and Malaysia all have been recording sustained economic growth rates of 7 percent a year or more; Japan has sustained a remarkable average of 9 percent a year since 1950, and an average 16.7 percent per year increase in exports over the same period. Thailand shifted into a period of rapid growth in 1958 and has averaged 7 percent a year since. South Korea, despite the unflattering estimates of its people's abilities by the average G.I. during the Korean War, is shooting ahead at a growth rate that has averaged 8 percent a year since 1963, with an average 42 percent a year increase in its exports.

These rapidly advancing countries vary widely in their social traditions and political systems, but their methods of economic management have certain traits in common: a prime reliance on private enterprise and on the pricing mechanisms of the market as the chief determinant of business decisions; a pacing of monetary expansion to match growth in output; receptivity to private capital investment, both domestic and foreign, including such incentives as tax advantages and quick government clearance of proposed projects; imaginative national programs for dealing with social problems; and, not least, a generally restrained posture in government planning, with the government's role suggestive rather than coercive. These nations have, in short, discovered and applied the lessons of America's own economic success.

IV

Any discussion of Asia's future must ultimately focus on the respective roles of four giants: India, the world's most populous non-Communist nation; Japan, Asia's principal industrial and economic power; China, the world's most populous nation and Asia's most immediate threat; and the United States, the greatest Pacific power. (Although the U.S.S.R. occupies much of the land map of Asia, its principal focus is toward the west and its vast Asian lands are an appendage of European Russia.)

India is both challenging and frustrating: challenging because of its promise, frustrating because of its performance. It suffers from escalating overpopulation, from too much emphasis on industrialization and not enough on agriculture, and from too doctrinaire a reliance on government enterprise instead of private enterprise. Many are deeply pessimistic about its future. One has to remember, however, that in the past five years India has fought two wars and faced two catastrophic droughts. On both the population and the agricultural fronts, India's present leaders at least are trying. And the essential factor, from the standpoint of U.S. policy, is that a nation of nearly half a billion people is seeking ways to wrench itself forward without a sacrifice of basic freedoms; in exceedingly difficult circumstances, the ideal of evolutionary change is being tested. For the most populous representative democracy in the world to fail, while Communist China—surmounting its troubles—succeeded, would be a disaster of worldwide proportions. Thus the United States must do two things: (1) continue its aid and support for Indian economic objectives; and (2) do its best to persuade the Indian Government to shift its means and adjust its institutions so that those objectives can be more quickly and more effectively secured, drawing from the lessons not only of the United States but also of India's more successful neighbors, including Pakistan.

Japan has been edging cautiously and discreetly toward a wider leadership role, acutely conscious at every step that bitter memories of the Greater East Asia Co-

Prosperity Sphere might rise to haunt her if she pressed too hard or too eagerly. But what would not have been possible ten, or even five, years ago is becoming possible today. Half the people now living in Asia have been born since World War II, and the new generation has neither the old guilts (in the case of the Japanese themselves) nor the old fears born of conquest.

The natural momentum of Japan's growth, the industry of her people, and the advanced state of her society must inevitably propel Japan into a more conspicuous position of leadership. Japan's industrial complex, expanding by 14 percent annually since 1950, already is comparable to that of West Germany or the United Kingdom. Japan's gross national product ($95,000,000,000) is substantially greater than that of mainland China, with seven times the population. Japan is expected soon to rank as the world's third-strongest economic power, trailing only the United States and the Soviet Union. Along with this dramatic economic surge, Japan will surely want to play a greater role both diplomatically and militarily in maintaining the balance in Asia. As the Prime Minister of one neighboring country put it: "The Japanese are a great people, and no great people will accept as their destiny making better transistor radios and teaching the underdeveloped how to grow better rice."

This greater role will entail, among other things, a modification of the present terms of the Japanese Constitution, which specifically provides that "land, sea, and air forces, as well as other war potential, will never be maintained." (Japan's 275,000 men presently under arms are called "Self-Defense Forces.") Twenty years ago it was considered unthinkable that Japan should acquire even a conventional military capability. Five years ago, while some Japanese thought about it, they did not talk about it. Today a substantial majority of Japanese still oppose the idea, but it is openly discussed and debated. Looking toward the future, one must recognize that it simply is not realistic to expect a nation moving into the first rank of major powers to be totally dependent for its own security on another nation, however close the ties. Japan's whole society has been restructured since World War II. While there still are traces of fanaticism, its politics at least conform to the democratic ideal. Not to trust Japan today with its own armed forces and with responsibility for its own defense would be to place its people and its government under a disability which, whatever its roots in painful recent history, ill accords with the role Japan must play in helping secure the common safety of non-Communist Asia.

Any American policy toward Asia must come urgently to grips with the reality of China. This does not mean, as many would simplistically have it, rushing to grant recognition to Peking, to admit it to the United Nations and to ply it with offers of trade—all of which would serve to confirm its rulers in their present course. It does mean recognizing the present and potential danger from Communist China, and taking measures designed to meet that danger. It also means distinguishing carefully between long-range and short-range policies, and fashioning short-range programs so as to advance our long-range goals.

Taking the long view, we simply cannot afford to leave China forever outside the family of nations, there to nurture its fantasies, cherish its hates, and threaten its neighbors. There is no place on this small planet for a billion of its potentially most able people to live in angry isolation. But we could go disastrously wrong if, in pursuing this long-range goal, we failed in the short range to read the lessons of history.

The world cannot be safe until China changes. Thus our aim, to the extent that we can influence events, should be to induce change. The way to do this is to persuade China that it *must* change: that it cannot satisfy its imperial ambitions, and that its own national interest requires a turning away from foreign adventuring and a turning inward toward the solution of its own domestic problems.

If the challenge posed by the Soviet Union after World War II was not precisely similar, it was sufficiently so to offer a valid precedent and a valuable lesson. Moscow finally changed when it, too, found that change was necessary. This was essentially a change of the head, not of the heart. Internal evolution played a role, to be sure, but the key factor was that the West was able to create conditions —notably in the shoring up of European defenses, the rapid restoration of European economies and the cementing of the Atlantic Alliance—that forced Moscow to look to the wisdom of reaching some measure of accommodation with the West. We are still far from reaching a full détente, but at least substantial progress has been made.

During the next decade the West faces two prospects which, together, could create a crisis of the first order: (1) that the Soviets may reach nuclear parity with the United States; and (2) that China, within three to five years, will have a significant deliverable nuclear capability—and that this same China will be outside any nonproliferation treaty that might be signed, free, if it chooses, to scatter its weapons among "liberation" forces anywhere in the world.

This heightens the urgency of building buffers that can keep the major nuclear powers apart in the case of "wars of national liberation," supported by Moscow or Peking but fought by proxy. It also requires that we now assign to the strengthening of non-Communist Asia a priority comparable to that which we gave to the strengthening of Western Europe after World War II.

Some counsel conceding to China a "sphere of influence" embracing much of the Asian mainland and extending even to the island nations beyond; others urge that we eliminate the threat by preemptive war. Clearly, neither of these courses would be acceptable to the United States or to its Asian allies. Others argue that we should seek an anti-Chinese alliance with European powers, even including the Soviet Union. Quite apart from the obvious problems involved in Soviet participation, such a course would inevitably carry connotations of Europe vs. Asia, white vs. non-white, which could have catastrophic repercussions throughout the rest of the non-white world in general and Asia in particular. If our long-range aim is to pull China back into the family of nations, we must avoid the impression that the great powers or the European powers are "ganging up"; the response should clearly be one of active defense rather than potential offense, and must be untainted with any suspicion of racism.

For the United States to go it alone in containing China would not only place an unconscionable burden on our own country, but also would heighten the chances of nuclear war while undercutting the independent development of the nations of Asia. The primary restraint on China's Asian ambitions should be exercised by the Asian nations in the path of those ambitions, backed by the ultimate power of the United States. This is sound strategically, sound psychologically, and sound in terms of the dynamics of Asian development. Only as the nations of non-Communist Asia become so strong—economically, politically, and militarily—that they no longer furnish tempting targets for Chinese aggression, will the leaders in Peking be persuaded to turn their energies inward rather than outward. And that will be the time when the dialogue with mainland China can begin.

For the short run, then, this means a policy of firm restraint, of no reward, of a creative counterpressure designed to persuade Peking that its interests can be served only by accepting the basic rules of international civility.

For the long run, it means pulling China back into the world community—but as a great and progressing nation, not as the epicenter of world revolution.

"Containment without isolation" is a good phrase and a sound concept, as far as it goes. But it covers only half the problem. Along with it, we need a positive policy of pressure and persuasion, of dynamic detoxification, a marshaling of Asian forces both to keep the peace and to help draw off the poison from the Thoughts of Mao.

Dealing with Red China is something like trying to cope with the more explosive ghetto elements in our own country. In each case a potentially destructive force has to be curbed; in each case an outlaw element has to be brought within the law; in each case dialogues have to be opened; in each case aggression has to be restrained while education proceeds; and, not least, in neither case can we afford to let those now self-exiled from society stay exiled forever. We have to proceed with both an urgency born of necessity and a patience born of realism, moving step by calculated step toward the final goal.

V

And finally, the role of the United States.

Weary with war, disheartened with allies, disillusioned with aid, dismayed at domestic crises, many Americans are heeding the call of the new isolationism. And they are not alone; there is a tendency in the whole Western world to turn inward, to become parochial and isolationist—dangerously so. But there can be neither peace nor security a generation hence unless we recognize now the massiveness of the forces at work in Asia, where more than half the world's people live and where the greatest explosive potential is lodged.

Out of the wreckage of two world wars we forged a concept of an Atlantic community, within which a ravaged Europe was rebuilt and the westward advance of the Soviets contained. If tensions now strain that community, these are themselves a byproduct of success. But history has its rhythms, and now the focus of both crisis and change is shifting. Without turning our backs on Europe, we have now to reach out westward to the East, and to fashion the sinews of a Pacific community.

This has to be a community in the fullest sense: a community of purpose, of understanding and of mutual assistance, in which military defenses are coordinated while economies are strengthened; a community embracing a concert of Asian strengths as a counterforce to the designs of China; one in which Japan will play an increasing role, as befits its commanding position as a world economic power; and one in which U.S. leadership is exercised with restraint, with respect for our partners and with a sophisticated discretion that ensures a genuinely Asian idiom and Asian origin for whatever new Asian institutions are developed.

In a design for Asia's future, there is no room for heavy-handed American pressure; there is need for subtle encouragement of the kind of Asian initiatives that help bring the design to reality. The distinction may seem superficial, but in fact it is central both to the kind of Asia we want and to the effectiveness of the means of achieving it. The central pattern of the future in U.S.–Asian relations must be American support for Asian initiatives.

The industrial revolution has shown that mass abundance is possible, and as the United States moves into the post-industrial world—the age of computers and cybernetics—we have to find ways to engineer an escape from privation for those now living in mass poverty. There can be no security, whatever our nuclear stockpiles, in a world of boiling resentment and magnified envy. The oceans provide no sanctuary for the rich, no barrier behind which we can hide our abundance.

The struggle for influence in the Third World is a three-way race among Moscow, Peking, and the West. The West has offered both idealism and example, but the idealism has often been unconvincing and the example non-idiomatic. However, an industrialized Japan demonstrates the economically possible in Asian terms, while an advancing Asia tied into a Pacific community offers a bridge to the underdeveloped elsewhere. During this final third of the twentieth century, the great race will be between man and change: the race to control change, rather than be controlled by it. In this race we cannot afford to wait for others to act, and then merely react. And the race in Asia is already under way.

October, 1967

THE LIBERAL, PERPLEXED

COLUMNIST NICHOLAS VON HOFF-
MAN DISCUSSES THE "BEFUDDLE-
MENT" ABOUT THE "NEW" NIXON
AND HOW IT GREW AFTER HE ENTERED
THE WHITE HOUSE.

PSYCHING NIXON
BY NICHOLAS VON HOFFMAN

The befuddlement about Nixon grows. Nobody can dope him out or find an internally consistent inner core. He sends his Secretary of Commerce to Russia to stimulate trade in order to right the balance of payments so we can use the money to pay for the troops who're going to fight the Russian Army when it invades Western Europe. He denounces isolationism while treating our allies and trading partners in a way that would have made Calvin Coolidge suck air.

People have already passed through the period when they thought he was nuts; now they're trying to psych him out.

One effort to find out about this little man who comes with the batteries not included appears in the current issue of *Transaction* magazine under the title "The Inner History of Richard Milhous Nixon—The best-kept secret of the Nixon administration is the missing person inside the President." Although written by two serious scholars, it reads like a parody with sentences like this: "The events of his adolescence must have reinforced Richard's emotional impoverishment, making anal control seem a safer road than oedipal rebellion or desire."

That almost explains what's going on in the Treasury Department, but not quite.

There are other folks who aren't interested in the pursuit of the real Richard Nixon; they just want him out. Among these are some of the deep conservatives who supported him in 1968. One of them, Hawaiian real estate man H. E. B. Shasteen, is reported to be thinking about suing Nixon for the return of a $1,000 campaign contribution.

He and some others of like persuasion are members of the National Taxpayers Union. The Union is hoping to send out a mailing to all of the 3,085 persons known to have given more than $500, asking them to reconsider before doing it again next year.

Since the members of the National Taxpayers Union are convinced and principled right-wingers and most campaign contributors give only to get a return on their investment, the letter will probably have little effect. Yet one suspects some of the words in it will evoke a small, sympathetic vibration even from the mass of Republicans who will doubtless stick with the President: "During his first three years in office, Mr. Nixon has demonstrated that he has no fixed principles. Apparently, there is no promise he would not break and no freedom he would not compromise in pursuit of his own success. He has already gone a long way toward remaking the Republican Party into the ideological twin brother of the liberal wing of the Democratic Party."

Programatically, Nixon appears to be far closer to a liberal Democrat than anything but a Rockefeller Republican. So why aren't liberals more pleased with him? By their lights he'd have to be judged as good or better at his job than John F. Kennedy.

In foreign policy there's hardly a comparison between the two men. Kennedy was an inflexible anti-Communist with none of Richard Nixon's talent for moving toward a worldwide accommodation with the other side. Of course, there is Cambodia, the Nixon finale to the war that Kennedy, as much as any man, started, but let's not forget the Bay of Pigs, an act of aggression against another nation for which there was less justification than Cambodia.

Domestically there's not much to choose between the two. Their economic policies are virtually identical save that Nixon applies them with more vigor and on a grander scale, bigger budget deficits and harsher controls. In the matter of judge-picking, Kennedy is ahead, although the qualitative difference between Kennedy's two Supreme Court guys, Whizzer White and Arthur Goldberg, and Nixon's Powell and Rehnquist may be difficult to appreciate in ten or twenty years.

In the lower federal courts Kennedy selected Thurgood Marshall to be a black federal judge in New York and balanced that by putting James Eastland's law partner, the ferocious Harold Cox, on the bench in Mississippi. That performance was characteristic of Kennedy's appreciation of the race question, which makes it more than ironic that many a poor black household hangs his picture in the same place that F.D.R.'s once hung.

By contrast Nixon doesn't look that bad. His handling of the bus issue has been appalling, but no worse than many Democratic liberals who've really earned the epithet "wishy-washy" on this issue. On other questions concerning race, Nixon has been up and down and in and out, but his family assistance program embodies and makes official one of the wildest liberal dreams of the 1950's.

Perhaps Nixon's problem is that he's giving us what so many of us have said we wanted. He's giving it to us like a technician, without betraying the smallest sign that he believes in it. Like Kennedy before him, he's counted our votes and gone with the prevailing sentiment.

We who squirm and fidget as this man does so many of the things we've always said we wanted can't forgive him for it. It's not just that we're finding out a lot of our ideas weren't so hot—we could live with that and learn to overlook it. It's the dispassionate, mechanistic way he's joined our side.

Soon we'll be yearning for Lyndon, that huge, flawed man who did believe. We'll be wanting him as our reform candidate.

December 3, 1971

SECTION

THE ROAD TO PEKING

"FEW EVENTS CAN BE CALLED HIS-
TORIC," NIXON SAID IN A MESSAGE TO
CONGRESS EXPLAINING THE BACK-
GROUND OF HIS FORTHCOMING VISIT
TO PEKING. WITHOUT DOUBT THE SIN-
GLE MOST DRAMATIC DEVELOPMENT
OF HIS PRESIDENCY WAS THE INITIA-
TION OF A NEW CHINA POLICY. IT
WAS ALL THE MORE REMARKABLE BE-
CAUSE IT TOOK PLACE WHILE THE WAR
IN VIETNAM STILL RAGED, AND WHILE
NIXON STILL MAINTAINED THAT A
"COMMUNIST TAKEOVER" WOULD
ENDANGER VITAL AMERICAN INTER-
ESTS. HUGH SIDEY'S BRIEF EVALUATIONS
OF THIS PARADOX ARE GEMS OF PO-
LITICAL REPORTING.

THE NEW CHINA POLICY
BY RICHARD M. NIXON

Few events can be called historic. The announcement which I read on July 15 merits that term:

Premier Chou En-lai and Dr. Henry Kissinger, President Nixon's Assistant for National Security Affairs, held talks in Peking from July 9 to 11, 1971. Knowing of President Nixon's expressed desire to visit the Peoples Republic of China, Premier Chou En-lai on behalf of the Government of the People's Republic of China has extended an invitation to President Nixon to visit China at an appropriate date before May, 1972.
President Nixon has accepted the invitation with pleasure. The meeting between the leaders of China and the United States is to seek the normalization of relations between the two countries and also to exchange views on questions of concern to the two sides.

This announcement could have the most profound significance for future generations. The course leading up to it was carefully navigated; the opening we have made is still fragile; the immediate concrete achievements may be limited. But our purpose, and now our potential, is to establish contact between the world's most powerful nation and the world's most populous nation, and to confine our future confrontations to the conference table. Contact now might help avert a disastrous catastrophe later. It should serve to enrich the lives of our two peoples. And it could lead to cooperative ventures between our countries in the future.

THE HISTORICAL SETTING

My meetings with the leaders of the People's Republic of China will be unprecedented.

103

The earliest Sino-American contacts developed in the early 1800's. At that time the ancient Chinese empire, secure and preeminent, was just beginning the painful process of adapting itself to the outside world. With the world's longest history of self-government, and as the dominant political and cultural force in their region, the Chinese were self-confident and self-contained as the "Middle Kingdom" of the world. Nevertheless they were exploited by technologically superior foreign powers. The United States—isolationist and bending its energies to national development—favored the territorial integrity of China; but our "open door" doctrine of equal treatment for all foreigners carried ambiguity in Chinese eyes.

The Communist leaders thus inherited a tradition marked by both pride and humiliation; the Chinese experience had not been one of dealing with the outside world as equals but one of either Chinese superiority or foreign exploitation. In recent years China has passed through a period of domestic turmoil and shifts in external relationships. China's leaders have decided to break the isolation that was partly self-chosen, to explore more normal relations with other countries, and to take their place in the international dialogue.

While the Chinese Revolution ran its long and tortured course the United States ended a long history of isolationism and plunged with zeal and idealism into worldwide responsibilities. We alone among the major powers emerged relatively unscathed from the Second World War. We provided the bulk of both the plans and resources for security and development around the globe. And we perceived the Communist countries, including China, as a monolithic bloc with central direction.

Today, two and a half decades after the war, new realities are reflected in a new American approach to foreign policy. The growing strength and self-confidence of others allow them to assume greater responsibilities and us to shift to a more restrained role. And with the time long past when one nation could speak for all Communist countries, we deal with individual nations on the basis of their foreign, and not their domestic, policy.

Thus, in February of 1972, after many vicissitudes, many achievements and our separate evolution, the U.S. and China enter this dialogue on a fresh foundation of national equality and mutual respect. We are both turning a new page in our histories.

Despite this hopeful beginning, we remain separated by profound differences in principle and the suspicions of decades. Until 1971 we had had little meaningful contact for most of a generation. The People's Republic's critical public statements and interpretations of history are well known to us. We have also made our position clear.

It serves no purpose to gloss over these sources of division. Neither side pretended during preparations for my journey, and neither will pretend afterwards, that we have solved our basic problems. We can expect our talks to be marked by the directness and candor which best serve leaders whose differences are deep but whose policies are rooted in realism.

A NEW APPROACH

My journey to the People's Republic of China marks both an end and a beginning. It is the culmination of three years of patient mutual effort to pierce the isolation of decades. And it represents the launching of a new process.

The July 15, 1971, statement on my trip was sudden and dramatic, but it was preceded and produced by a carefully developed series of steps. In fact, no other U.S. foreign policy move in the past three years has been approached more meticulously.

As far back as October, 1967, I had written in the journal

Foreign Affairs that "any American policy toward Asia must come urgently to grips with the reality of China," while pointing out that bold new initiatives without preparation were inappropriate.

In January, 1969, I entered office convinced that a new policy toward the People's Republic of China was an essential component of a new American foreign policy. I was, of course, fully aware of the profound ideological and political differences between our countries, and of the hostility and suspicion to be overcome. But I believed also that in this era we could not afford to be cut off from a quarter of the world's population. We had an obligation to try to establish contact, to define our positions, and perhaps move on to greater understanding.

Recalling our historical experience and contemplating tomorrow's world, I saw the present period as a unique moment. The shifting tides in international relations, our new foreign policy perspectives, the changing face of China—these were the factors, at work in Peking as well as Washington, that beckoned our two nations toward a dialogue.

The following considerations shaped this Administration's approach to the People's Republic of China:

—Peace in Asia and peace in the world require that we exchange views, not so much despite our differences as because of them. A clearer grasp of each other's purposes is essential in an age of turmoil and nuclear weapons.

—It is in America's interest, and the world's interest, that the People's Republic of China play its appropriate role in shaping international arrangements that affect its concerns. Only then will that great nation have a stake in such arrangements; only then will they endure.

—No one nation should be the sole voice for a bloc of states. We will deal with all countries on the basis of specific issues and external behavior, not abstract theory.

—Both Chinese and American policies could be much less rigid if we had no need to consider each other permanent enemies. Over the longer term there need be no clashes between our fundamental national concerns.

—China and the United States share many parallel interests and can do much together to enrich the lives of our peoples. It is no accident that the Chinese and American peoples have such a long history of friendship.

On this basis we decided that a careful search for a new relationship should be undertaken. We believed that the Chinese could be engaged in such an effort.

THE UNFOLDING OF U.S. POLICY

Both political and technical problems lay in the way of such a search. When this Administration assumed responsibility, there had been virtually no contact between mainland China and the American people for two decades. This was true for our governments as well, although sterile talks in Geneva and Warsaw had dragged on intermittently since 1955. A deep gulf of mistrust and noncommunication separated us.

We faced two major questions. First, how to convey our views privately to the authorities in Peking? Second, what public steps would demonstrate our willingness to set a new direction in our relations?

Within two weeks of my inauguration we moved on both of these fronts. I ordered that efforts be undertaken to communicate our new attitude through private channels, and to seek contact with the People's Republic of China.

This process turned out to be delicate and complex. It is extremely difficult to establish even rudimentary communications between two governments which have been completely isolated from one another for twenty years. Neither technical nor diplomatic means of direct contact existed. It was necessary to find an intermediary country which had the full trust of both nations, and could be relied upon to promote the dialogue with discretion, restraint, and diplomatic skill.

The two sides began clarifying their general intentions through mutually friendly countries. After a period of cautious exploration and gathering confidence, we settled upon a reliable means of communication between Washington and Peking.

In February, 1969, I also directed that a comprehensive National Security Council study be made of our policy toward China, setting in motion a policy review process which has continued throughout these past three years. We addressed both the broader ramifications of a new approach and the specific steps to carry it out.

Drawing on this analysis, we began to implement a phased sequence of unilateral measures to indicate the direction in which this Administration was prepared to move. We believed that these practical steps, progressively relaxing trade and travel restrictions, would make clear to the Chinese leaders over time that we were prepared for a serious dialogue. We had no illusion that we could bargain for Chinese goodwill. Because of the difficulties in communication we deliberately chose initiatives that could be ignored or quietly accepted; since they required no Chinese actions, they were difficult to reject. We purposely avoided dramatic moves which could invoke dramatic rebukes and set back the whole carefully nurtured process.

Throughout 1969 and 1970 we underlined our willingness to have a more constructive relationship:

—In July, 1969, we permitted noncommercial purchases of Chinese goods without special authorization by American tourists, museums, and others. We also broadened the categories of U.S. citizens whose passports would be validated automatically for travel to China.

—In December, 1969, we allowed subsidiaries of

American firms abroad to engage in commerce between mainland China and third countries.

—In January and February, 1970, the two sides held ambassadorial meetings in Warsaw, which in turn had been set through private exchanges. These sessions underlined the handicaps of this formal discourse. The two sides' representatives had minimum flexibility; they could do little more than read prepared statements and refer back to their capitals for instructions for the next meeting. This cumbersome exchange between wary adversaries reinforced the need for a new approach.

—In March, 1970, we announced that U.S. passports would be validated for travel to mainland China for any legitimate purpose.

—In April, 1970, we authorized selective licensing of non-strategic U.S. goods for export to mainland China.

—In August, 1970, we lifted certain restrictions on American oil companies operating abroad so that most foreign ships could use American-owned bunkering facilities on trips to and from mainland Chinese ports.

By the end of 1970, therefore, we had laid out a careful record of unilateral initiatives. Throughout these two years we had accompanied these steps with a series of public statements which delineated our general attitude:

—Secretary Rogers in a speech in Canberra, Australia, on August 8, 1969, noted the barriers between our countries but added, "We nonetheless look forward to a time when we can enter into a useful dialogue and to a reduction of tensions."

—In my February, 1970, Foreign Policy Report, I stated that ". . . it is certainly in our interest, and in the interest of peace and stability in Asia and the world, that we take what steps we can toward improved practical relations with Peking. . . . We will seek to promote understandings which can establish a new pattern of mutually beneficial actions."

—On October 26, 1970, in a toast to visiting President

Ceausescu of Romania, I deliberately used Peking's official title, "the People's Republic of China." This was the first time an American President had ever done so.

By the time of my second Foreign Policy Report in February, 1971, we had reason to believe that our moves were being noted and evaluated by the Chinese. In that report, I cited the importance of China's participation in world affairs, reiterated that we were ready for a dialogue with Peking, and stated that we hoped to see the People's Republic of China assume a constructive role in the family of nations. I looked toward the immediate future:

In the coming year, I will carefully examine what further steps we might take to create broader opportunities for contacts between the Chinese and American peoples, and how we might remove needless obstacles to the realization of these opportunities. We hope for, but will not be deterred by a lack of, reciprocity.

THE BREAKTHROUGH

By the fall of 1970, in private and reliable diplomatic channels, the Chinese began to respond. Both sides were now working to launch a process. The spring of 1971 saw a series of orchestrated public and private steps which culminated in Dr. Kissinger's July trip to Peking and the agreement for me to meet with the leaders of the People's Republic of China:

—On March 15, 1971, we announced that U.S. passports no longer needed special validation for travel to mainland China.

—On April 6, 1971, in Nagoya, Japan, the U.S. table tennis team competing in the world championships received an invitation from the Chinese team to visit mainland China. This was accepted the next day. The Chinese also granted visas to seven Western newsmen to cover the team's tour. The U.S. team traveled extensively in China, and was received on April 14 by Prime Minister Chou En-lai, who told them: "with your acceptance of our invitation, you have opened a new page in the relations of the Chinese and American people."

—On that same day, we moved to further the momentum that had clearly developed. I decided on the following measures which had been under governmental study since December, 1970: (1) We would expedite visas for visitors from the PRC; (2) U.S. currency controls would be relaxed to permit the PRC to use dollars; (3) Restrictions on U.S. oil companies providing fuel to ships or aircraft en route to or from China (except those bound to or from North Korea, North Vietnam, and Cuba) were eliminated; (4) U.S. vessels or aircraft would be permitted to carry Chinese cargoes between non-Chinese ports, and U.S.-owned foreign-flag carriers could call at Chinese ports; and (5) A list of items of a non-strategic nature would be compiled for direct export to the PRC.

—In the April 30 issue of *Life* magazine, the author, Edgar Snow, reported a conversation he had had earlier with Chairman Mao Tse-tung which confirmed private signals we had already received of Chinese interest in my visiting China.

—On May 7, 1971, we removed U.S. controls on dollar transactions with China (except those in previously blocked accounts) and certain controls on U.S. bunkering facilities and flagships.

—On June 10, 1971, we announced the end of the twenty-one-year embargo on trade with the PRC. We issued a general export license for a long list of non-strategic items for China and designated other items to be considered on a case-by-case basis. Restrictions on the import of Chinese goods were simultaneously lifted.

The stage was thus set for Dr. Kissinger's secret visit to

Peking. From July 9 to July 11, Dr. Kissinger held very extensive and important discussions with Premier Chou En-lai which produced the agreement that I would visit China before May, 1972.

From October 20 to 26, Dr. Kissinger again visited Peking to reach agreement on the major arrangements for my trip. Further lengthy talks with Prime Minister Chou En-lai and other Chinese officials produced the basic framework for my meetings with the leaders of the People's Republic of China—including the February 21, 1972, date, the duration and itinerary, the broad agenda, and the approximate composition and facilities for the accompanying party and representatives of the media. The major elements were announced at the end of November.

On December 13, 1971, the Chinese released two Americans whom they had been holding prisoner, and commuted the life sentence of a third American to five more years. This welcome gesture came after Dr. Kissinger transmitted my personal concern during his two visits to Peking. It was both a concrete result of our efforts to establish a dialogue and a hopeful sign for future progress in our relations.

INTERNATIONAL IMPACT

No major step in international relations is taken without some painful adjustments and potential costs. Indeed, the tendency is to focus on the risks that might flow from a departure from familiar patterns and to lose sight of its possible benefits. It is precisely this tendency that inhibits major initiatives and perpetuates established policies which sustain the status quo.

We undertook our initiatives toward the People's Republic of China aware of the problems as well as the opportunities. Such a dramatic move was bound to stir great changes in the world. The news of my forthcoming trip had an expectedly galvanic impact and set in motion new currents in international relations.

We were able to inform our friends only shortly before this announcement, and we understand the complications this caused for them. There were overriding reasons for keeping Dr. Kissinger's July visit secret. We could not risk advance public disclosure of these conversations whose outcome we could not predict. This would have risked disillusionment by inflating expectations which we could not be certain of meeting. And it would have created pressures on both the Chinese and American sides, forcing both of us to take public positions which could only have frozen discussions before they began. Moreover, we knew the July discussions would not settle anything directly concerning third parties; neither we nor Peking would set or accept any preconditions.

Regardless of how it was achieved, the change in the U.S.–Chinese relationship after twenty years of animosity was bound to be unsettling. Indeed, once Peking had decided to improve relations with the U.S., it had the capability to shake our relations with our friends through its own unilateral moves; the mere invitation to an American table tennis team had major repercussions.

The price we paid for secrecy was therefore unavoidable. It should prove transitory. The important task was to move swiftly to explain our purposes to our friends and to begin meaningful exchanges about the prospects for the future.

This we have done. Since July we have consulted with interested nations, outlining our objectives and expectations, and making clear we would not negotiate to the detriment of their interests. Secretary Rogers was extremely active in explaining our China policy to foreign ministers and other leaders of foreign countries. Secretary Connally and Governor Reagan traveled through Asia as my personal representatives, and carried my views on our China initiative and Asian policies in general. I sent personal messages to many of our friends and allies. Our Ambassadors were instructed to explain our views and solicit those of their host governments. The prospects of my meetings in Peking and in Moscow were among the primary topics of my series of talks with allied leaders in December, 1971, and January of this year.

We shall continue this process of consultation as we move forward in our relationship with the People's Republic of China. Our talks with our friends have focused on the longer term implications for U.S. policy. Questions have been raised which we have been careful to address publicly as well as privately.

How should our Asian friends interpret this initiative in terms of our commitments and their direct interests? There are, first of all, some general principles which apply to our relations with all concerned countries. Neither we nor the People's Republic asked, or would have accepted, any conditions for the opening of our dialogue. Neither country expects the other to barter away its principles or abandon its friends. Indeed, we have moved jointly in the conviction that more normal relations between us will serve the interests of all countries and reduce tensions in the Far East.

My conversations with the Chinese leaders will focus primarily on bilateral questions. Either side is free to raise any subject it wishes, and, of course, issues affecting the general peace are of bilateral concern. But we have made it clear to our Asian friends that we will maintain our commitments and that we will not negotiate on behalf of third parties. We cannot set out to build an honorable relationship of mutual respect with the PRC unless we also respect the interests of our long term friends.

Should our moves be read as shifting our priorities from Tokyo to Peking? They should not. With the Chinese we are at the beginning of a long process. With the Japanese we have enjoyed over two decades of the closest political and economic cooperation. It would be shortsighted indeed to exchange strong ties with a crucial ally for some mitigation of the hostility of a dedicated opponent. But it would be equally shortsighted not to seek communication and better understanding with a quarter of the world's people. We see no conflict in these two aims.

The preservation of our close relationship with Japan during this effort to broaden communications with China will call for wisdom and restraint on all sides. Each of us will have to avoid temptations to exacerbate relations between the other two. Despite the uneasy legacies of history, there can be more room for progress through cooperative interchange than through destructive rivalry.

What are the implications for our long-standing ties to the Republic of China? In my address announcing my trip to Peking, and since then, I have emphasized that our new dialogue with the PRC would not be at the expense of friends. Nevertheless, we recognize that this process cannot help but be painful for our old friend on Taiwan, the Republic of China. Our position is clear. We exerted the maximum diplomatic efforts to retain its seat in the United Nations. We regret the decision of the General Assembly to deprive the Republic of China of its representation although we welcomed the admission of the People's Republic of China. With the Republic of China, we shall maintain our friendship, our diplomatic ties, and our defense commitment. The ultimate relationship between Taiwan and the mainland is not a matter for the United States to decide. A peaceful resolution of this problem by the parties would do much to reduce tension in the Far East. We are not, however, urging either party to follow any particular course.

What does our China initiative mean for our relations with the Soviet Union? Our policy is not aimed against Moscow. The U.S. and the U.S.S.R. have issues of paramount importance to resolve; it would be costly indeed to impair progress on these through new antagonisms. Nevertheless some observers have warned that progress toward normalization of relations with Peking would inevitably jeopardize our relations with its Communist rival. There is no reason for this to be the case. Our various negotiations with the Soviet Union, for example on Berlin and SALT, made major progress subsequent to the July 15 announcement; and the agreement to meet with the Soviet leadership in May, 1972, was announced on October 12, 1971.

Others have suggested that we should use our opening to Peking to exploit Sino-Soviet tensions. We have consistently explained to all parties that we will not attempt to do so because it would be self-defeating and dangerous. We did not create the differences between the two Communist powers. They disagree over the proper interpretation of Communist philosophy, a subject in which we have no competence and little interest. And they dispute the lines of their common border, which can hardly be susceptible to our manipulation. In any event we will try to have better relations with both countries. In pursuing this objective we will conduct our diplomacy with both honesty and frankness.

THE JOURNEY TO PEKING

The record of the past three years illustrates that reality, not sentimentality, has led to my journey. And reality will shape the future of our relations.

I go to Peking without illusions. But I go nevertheless committed to the improvement of relations between our

two countries, for the sake of our two peoples and the
people of the world. The course we and the Chinese have
chosen has been produced by conviction, not by personalities or the prospect of tactical gains. We shall deal with
the People's Republic of China:

—Confident that a peaceful and prospering China is in
our own national interest;

—Recognizing that the talents and achievements of its
people must be given their appropriate reflection in world
affairs;

—Assured that peace in Asia and the fullest measure of
progress and stability in Asia and in the world require
China's positive contribution;

—Knowing that, like the United States, the People's
Republic of China will not sacrifice its principles;

—Convinced that we can construct a permanent relationship with China only if we are reliable—in our relations with our friends as well as with China;

—Assuming that the People's Republic of China will
shape its policy toward us with a reciprocal attitude.

These principles will guide my approach to my forthcoming conversations with Chairman Mao Tse-tung and
Premier Chou En-lai. The tenor of these discussions and
of our future relations, of course, does not depend on us
alone. It will require a mutual understanding of perspectives and a mutual willingness to combine a principled
approach with a respect for each other's interests.

At this point in history we need talks at the highest level.
Eighteen years of desultory ambassadorial discussions in
Geneva and Warsaw demonstrated that subsidiary problems could not be cleared away at lower levels. Authorita-
tive exchanges between our leaders, however, now hold
hope of genuine communication across the gulf and the
setting of a new direction.

The trip to Peking is not an end in itself but the launching of a process. The historic significance of this journey
lies beyond whatever formal understandings we might

reach. We are talking at last. We are meeting as equals. A prominent feature of the postwar landscape will be changed. At the highest level we will close one chapter and see whether we can begin writing a new one.

Both sides can be expected to state their principles and their views with complete frankness. We will each know clearly where the other stands on the issues that divide us. We will look for ways to begin reducing our differences. We will attempt to find some common ground on which to build a more constructive relationship.

If we can accomplish these objectives, we will have made a solid beginning.

Over the longer term, we will see whether two countries —whose histories and cultures are completely different, whose recent isolation has been total, whose ideologies clash, and whose visions of the future collide—can nevertheless move from antagonism to communication to understanding.

On January 20, 1969, in my Inaugural Address, I defined our approach toward all potential adversaries:

After a period of confrontation, we are entering an era of negotiation.

Let all nations know that during this Administration our lines of communication will be open.

We seek an open world—open to ideas, open to the exchange of goods and people—a world in which no people, great or small, will live in angry isolation.

We cannot expect to make everyone our friend, but we can try to make no one our enemy.

When I spoke those lines, I had the People's Republic of China very much in mind. It is this attitude that shaped our policy from the outset and led to the July 15, 1971, announcement. It is in this spirit that I go to Peking.

March 13, 1972

MAKING HISTORY IN PEKING
BY HUGH SIDEY

There is at this moment a Peking White House, a stolid building that sits near a lake in the western suburbs of the Chinese capital, ten minutes from the Great Hall of the People. It is occupied by Richard Nixon, the former nemesis of all Communists, and it exudes the same fragrance of power that one can whiff from Lafayette Park on Pennsylvania Avenue in Washington: the Secret Service agents with knife creases in their pants and wing-tip shoes; the omnipresent organizational aide H. R. ("Bob") Haldeman with his crew cut, Canon movie camera, and the air of ownership; the great big brain of Henry Kissinger coming through in German accent; and those white telephones which can connect Nixon with anyone, anywhere, at any time.

Last week in Washington it was as if two decades of assumptions had been ripped out and thrown away and we were beginning again. A singular spell lay over the city in the days before Nixon left. This reporter picked up his phone early one morning to hear a warm but utterly strange Chinese American voice say that he had been born in China and his father-in-law had been a friend of Henry Luce, *Life's* founder, whose father was a missionary in China, and, well, said the caller, how he wished he could go, and, well, "good luck." There was the sudden discovery that a contractor putting a couple of rooms on my house had spent two boyhood years in Tientsin when his father served in the army there. He envied my opportunity to go. It was the same with a housewife just down the street. And a neighborhood stroller who stopped to see the construction explained how he had been born in Peking and lived there until he was fifteen. There is apparently an army of people who touched China or were touched by it in some way. Those decades of isolation seem almost meaningless to them. And to the rest of us: the whole idea of "containing" the Chinese Reds, an axiom of United States foreign policy for more years than one can recall, has apparently joined the skeletal Joe McCarthy in our national closet.

There were other echoes of the past in Nixon's departure. In a way, he seemed to be the scrubbed and wholesome American missionary every Sunday-school boy gave his dimes to support a few decades ago. But the cool efficiency of his entourage recalled another image—the Yankee trader out to sell locomotives and bulldozers. The true character of the enterprise was still to be revealed. Nixon knew what he wanted it to be. In the countdown hours in the Oval Office, on the plane looking out at those towering cumulus clouds that shroud the Pacific, he had done his best to make the trip transcend politics, most of which is forgotten in a generation, and to cast it in a more lasting form.

"It can be a historical event," Henry Kissinger insisted. As planner and arranger, for him as for his boss there is really only one objective. It is for Nixon and Mao Tse-tung (and Chou En-lai) to take the measure of each other and establish some common base. It is to discover, in some hours of intimacy, that each is an essentially reliable man, and on that understanding found a new relationship. "For the first time," says Kissinger, "the two cultures and two societies are meeting on a level of equality. When America first got to know China, America was a small country and China was a great civilization. When we became a great power, China was being exploited by foreign powers—even our Open Door policy was seen by the Chinese in this light."

In the last hours before leaving, by candlelight, with a fire crackling in the fireplace of the family dining room,

Nixon met with the seventy-year-old André Malraux, French writer, thinker, and political activist, Charles de Gaulle's minister of culture. They talked of the nature of greatness in men. Malraux insisted there were only three great men in recent history—Mao, Gandhi, and de Gaulle. With an aplomb that only a Frenchman could muster (and perhaps only Malraux among Frenchmen), he ruled out Churchill and Nehru. Mao, Gandhi, and de Gaulle, he told Nixon, "were great men because they molded the conditions which they faced."

"Yes," replied Nixon, "but to mold the conditions you have to have a big nation in an important geographical location. If greatness depended only on the skill and intelligence of the person, a man like Australia's Robert Menzies would have been great."

Nixon turned to discuss the trip and struck a strangely melancholy note. He was reminded of the story one of Lincoln's biographers told. The day before Lincoln's assassination, Nixon said, Lincoln had come into the Cabinet Room and told the people there he had a feeling something important was going to happen. He had had a dream, the story goes, that he had embarked on a voyage on a boat and he could see only a strange, indefinable shore ahead.

"Perhaps I, too, am embarked on a strange voyage," Nixon said quietly. "But my purpose is to try to manipulate the boat, avoid the reefs, and arrive at my destination, which is better understanding of China."

"No one will know if you succeed for at least fifty years, Mr. President," answered Malraux. "The Chinese are very patient."

"I know that," said Nixon. "But I believe, as you believe, that relations should be restored. The American people and I can be patient too."

Over the brandy, as the candles burned low, Malraux

suddenly looked at the man beside him. "When you face Mao you will be meeting a colossus," he said. "But a colossus facing death. Do you know what the most important thing about you will be to Mao? Your youth."

February 25, 1972

ON THE *WAY* TO PEKING: THE NIXON DOCTRINE

THE SO-CALLED NIXON DOCTRINE
IS SUBJECTED TO LENGTHY ANALYSES BY
JOHN DOWER AND EARL RAVENAL.

TEN POINTS OF NOTE: ASIA AND THE NIXON DOCTRINE
BY JOHN DOWER

Although the President first enunciated the "Nixon Doctrine" informally on Guam in July, 1969, the precise meaning of that doctrine has remained ambiguous ever since. Transcripts of this initial briefing exist, but have never been published and cannot be quoted directly. As Administration supporters explain it, such ambiguity is deliberate and essential; any greater spelling out of American intentions would place the United States in a straitjacket and prevent it from pursuing a flexible and responsive diplomacy in the future. As some critics see it, the doctrine is little more than a political accordion; the Administration's traveling minstrels, playing by ear, can stretch it out or squeeze it tight depending on their particular audience.

Despite this ambiguity, however, the general parameters of the doctrine seem fairly clear. In the first place, it projects the partial "disengagement" of American military personnel from Asia in the near future. This includes not only troop withdrawals from Vietnam, but from other countries as well. Thus a substantial reduction of the large American garrison which has been maintained in South Korea since the Korean War has already been announced. The November, 1969 Sato-Nixon communiqué calling for return of Okinawa to Japanese rule by 1972 was described as part of the Nixon Doctrine, and since then it has been emphasized that the Japanese military is beginning to assume functions hitherto performed by the American forces in Japan. The Thai government has indicated that it expects the number of American soldiers stationed in Thailand to be reduced "after" the present Indochina conflict. And so on. The essential ingredient in the

new "low posture" or "low profile," in short, is that the
most visible American presence in Asia—almost a million U.S. troops—will be partially reduced.

The other side of disengagement, and a side which the
Administration also stresses, is Asian self-help. In the
President's phrase, "Asian hands must shape the Asian
future." More specifically, pro-American regimes are to
be strengthened militarily so that in the suppression of future "insurgencies" they can shoulder a major part of the
burden borne up to now by the United States (notably in
the Korean and Indochina wars). At the same time, the
United States will stand by with its nuclear arsenal and
tactical air and sea support, honoring its commitments
and vigilant against external aggression. In the President's words:

First, the United States will keep all of its treaty commitments.

Second, we shall provide a shield if a nuclear power
threatens the freedom of a nation allied with us, or of a nation whose survival we consider vital to our security.

Third, in cases involving other types of aggression we
shall furnish military and economic assistance when requested in accordance with our treaty commitments. But we
shall look to the nation directly threatened to assume the
primary responsibility of providing the manpower for its defense.

Finally, while the primary thrust of the doctrine is military, the economic side is not ignored. Here the President
stresses interregional cooperation—"Asian initiatives in
an Asian framework"—abetted by "multinational" corporations and organizations. At the same time, however,
he acknowledges that in both military and economic matters, "Japan's partnership with us will be a key to the success of the Nixon Doctrine in Asia."

The metaphor of the "low profile" has generally proven

effective from a public relations point of view. It conveys the image of the wise man—balanced in perspective, powerful but restrained—and such connotations are all the more grasped at now since they have been so lacking in past American policy. Yet it would seem more reasonable if the experience of this recent past prompted, at the very least, a suspension of faith—and indeed closer analysis provides good reasons for such skepticism.

The Nixon Doctrine is not new.

Rather, like many of the President's basic views, it can be traced back to the early years of the cold war, particularly the late 1940's and the early 1950's. The Korean war presumedly converted a generation of America's military and political planners to a belief in the absolute necessity of avoiding a land war in Asia; the "lesson" of Vietnam in this respect is the irrelevance of lessons to the decision-making process. It was Eisenhower himself who during the Korean war stated that "If there must be a war there in Asia let it be Asians against Asians." This notion of letting Asians fight Asians ("Asian self-help," "regional security") can be traced through John Foster Dulles' application of "pactomania" to Asia, beginning with the Japanese security treaty and extending through SEATO. Japan's projected role as America's military and economic partner in Asia also has deep roots. As Vice-President in the early 1950's, Nixon was one of the first prominent American officials to publicly criticize Article 9, the "no-war clause" of Japan's new constitution. And of course the United States has been preparing clients in Saigon for "self-help" ever since Diem. No post-war American administration has ever claimed that it was performing anything other than temporary military tasks in Asia, and all have supported huge military investments in

Asia in anticipation of that day when Asian allies would be able to shoulder the bulk of the burden themselves.

With regard to outright American military intervention in Asia in the future, it should be noted that nothing in the President's various formulations of the doctrine would have been rejected by the policy-makers (including Mr. Nixon himself in the early 1950's) who encouraged and planned American intervention in Indochina over the past decade. Following the "State of the World" message of February 18, 1970, for example, Max Frankel noted that

Mr. Nixon's aides concede . . . that there is nothing in his new doctrine that excludes a Dominican-style intervention in defense of vital interests. They say that the document is a call to the nation and government to define those interests more precisely and prudently than in the past, but they have only begun that job and it is never really finished until the moment of crisis.

Despite new considerations and emphases, the basic analysis of the situation in Asia, and of America's proper relation to it, has not changed.

In his frequently cited 1967 *Foreign Affairs* article, Nixon argued that "Both our interests and our ideals propel us westward across the Pacific." He has repeated this as President: "We remain involved in Asia. We are a Pacific power." The Nixon Doctrine denies any intention of re-evaluating present American "commitments" in Asia, and does not pretend to offer a fundamental redefinition of American "national interests" in the area. Significantly, it also does not seriously question the discredited goals of containing China, checking "Communism," suppressing "insurgencies," and bolstering pro-American Asian regimes, however corrupt or unrepresentative they may be.

In the State of the World message, the President did acknowledge that nationalism had proven itself destructive of "international Communist unity," and he also called for "improved practical relations with Peking." Much has been made of this seemingly conciliatory attitude toward China, particularly since it comes from a President whose early political successes derived from a striking aptitude for Red-baiting. Specific deeds, furthermore, can be cited to illustrate the new attitude toward Peking: the United States, for example, has recently eased trade and travel restrictions relating to the People's Republic, virtually eliminated its naval patrol of the Taiwan Straits, and significantly downgraded its military mission in Taiwan. There is less serious talk recently of the Kuomintang as the only legitimate government of China, or as a viable "alternative regime" for the mainland; stated differently, there is grudging recognition of the viability of the People's Republic. Furthermore, it appears that some U.S. military advisers are engaged in attempting to revise the orthodox apocalyptic version of the "Chinese threat." This is a rather curious exercise in which the most significant change lies in the psyche of the American planners rather than in China itself; what is involved is primarily a shucking of the shell of paranoia which has encased American China-watchers ever since the "loss of China." Some observers maintain that this new evaluation of China's intentions is crucial to understanding the President's willingness to maintain existing commitments while reducing force levels in Asia.

Perhaps so, but this remains to be seen. In the same address in which he called for improved relations with Peking, the President reaffirmed America's military commitment to the Nationalist regime in Taiwan and reiterated the familiar condescending hope that "sooner or later Communist China will be ready to re-enter the international community." A key theme in the Nixon *Foreign Affairs* article mentioned above was that China poses the greatest threat in Asia today. Despite the restraint China has shown in the face of the Indochina bloodbath on her borders it would appear that both the Pentagon and State Department continue to adhere to this view. In his budget address to Congress last March, Secretary of Defense Melvin Laird stressed China's nuclear potential and "ambitions for great power status and regional hegemony," and described the People's Republic as posing "a pervading psychological and actual threat to the peace and security of the Asian arena." Laird also, it will be recalled, attempted to sell the ABM to the American public on the grounds that "we do not want to become hostage to the Chinese." As recently as July 9, scarcely two months after the U.S. invasion of Cambodia, Secretary of State William Rogers appeared on a television interview in Tokyo and blandly urged China to abandon its "belligerent attitude" toward the world and play "a sensible role in the international community." Along similar lines, the new official version of polycentric Communism has not prevented the President from reviving and reemphasizing the domino theory, most notably in his television interview of July 2.

Focus upon the administration's China policy has had the effect of obscuring an equally significant concern, namely the reluctance of American officials (and academics) to revise the accepted stereotype of insurgency and guerrilla warfare, a stereotype, of course, which is intertwined with an image of China's role in revolutionary movements in Asia. While the military effectiveness of the insurgency movements of Indochina can no longer be denied, neither the political nor social viability of the NLF and Pathet Lao—nor the sharply contrasting, and endemic, corruption and inefficiency of the regimes the U.S. supports against them—have been acknowledged and used as the basis for a truly fundamental policy reappraisal. Opposition to popular revolutionary movements in Asia remains, in fact, a bedrock of the Nixon Doctrine. In Laird's words:

The principal threat to the independent nations in Asia is internal insurgency supported by external assistance. This is an important aspect of the threat to which our General Purpose Force planning for Asia should be oriented.

In the future as in the past—as seen in American responses to the Chinese revolution and the Korean War, as well as to events in Indochina—it seems probable that American officials will continue to place unwarranted emphasis on the role of "external assistance" while minimizing the strength, legitimacy, and popular support of national movements. As has been the case since before World War II, fundamental American objectives in Asia remain containment and counterrevolution.

The Nixon Doctrine is fundamentally a cost-conscious policy, aimed at maintaining a major U.S. role in Asia at less cost in both dollars and American lives.

This emerges vividly in Ambassador Bunker's notorious comment that Vietnamization simply means changing "the color of the corpses." Viewing the issue from a slightly different vantage, former Defense Secretary Clark Clifford informed Congress in January, 1969, that "an Asian soldier costs about one-fifteenth as much as his American counterpart." The present Secretary of Defense has described the Nixon Doctrine as a balance of withdrawal-plus-Vietnamization, and argued that the success of this will depend greatly upon the effectiveness of the U.S. Military Assistance Program (MAP)—a program which embraces military grants, training, and "some of the needed weapons, and, in some circumstances, specialized military support." In Laird's words:

The Military Assistance Program is the key to this approach. It is the essential ingredient of our policy if we are to honor our obligations, support our allies, and yet reduce the likelihood of having to commit American ground combat units. When looked at in these terms, a MAP dollar is of far greater value than a dollar spent directly on U.S. forces.

The proposal to disengage from Asia militarily is itself highly qualified.

In the first place, the emphasis thus far has been placed primarily on ground combat troops, while support forces, particularly the devastating aviation units, will continue to be maintained in Asia indefinitely. This is openly acknowledged. As Laird explained it last March:

In Asia, we seek to help our allies develop the capability to defend themselves with the United States providing materiel and logistic support. However, most of these countries lack adequate air and sea power. Considerable time and resources will be required to solve this problem.

In the case of Vietnam itself, there is still no reason to believe that the United States seriously contemplates anything other than a "Korean solution," that is, indefinite maintenance of large American garrisons in key bases throughout South Vietnam.

In the rest of Asia, the U.S. has given little indication of which of its nearly two hundred major bases it intends to relinquish. While some will indeed be phased out as obsolete or uneconomical (Tachikawa in Japan is a recent example), and others will be turned over to local forces for maintenance (as is presently taking place in Japan and

Vietnam), there is no intention of abandoning the "ring of steel" around China. Official announcements of the phasing out of U.S. military "installations" in Asia must be heard with the awareness that most often these are golf courses or firing ranges or the like, and also with a recognition of the immensity of the present physical presence of the American military in Asia. At the time the President announced his doctrine on Guam, the United States maintained roughly 63,000 troops in Korea, 40,000 in Japan, 45,000 in Okinawa, 10,000 in Taiwan, 30,000 in the Philippines, and 49,000 in Thailand. Another 389,000 were with the Pacific Fleet, with over 200,000 of these in the Western Pacific with the Seventh Fleet. American bases in Asia officially classified as "major" totaled fifty-four in Korea, forty in Japan, sixteen in Okinawa, three in Taiwan, six in the Philippines, seven in Thailand, and nine in the islands of Micronesia (the Marianas, Marshall Island, and Midway). The generally accepted number of major bases in Vietnam is fifty-nine.

Exactly what will be done with these bases in the future remains unclear, but obviously it will be possible to trim an impressive amount of fat without touching the real bones of the American military posture toward Asia. Moreover even as certain facilities are being closed or cut back, other major Asian bases are presently being expanded and new sites and facilities acquired. In two perceptive articles, Michael Klare has suggested that among the key bases which will probably assume a pivotal role in post-Vietnam strategic planning are the huge logistical bases at Cam Ranh Bay (South Vietnam) and Sattahip (Thailand); the Air Force complexes at Tan Son Nhut (Saigon) and U-Taphao and Khorat (Thailand); and probably counterinsurgency or paramilitary centers such as those located at Nhatrang (South Vietnam), Kanchanaburi and Udorn (Thailand), and Vientiane (Laos).

The Philipines, Japan, and Guam remain of central importance to Pacific planning; they house, in addition to major airfields and supply depots, the four major naval facilities used by the Seventh Fleet (Guam, Subic Bay in the Philippines, Sasebo and Yokosuka in Japan). The $2,-000,000,000 American complex on Okinawa, with 120 separate military installations on this island alone, poses particular problems because its present use as a site for nuclear MACE-B missiles (specially designed against China), as a berth for nuclear-armed Polaris submarines, and as a storage arsenal for nuclear bombs will probably have to be modified when sovereignty over the island reverts to Japan in 1972. Two fall-back sites have been suggested as alternatives to handle Okinawa's present nuclear functions. Most frequently mentioned is the Mariana island chain, which includes Guam and Saipan. Pentagon insiders, however, suggest that a more probable alternative site will be South Korea. Whatever readjustment is made in this respect, it can be anticipated that Okinawa and the four main islands of Japan (which now have over 125 U.S. military installations, of which twenty-eight Army, six Navy, and six Air Force bases were classified as "major" in September, 1969) will continue to be utilized by the U.S. Navy and Air Force, with the Japanese military gradually assuming a more direct role in their upkeep during the decade of the 1970's.

In the Indian Ocean the thrust of American concerns seems to imply not continued disengagement, but rather the assumption of new missions. In January, 1969, Britain announced that it would withdraw its troops east of Suez by the end of 1971, thus threatening to leave what Western geopoliticians refer to as a "power vacuum" in the Indian Ocean—a term commonly used here to mean an absence of Anglo-Saxons. This, coupled with the Soviet Union's recent growth in naval strength, has prompted administration advisers such as Arleigh Burke of Georgetown's Center for Strategic and International

Studies to urge creation of a permanent U.S. task force in the Indian Ocean. Whatever may come of this proposal, steps have already been taken to increase U.S. naval capabilities in the area. Probably of greatest significance are the sophisticated communications facilities being established at Northwest Cape (Australia), Canterbury (New Zealand), and Asmara (Ethiopia), which together can provide the electronic network necessary for operations in the entire Indian Ocean area. As Klare has pointed out, the Australian facility, one of the largest in the world, will house the most powerful VLF (very low frequency) transmitter in existence, which will function as part of the "Omega" system for radio transmission with submerged nuclear submarines.

On the eastern rim of the South Asian theater, interest is also focused on the great naval facilities in Singapore, which Britain will turn over to the Singapore government in 1971. In keeping with the new soft-shoe approach to military choreography in Asia, a recent (1969) issue of the *Naval War College Review* offered this suggestion concerning Singapore:

U.S. interest in that excellent facility, if deemed feasible, should be approached in low-profile, and negotiations for U.S. interests could be pursued through its allies such as Japan or Australia, both of whom have principal interests there. Arrangements could provide for joint utilization on a cost- and maintenance-sharing basis. The availability of this facility would provide a superior logistical capability for the U.S. Navy than it has at present.

Whatever form the future American military presence may take in Asia, the essentials of the containment policy remain. The Seventh Fleet will continue to prowl Asia's shores, with various styles of nuclear and conventional death amidst its arsenal. Polaris submarines will continue to glide beneath the Pacific, systematically undergoing a sea-change to the "Poseidon configuration." SAC will continue to be guaranteed runways which will permit it to rain an ingenious variety of destruction from the skies. Asian real estate will continue to be made available on which America can store and position the conventional weapons, missiles, nuclear devices, gases, poisons, vehicles, computers, provisions, and other items required to eradicate Asians should the occasion arise. While elsewhere 1,000 ICBM's will continue to nestle in their silos, gradually being "MIRV-ed" and awaiting the turn of the key.

Client armies are to assume some of the functions now carried out by the U.S. military.

Vietnamization, the brutalizing policy under which the South Vietnamese Army (ARVN) is now being trained to continue the war, is commonly cited as a model of the Nixon Doctrine in action. Similarly, the unleashing of South Vietnamese troops in Cambodia "to assure the survival of the government of Lon Nol in Phnompenh and prevent the return to power of Prince Sihanouk" was justified by Secretary of State Rogers on the grounds that "the whole Nixon Doctrine as pronounced at Guam is that Asians should work with each other to take care of their common problems." In this latter case, the most obvious common problem shared by Lon Nol and the South Vietnamese government was that neither had much popular support.

Despite the fact that the 1,000,000-man ARVN has been wet-nursed by the United States for a decade and still cannot hold its own without decisive American air and combat support against numerically and technologically inferior NLF and North Vietnamese forces, this appears to be the path of the future for America's allies: more U.S.

military aid (note the accelerating commitment to the Lon Nol regime in Cambodia); more U.S. military advisers (witness the new John F. Kennedy Center for Military Assistance at Fort Bragg); more military training for Asian nationals (Thai soldiers, for example, are already receiving CBW training in the U.S. in preparation for the day when they too can participate in the defoliation of their land); a larger policy-making role for the Pentagon and CIA (this seems to be the implication of the recent proposal to turn AID functions over to the Pentagon); emphasis upon police functions and control mechanisms within the client society (close to 50 percent of the "civilian" aid budget to Thailand, for example, is now being spent on police stations and specially trained Special Police); and so on. In effect the U.S. seeks to defend its ambitions in Asia through proxy armies and client regimes.

There is little new in this approach. Military aid in various forms has comprised the preponderant part of U.S. aid to Asia throughout the post-war era, despite the often humanistic rhetoric of "nation building." The Nixon Doctrine expresses established priorities more bluntly, but the prospect it offers is none the less grim. South Korea, heralded as "the first application of the so-called Nixon Doctrine aside from Indochina," can be taken as a case in point. In June of 1970 the Defense Department announced that over the course of the next few years, the U.S. intended to withdraw all but a token contingent of its 63,000 troops (53,000 Army and 10,000 Air Force) now stationed in South Korea. This has since been qualified following expressions of concern on the part of the South Korean government, but the U.S. remains committed to the withdrawal of roughly 15,000 or 20,000 American men in the near future. They will leave behind them a 620,000-man South Korean military establishment, a projected paramilitary "home guard" of 2,000,000 men, and a 1968 congressional appropriation which included funds for a squadron (around 54 planes) of Phantom F-4D fighter-bombers. In addition to continuing the annual military aid program to the ROK, administration officials have also indicated that they intend to request a $1,000,000,000 appropriation from Congress to be used in further modernizing the Korean military over the course of the next five years. While South Korea will not be provided with its own air sufficiency (partly because it is feared that the Seoul government will then attack the North), bids have been opened to American defense contractors for a proposed short-range jet fighter appropriate for use by Korea and other allies such as Taiwan and Thailand; some $28,-000,000 for such a study was made available by the U.S. government in fiscal year 1970, and another $30,000,000 was requested for FY 1971. In addition, the United States has privately agreed to advance credits for the construction of a factory to manufacture modern rifles.

As an example of regional military cooperation, South Korea has sent 50,000 troops to Vietnam at an estimated cost to American taxpayers of $1,000,000,000 since 1965. In Vietnam, the South Koreans have distinguished themselves by their ferocity and have been charged with carrying out systematic atrocities by a number of journalists, as well as by researchers under contract to Rand Corporation and the Defense Department.

In his State of the World address, the President pointed proudly to South Korea as an example of regional development and Asian capitalist prosperity. In his words, "Korea's annual growth rate of 15 percent may be the highest in the world." He neglected to note that Korea's boom since 1965 has been intimately tied in to war profits derived from Korean exports to Vietnam, fees to Korean civilian contractors there, dollar remittances from the earnings of the 50,000 American-paid Korean soldiers and 16,000 Korean civilians employed by the U.S. in Vietnam, and direct and indirect earnings from the American military presence in South Korea itself. It is estimated that in 1969, twenty percent of South Korea's foreign currency revenue came from Vietnam.

"Koreanization," like "Vietnamization," is a cover phrase for militarization. And it is a striking commentary upon both the Nixon Doctrine and its apologists that the two Asian client states which have been most distorted by American policy in the past are now blandly offered as models for the future.

American military planners also anticipate that much of the slack of disengagement will be taken up by major technological advances in warfare.

While Asian land forces will assume some of the burden left by the withdrawal of American manpower, a less propagandized but potentially more significant surrogate development lies in the new technology of death now under development. Richard Barnet has calculated that thirteen new weapons systems are now "waiting in the Pentagon wings" and scheduled for production following the termination of hostilities in Indochina. Of particular interest insofar as the Nixon Doctrine is concerned are two rather dramatized projects: (1) the concept of rapid transport and the fire brigade, first popularized by Secretary of Defense Robert McNamara; and (2) the electronic battlefield recently rhapsodized by General Westmoreland.

McNamara explained his concept of rapid transport and brushfire wars as follows in 1965:

Either we can station large numbers of men and quantities of equipment and supplies overseas near all potential trouble spots, or we can maintain a much smaller force in a central reserve in the United States and deploy it rapidly where needed. . . . A mobile "fire brigade" reserve, centrally located . . . and ready for quick deployment to any threatened area in the world, is, basically, a more economical and flexible use of our military forces.

One key to the brushfire concept lies in the new capabilities of air transport, primarily as exemplified in the now notorious C-5A. Six stories tall and nearly as long as a football field (dubbed "Moby Jet" by a metaphysical PR man), each of these superjets can carry 600 men and their equipment, or the equivalent of this. The plane is also capable of taking off and landing on short runways, thus enabling it to set down almost anywhere. In addition, it is equipped with lifts, ramps, and the like which make it "self-unloading," thus permitting use of poorly equipped airfields. The supertransport is a key component of what is known to military planners as "rapid deployment strategy" or "rapid response capability." It has been described by high officials as the pivot of logistics planning for the decade of the 1970's. One Air Force officer, speaking less formally, has called it an advanced form of gunboat diplomacy. Lockheed, the manufacturer, advertises its product in these terms:

The C-5A Galaxy is more than the world's largest airplane. It's a new kind of defense system. It's like having a military base in nearly every strategic spot on the globe.

And Senator Stuart Symington, a critic of certain kinds of military spending, defended funding of the C-5A on grounds which neatly sum up the crucial relationship between the transport revolution and the Nixon policy of disengagement:

I want to say here and now, that people who really mean it when they say we should bring these troops home, had better provide for the airlift because you are not going to be able to bring them home until you have some means to send them back.

Just as new potentialities of transportation make it possible to reevaluate the entire concept of permanent garrisons abroad without necessarily reevaluating commitments or definition of "national security" or "national interest," so in a similar manner new developments in tactical warfare promise to make it possible to kill on the old scale and for the old goals but with new and impersonal dispatch. As America's young men march out of Asia their place will be taken by America's client armies, with the menacing presence of Moby Jet ever in the background. But that is only half of it. If General Westmoreland's vision holds true, in the future it may be possible to respond militarily to Asia's protesting peasants largely by computer and the touch of a few select buttons.

Like the concept of the fire brigade, the "electronic battlefield" also had its inspiration during the McNamara tenure. It derives from studies undertaken in 1966 by the Institute for Defense Analyses for creation of an "electronic fence" for Vietnam—the so-called "McNamara Wall"—and some of its components have been tested and used in Vietnam, Laos, and Cambodia since 1968. Its potential is sufficient to quicken the prose of even as stiff and prosaic a warrior as Westmoreland, as witness the General's classic address of October 14, 1969, on "The Army of the Future":

. . . In mid 1968, our field experiments began. . . . We are on the threshold of an entirely new battlefield concept.

. . . On the battlefield of the future, enemy forces will be located, tracked, and targeted almost instantaneously through the use of data links, computer assisted intelligence evaluation, and automated fire control. With first round kill probabilities approaching certainty, and with surveillance devices that can continually track the enemy, the need for large forces to fix the opposition physically will be less important.

. . . Based on our total battlefield experience and our proven technological capability, I foresee a new battlefield array.

I see battlefields or combat areas that are under 24-hour real or near-real time surveillance of all types.

I see battlefields on which we can destroy anything we locate through instant communications and the almost instantaneous application of highly lethal firepower.

I see a continuing need for highly mobile combat forces to assist in fixing and destroying the enemy.

The changed battlefield will dictate that the supporting logistics system also undergo change.

I see the forward end of the logistics system with mobility equal to the supported force.

I see the elimination of many intermediate support echelons and the use of inventory-in-motion techniques.

I see some Army forces supported by air—in some instances directly from bases here in the continental United States.

. . . With cooperative effort, no more than ten years should separate us from the automated battlefield.

Senator Proxmire recently pointed out that $2,-000,000,000 worth of research had still not made the electronic detection system capable of sorting out the friendly and the enemy on the battlefield of the future:

. . . the sensors could not differentiate between friend and foe, women and children.

All we know is that something is moving out there. It could be the wind, an elephant or an enemy soldier. We really have almost no idea what we are shooting at.

That is probably not an entirely relevant concern, however, since the fundamental principle of counter-insurgency which has most obviously emerged in the course of the war in Indochina is that of "emptying the countryside" —in military parlance, turning about Mao's phrase: to dry up the ocean of people in which the guerrillas move as fish. Drawing fine distinctions among "Oriental human beings" in the countryside has not been of particular importance previously, and there is no reason to expect it to become important in the future. What is important to the administration and military is the capability of killing more at less cost and less loss of American lives. The old Eisenhower ideal of a bigger bang for a buck has been revived in the guise of a bigger bag for a buck, and in this respect the new instrumented battlefield plays a significant part in American planning for future "disengagement" from Asia. A prototype system (SEEK DATA II) is already being installed in Vietnam, and Westmoreland suggests that instrumentation is indeed already taking over roles formerly requiring manpower:

Firepower can be concentrated without massing large numbers of troops. In Vietnam where artillery and tactical air forces inflict over two-thirds of the enemy casualties, firepower is responsive as never before. It can rain destruction anywhere on the battlefield within minutes . . . whether friendly troops are present or not.

More bluntly, one can afford to disengage combat forces because they are no longer the big killers. Dr. John S. Foster, Jr., Director of Defense Research and Engineering, notes that "each few years often sees a tenfold improvement" in military electronics technology, with these advances:

Flexibility of installation and operation and increased survivability will also be realized. New equipment will be considerably smaller in size, lighter in weight, more reliable, more easily maintained and, in some cases, less expensive. Greater power output will be possible with reduced power consumption.

Among the capabilities which it is hoped these developments will bring, Foster goes on to note that they may:

Permit the development of ultrareliable equipment and systems (thousands vs. hundreds of hours between failures) that will drastically reduce supporting logistics costs (maintenance personnel, spare parts inventory, training) and increase operational availability.

Reduce the number of people overseas operating intelligence collection systems, thus reducing gold flow as well as certain risks in intelligence collection.

Where it will all end is anyone's guess, although those with a more macabre sense of destiny would seem to be on the right track. Insofar as the financing of the new technology of death is concerned, Proxmire speculates that the automated battlefield may eventually carry a price tag in the neighborhood of $20,000,000,000—in his words, "almost twice as much as we are spending on the ABM and four times as much as we have spent on the C-5A." This, of course, is in addition to the development of more conventional new weapons systems for use in local or insurgency situations—new helicopters, tanks, missiles, etc. In addition, the Defense Department requested $68,-000,000 for FY 1971 research in chemical and "defensive biological" research, and another $381,000,000 for a special program known as "Southeast Asia RDT&E (Research, Development, Test & Evaluation)."

Both the C-5A and the "electronic battlefield" still pose technological problems which cannot be ignored. While recognizing this, however, it still can be argued that even without a Nixon Doctrine, the logic of increasingly sophisticated military technology would have dictated a gradual "disengagement" of American manpower from Asia.

The combination of old objectives, cost-consciousness, and reluctance to become mired in another counterinsurgency war in Asia may well increase the possibility of resort to nuclear weapons in the future.

The nature of popular resistance to the military machines of the French and Americans over the past decades in Indochina indicates that neither client armies nor American air and sea support nor supertransports nor still unperfected computerized battlefields will turn the tide decisively against future "insurgencies." At this point it becomes necessary to speculate on the role of the nuclear alternative in the Nixon Doctrine for Asia. Here it is instructive to recall Vice-President Nixon's public position on the issue of nuclear weapons as expressed in 1955:

It is foolish to talk about the possibility that the weapons which might be used in the event war breaks out in the Pacific would be limited to the conventional Korean and World War II types of explosives. Our forces could not fight an effective war in the Pacific with those types of explosives if they wanted to. Tactical atomic explosives are now conventional and will be used against the military targets of any aggressive force.

Among those who debate the issue, there is at the present time considerable disagreement as to whether or not the present leadership in Washington is more willing to consider the use of nuclear weapons in certain situations than has been the case in the past. Those who disagree with this view defend their position on a number of grounds. They point out that world opinion would not tolerate resort to the nuclear option; that among American military planners, interest in tactical nuclear weapons has declined during the last decade when compared to that shown other systems; that intolerable radiation levels plus undesirable wind patterns mitigate against the resort to nuclear weapons in Asia—particularly since prevailing winds might expose Japan to fallout; that once the barrier to use of nuclear weapons is violated, it is recognized that the potential for use elsewhere (for example the Middle East or Europe) is increased; and so on. Such arguments are fairly persuasive if one assumes that pivotal military decisions are taken after careful, rational deliberation—an assumption which hardly seems tenable any longer. Neither the President's past attitude toward nuclear weapons, his recent pledge to "move decisively and not step by step" if challenged in Indochina, his reliance upon advisers known to be especially tolerant of using tactical nuclear weapons in certain situations, nor his personal propensity for equating virility with force dispel this concern.

Precise information on present American nuclear deployment in Asia is understandably difficult to come by. American use of Okinawa as a nuclear arsenal and site of nuclear missiles is generally taken for granted; in addition, nuclear weapons are maintained in Korea, Thailand, the Philippines, and within the Seventh Fleet. The most suggestive studies on these matters have emanated from the independent Institute for Policy Studies in Washington. Richard Barnet reports that as of 1968 the United States maintained more than 5,500 nuclear weapons in Southeast Asia, mostly on aircraft carriers, and that "Until 1965 the Commander in Chief of the Pacific (CINCPAC) had no plans or weapons capabilities to fight other than a nuclear war in Southeast Asia." He also notes that since the Second World War, the U.S. military has proposed the use of nuclear weapons in Indochina on two occasions: at the time of the French debacle at Dienbienphu in 1954 and during the siege of the American garrison at Khe Sanh in 1968. It might also be noted that in December, 1950, the staffs of both the Eighth Army and the Fifth Air Force gave serious thought to the use of atomic weapons in Korea.

One of the most precise and chilling examples of the interrelationship which some planners undoubtedly envision as existing between the Nixon Doctrine, technological advances, and nuclear weapons, is to be found in a recent, Strangelovian article by Hanson Baldwin, former military editor of *The New York Times.* "There must be no hesitancy in equipping" America's bases in the Western Pacific "with nuclear weapons for their own defense," Baldwin argued, and went on to note that:

. . . We appear to have forgotten that, in the atomic age, a limited war, a counterinsurgency war, a conventional war of any kind, can be fought only under the umbrella of a superior strategic nuclear-delivery capability. Unless the right fist of tremendous power is cocked, our conventional forces are hostages. . . . The *sine qua non* of any sound United States political or military policy in Asia is a superior nuclear-delivery capability; only if we are prepared to fight World War III can we deter it.

Having concluded that the great lesson of Vietnam has been the folly of "overcaution" and "gradualism," Baldwin goes on to argue that if the United States should decide to "scotch" an Asian insurgency in the future, it must do so with "instantaneous and overwhelming application of superior power." In this view, China and "creeping Communism" have no identity other than that of the "enemy":

If the United States cannot, in the future, bolster governments under attack and secure them against creeping Com-

munism with a United States troop commitment of—for
instance—fewer than 100,000 men, then it had better do
one of two things: either call it quits, or escalate technologically rather than with manpower. Certainly any direct involvement with massed Chinese Communist ground forces
on the Asiatic mainland should imply immediate technological escalation. Such escalation might involve the use of ex-
otic new conventional weapons, or the utilization under
carefully restricted conditions, where targets and geogra-
phy are favorable, of small nuclear devices for *defensive*
purposes.

Baldwin acknowledges that this might have undesirable
consequences, such as escalation into a nuclear confla-
gration, but in the short run—that is, while China still has
no tactical nuclear weapons of her own—"the likelihood
of this would be less dangerous than the adverse political
and psychological consequences." The nuclear option
would of course be a "last resort," but a curiously attractive one when one thinks about it, and certainly conducive
to colorful paragraphs:

On the other hand, the careful and precise use of an atomic
shell, fired from an 8-inch howitzer, the utilization of atomic
land mines to guard a frontier (as now proposed by Turkey),
the creation of a restricted and carefully controlled radio-
active belt in virtually uninhabited country through which any
aid from outside the country would have to pass, or the use
of atomic demolition devices in thick jungle areas or in pre-
cipitous defiles to cause tangled "blow-downs" or land-
slides to block trails, roads or natural approach routes
could substitute for manpower and add great power to the
defense.

The Baldwin version of military imperatives is in fact
quite logical if one accepts his assumptions—and indeed
the Nixon Doctrine does embody those premises: that
America is in Asia and the Pacific to stay; that insurgency
and revolution anywhere in Asia are to be seen first and

foremost as "creeping Communism" and checked wherever possible; that China rather than the United States represents aggressive expansionism in Asia and must continue to be rigorously "contained"; that the best interests of the peoples of Asia as well as of the United States (happy coincidence) lie in the preservation and strengthening of those regimes presently allied with the U.S.; and so on. These are traditional assumptions, and if the United States is to defend them militarily while reducing its own manpower commitments to Asia, then it is only natural to assume that something must take the place of that manpower. In fact, as has been seen, several things are to take its place: beefed-up Asian client armies; new technology; and a new commitment to prompt and strong response. In Baldwin's words:

In any case, tactical atomic weapons cannot be automatically foresworn if Asia is to be stabilized, for even their tacit invocation contributes to the "balance of terror' which —whether we like it or not—now governs the world we live in. And in any case, it is only by technological escalation, rather than by manpower escalation, that United States military forces can, without excessive cost in United States blood, redress within the immediate time frame of the near tomorrows the unfavorable manpower balance in Asia. And only thus can the power of the deterrent to aggression be maximized.

By "the unfavorable manpower balance in Asia," Baldwin means that there are unfortunately more Asians than Americans there.

In the economic realm, the Nixon Doctrine offers no real alternative to policies which have been of dubious merit up to now.

Economically as well as militarily, the low-profile role projected for the U.S. in Asia involves an attempt to cloak

American involvement in a multinational guise. The new vocabulary of multinationalism, however, fails to obscure the fact that the development of the area will be dominated by the United States, its white allies (notably Australia and New Zealand), and Japan.

Though there are several views about what Southeast Asia offers the more developed countries, differing approaches suggest that the following factors must be seriously considered: (1) raw materials (especially minerals, petroleum, rubber, and timber); (2) cheap labor for foreign-controlled light industries, including both manufacture of parts to be assembled in the home country and assembly plants for parts manufactured in the home country —neither process contributing much to the local economy (Japan, ironically, is particularly eager to exploit this human resource as its own wage levels rise); (3) a potential market for the products of the more industrialized countries (U.S. trade, as opposed to direct investment, is increasing faster in the Pacific than in Europe); and (4) the opportunity for an early and potentially lucrative role in the basic economic and financial institutions of the area (to take Indonesia as an example, since the coup of 1966, fifteen American banks have opened offices in the country and it is estimated that two-thirds of the planned investments will be American-owned.

When one addresses the question of whether the advanced capitalist countries offer a real hope to the *peoples* of Southeast Asia, however, the answers are less easily forthcoming. Past examples and present trends, in Latin America as well as Asia itself, suggest that reliance upon multinational aid, trade, and investment along the lines Mr. Nixon seems to have in mind will create or consolidate native elites more intent upon personal aggrandizement than on public works; will exacerbate rather than resolve existing schisms between city and countryside and between rich and poor; will foster a system of "industrial dualism" in which a favored sector of manufactures is encouraged and protected to the neglect of a far larger sector of native crafts and cottage industries; and will lock the recipient countries into a permanently inferior and dependent relationship with the advanced capitalistic countries. These distortions—and the corruption and glut of services and luxury consumer items for the native elite which invariably accompanies them—are already apparent in the Philippines, Thailand, South Vietnam, and elsewhere in "free" Asia. Thus two economists observe that "In human terms, the result of the last twenty-five years has meant abysmally low levels of consumption, education, health and welfare for about two-thirds of the people" of Southeast Asia. A United Nations report of 1965 describes the situation as presenting "a scene of contrast, with some indications of considerable progress standing out against a background of extensive poverty, hunger, illiteracy, and sickness." And Gunnar Myrdal notes that "the extent of inequality has either remained constant over the past decade (or longer) or has increased."

By assigning the countries of Southeast Asia a specific role in the international capitalist system as suppliers of raw materials and recipients of advanced manufactured goods, the grave danger exists that these economies will be skewed in such a way as to relegate them to a state of permanent underdevelopment. Since the world market price of raw materials has been steadily declining, while the price of consumer and capital goods is rising, the underdeveloped nations drawn into the capitalist system in this manner face the prospects of a chronic trade imbalance; a drain on foreign exchange reserves; and a permanent inability to develop their own light or heavy industries in the face of Western and Japanese competition, pressure, and priorities. Nor do past trends in foreign investment and aid offer real hope that future multinational efforts will provide underdeveloped countries the capital necessary to establish a balanced base for future economic development. Between 1950 and 1965, for example, direct U.S. investment in underdeveloped countries totaled $9,000,000,000, while the return to the U.S. from these countries was $25,600,000,000 for a net inflow of $16,600,000,000 or about $1,000,000,000 a year. Similarly, most U.S. foreign aid has been structured so that in one way or another it benefits the U.S. in the end (whether given as interest-bearing loans, or tied to purchases of U.S. goods or transportation in U.S. carriers, or directed to projects which will benefit U.S. investors in the long run). Japan, America's major partner in future development projections for Asia, is proving itself adept at the same game. Already established in Southeast Asia as a major importer of raw materials and salesman of everything from caramels to buses, Japan's leaders now regularly reaffirm their intention of increasing their "aid" to their poor neighbors. But selectively. As the *Far Eastern Economic Review* recently noted, to no one's surprise, "the Japanese admit that one purpose of their aid program is to develop markets capable of absorbing their products." The prospect, in a word, is that the underdeveloped countries of "free Asia" face the danger of remaining the neo-colonies of the West and also of becoming, at last, Japan's long dreamed of "co-prosperity sphere."

The problem of development is further compounded by the peculiar relationship between American military spending and the growth of Asian capitalism ever since 1945. The post-war economic growth of South Korea, South Vietnam, Taiwan, Thailand, Singapore, Japan, and the Philippines has been greatly accelerated by American expenditures for the wars in Korea and Vietnam, by maintenance of the huge American network of bases in Asia; and by growth in the domestic U.S. market sparked by American defense spending. As of 1968, for example, Japan was taking in an estimated $850,000,000 annually just from purchases directly or indirectly related to U.S. military activities in Asia. In Thailand, since 1961 the U.S. has invested $500,000,000 in the construction of six major air bases for the bombing of Laos and Vietnam, with extensive additional funds going into the construction of the deepwater port of Sattahip on the Gulf of Siam. Half of the increase in the gross domestic product of Thailand between 1965 and 1967 derived from U.S. military spending within the country, and early this year *The New York Times* noted that "The closing of the air bases, and the withdrawal of the airmen stationed on them, would have a shattering impact on the Thai economy, just as their construction and the presence of the men has worked profound changes in the economic and cultural patterns in rural Thailand." As mentioned above, in South Korea dollar earnings directly connected with the Vietnam war totaled almost $400,000,000 in 1968 and 1969 alone; this was in addition to $403,000,000 in U.S. military assistance funds in fiscal 1968, $140,000,000 in fiscal 1969, and in the neighborhood of $200,000,000 in fiscal 1970. According to a recent report prepared under Professor Franz Schurmann at the University of California, Berkeley:

. . . the Korean economy finds itself in a rather precarious position. While her trade deficit has thus far been covered by loans from the U.S. and Japan, these loans must now be paid back. By 1972 repayments will reach over $200 million. This in turn promises to strip her of much needed future growth capital. As long as Korea is involved in Vietnam she can earn enough foreign exchange to meet these commitments but with the eventual conclusion of the war she must either default, renegotiate, or find new sources of capital.

The road to Asian capitalism has been paved by the American military, and it remains a serious but generally unstated question as to whether the growth rate of America's "Free World" allies in Asia has not become to a greater or lesser extent dependent upon such war-related stimulants. The predominantly military focus of the Nixon Doctrine, with its stress on military assistance and strengthening of the military capacities of the various pro-American regimes in Asia, is not inconsistent with this trend. To Asians, whatever their political persuasion, capitalism and militarism are openly and inseparably linked.

Considerations such as these lock into the more purely military dimension of the Nixon Doctrine. If the economic development of the countries of Southeast Asia proceeds in such a way as to exacerbate impoverishment and hardship among the majority of the people, insurgency can be expected to increase, with an increasingly high content of revolutionary nationism directed against the foreign presence. The primary focus of U.S. aid to its client governments is already military to begin with. This would increase even more, particularly as the stakes of the "multinational" corporations and organizations in preserving the political, social, and economic status quo in the various countries increase. And one can anticipate that such a rise in tensions would also be accompanied by a rise in the number of those advocating solution by a quick resort to the new technology of death.

In the political and social realms, the Nixon Doctrine continues to offer support to the same type of generally corrupt, repressive, exploitative—but pro-American— regimes which the United States has supported in the past.

Implicit in much of the preceding discussion is the belief that the poverty and misery under which many of Asia's peasant millions toil derives as much from a social and political malaise as from an economic dilemma; that the military issue is branch and not root. Many policy-makers and academics would probably agree with this, yet few are willing to seriously face the dilemma which has been consistently posed by American reliance upon "anti-Communist reformist elites." In the Nixon Doctrine also, the focus remains upon attempting to bring about change through a military or urban elite which, as case after case has shown, can rarely carry out thoroughgoing and meaningful reforms without undermining its own privileged position. In Indochina, this is readily apparent in the venal puppet regimes in Saigon and Vientiane. Outside the war theater it is equally obvious although less publicized. Consider, for example, the Philippines, where seven decades of intimate American involvement culminated in the "democracy" of the 1969 elections:

Filipinos view elections as a confirmation of the power of the wealthy business and landed interests who back both parties but usually pick the winners before Election Day and quietly give them the most support. In this case they picked President Marcos.

For the Philippine peasantry, three-fourths of the population, living standards have not risen since the Spanish occupation.

The Nixon Doctrine glosses over this side of the Asian dilemma. Also ignored or disparaged is the other and more hopeful side of the dilemma, namely, the dynamic of social and political change which has thus far proven itself most viable in underdeveloped, largely peasant societies: change initiated in the countryside, calling upon the energies of the people themselves, and motivated not by an attempt to siphon off discontent which might feed "insurgency," but rather by a fundamental desire to alleviate misery.

In international as well as internal affairs, the Nixon Doctrine enforces bipolarization.

Whatever allegations the administration may make to the contrary, the record clearly indicates that American support invariably goes to those elements in a country who in external affairs support the United States and in internal affairs endorse private enterprise and are tolerant of considerable foreign investment. The result is to exacerbate polarization within the society on the one hand (as seen in South Vietnam), and on the other hand to make adherence to an independent role in diplomacy extremely difficult for nations caught in the path of the American juggernaut (as witness the effect of American actions on Cambodia, Laos, and both North [and South] Vietnam). The attitude that neutrality is inherently immoral has its roots in the moral globalism of the Dulles period, but whatever its origins, the fact remains that there is a greater degree of national sovereignty and greater independence in foreign affairs within the so-called "Communist camp" in Asia than exists among the nations of what the administration calls "free Asia." The latter remains an alliance heavily reliant upon American aid; greatly indebted to America's post-war military spending and wars in Asia for much of its economic growth; increasingly dependent upon a market system dominated by the United States and Japan; and predominantly judged not by its contribution to the well-being of its peoples, but rather by its anti-Communist credentials and its contribution, real or potential, to American military objectives in Asia.

In saying this, there is no intention of denying present trends toward a multipolar configuration in contemporary Asia, with China, the Soviet Union, the United States, and Japan playing the leading power roles. This must, in fact, be a key point of focus in any attempt to comprehend Asia's future, and it would be foolish to assert that the administration does not recognize this. At best, however, this recognition can only be described as a grudging one, a rather technocratic endeavor to reconcile new power realities in Asia with other changing political, economic, and military considerations—and to do so with the least possible sacrifice of old, often killing, but generally comfortable shibboleths concerning the nature and needs of Asia's peoples and America's proper role toward them. The Nixon Doctrine is good domestic politics, perhaps; it is obviously high time for the low posture at home. It is hardly statesmanship, however, and indeed little more than one would have expected to be tossed up in any case by the normal momentum of time, technology, bureaucracy, and imperial pride.

Fall, 1970

THE NIXON DOCTRINE AND OUR ASIAN COMMITMENTS
BY EARL C. RAVENAL

Eighteen months after its enunciation at Guam the Nixon Doctrine remains obscure and contradictory in its intent and application. It is not simply that the wider pattern of war in Indochina challenges the doctrine's promise of a lower posture in Asia. More than that, close analysis and the unfolding of events expose some basic flaws in the logic of the administration's evolving security policy for the new decade. The Nixon Doctrine properly includes more than the declaratory policy orientation. It comprises also the revised worldwide security strategy of "one and a half wars" and the new defense decision-making processes such as "fiscal guidance budgeting." These elements have received little comment, especially in their integral relation to our commitments in Asia. But the effects of this administration's moves in these areas will shape and constrain the choices of the United States for a long time to come.

The President's foreign policy declaration of February, 1970, promised that "our interests, our foreign policy objectives, our strategies and our defense budgets are being brought into balance—with each other and with our overall national priorities." After a decade of burgeoning military spending and entanglement in foreign conflict, the nation has welcomed the vision of lower defense budgets balanced by a reduction in American involvement overseas, particularly in Asia. Actually, however, the administration's new policies and decision processes do not bring about the proposed balance; in fact, they create a more serious imbalance. Essentially we are to support the same level of potential involvement with smaller conventional forces. The specter of intervention will remain, but the risk of defeat or stalemate will be greater; or the nuclear threshold will be lower. The fundamental issues of interests, commitments, and alliances are not resolved.

II

The objectives of close-in military containment and the forward defense of our Asian allies present us with a series of bleak choices:

With regard to deterrence: (1) perpetuation of a high level of active conventional forces, conspicuously deployed or deployable; (2) fundamental and obvious reliance on nuclear weapons; or (3) acknowledgment of the higher probability of an enemy initiative.

With regard to initial defense: (1) maintenance or rapid deployment of large armies in Asia; (2) early recourse to tactical nuclear weapons; or (3) acceptance of the greater risk of losing allied territory.

With regard to terminating a war: (1) large commitments of troops and heavy casualties; (2) use of nuclear weapons, either tactical or strategic; or (3) resignation to an indefinite and wasting stalemate, tantamount to defeat.

The only solution that transcends the triangle of unsatisfactory choices is to reevaluate our interests in Asia; restate those objectives that implicate us in the possibility of war on the Asian mainland and diminish our control over our actions; resist the grand and vapid formulas of our role in Asia—such as the existential platitude that "we are a Pacific power"—that perpetuate the illusion of paramountcy; retreat from the policy of military containment of China; and revise the alliances that have come to represent our commitment to containment.

But this course the President has consistently rejected:

". . . we will maintain our interests in Asia and the commitments that flow from them. . . . The United States will keep all its treaty commitments." Thus the root problem of the Nixon Doctrine is its abiding commitment to the containment of China. In the furtherance of this policy our government hopes to maintain all our present Asian alliances and de facto commitments, profiting from their deterrent value but avoiding their implications. Yet it also intends to scale down our conventional military capability. The result is that the Nixon Doctrine neither reduces our potential involvement in Asian conflicts nor resolves the resulting dilemma by providing convincingly for a defense that will obviate reliance on nuclear weapons.

Let us examine the prospect of the Nixon Doctrine as a relief from involvement in Asian contingencies. The trauma that has resulted from our inability to win decisively in Vietnam has caused our policy-makers to suggest a limitation of future involvement on the basis of a distinction between external or overt aggression on the one hand, and insurgency, political subversion and civil war on the other. The President attempts in this way to avoid the strategy dilemma by altering the criteria for intervention and thus understating the probability of involvement:

. . . we cannot expect U.S. military forces to cope with the entire spectrum of threats facing allies or potential allies throughout the world. This is particularly true of subversion and guerrilla warfare, or "wars of national liberation." Experience has shown that the best means of dealing with insurgencies is to preempt them through economic development and social reform and to control them with police, paramilitary and military action by the threatened government.

But this is nothing more than a postulation that the unwished contingency will not arise. The hard question remains: What if these "best means" are not successful? Under *those* conditions what kind of solutions does the Nixon Doctrine envisage? Might the United States be impelled to intervene with combat forces? The President states:

. . . a direct combat role for U.S. general purpose forces arises primarily when insurgency has shaded into external aggression or when there is an overt conventional attack. In such cases, we shall weigh our interests and our commitments, and we shall consider the efforts of our allies, in determining our response.

But this formula for discrimination and discretion seems both unclear and unrealistic. At what point does an insurgency become "external aggression"? A definition sometimes proposed is the introduction of enemy main-force units, rather than mere individual fillers. But, even apart from the difficult question of verification, this event might be well beyond the point where our intervention became critical to the situation. The paradox is that in critical cases we might not wish to define the situation to preclude intervention; in less than critical cases we would not need to invoke nice distinctions to justify it. In any case, relying on formulas and distinctions misses the point: it is simply not credible that we would sacrifice our still-held objectives to the vagaries of circumstance.

Indeed, as long as our policy remains the containment of China and the repression of Asian Communism, we are inclined to view even largely indigenous revolutions as objective instances of the purposes of Peking or Hanoi or Pyongyang. Consequently, if an insurgency in an allied or even a neutral country began to succeed, we would probably first increase logistical aid, then extend the role of advisers and provide air support. Since such moves might bring a countervailing response from the Asian Communist sponsors of the insurgency, we might have to choose between sending ground forces and allowing an ally to lose by our default. In certain extremities we might be forced to the final choice among unlimited conventional escalation, defeat of our own forces, or "technological escalation" to the use of nuclear weapons.

Thus, with our formal or implied commitments and the President's open-ended prescription, the United States might yet be drawn into a land war on the Asian mainland or have to confront equally dire alternatives. In this respect the Nixon Doctrine does not improve on the policy that led to Vietnam. And, of course, our exposure to involvement in the case of more overt aggression, such as a Chinese-supported invasion in Korea or Southeast Asia, remains undiminished.

The only proposition that has become clear about the Nixon Doctrine is that its most advertised hope of resolving the strategy problem—both reducing the forces we maintain for Asian defense and avoiding involvement in conflict—is Asianization; *i.e.,* the substitution of indigenous forces, equipped through enlarged U.S. military assistance, for American troops. The case for expanded military assistance has been stated with unprecedented urgency by Secretary Laird in preparation for vastly increased Military Assistance Program (MAP) budget requests for 1972 and succeeding fiscal years. Secretary Laird has characterized MAP as "the essential ingredient of our policy if we are to honor our obligations, support our allies, and yet reduce the likelihood of having to commit American ground combat units."

But the Secretary recognizes the declining level of popular and congressional support for military assistance. His solution, considered perennially within the Defense and State departments but proposed for the first time in a secretarial posture statement to the Congress, is that "military assistance should be integrated into the Defense Budget so that we can plan more rationally and present to the Congress more fully an integrated program." Military aid for certain "forward defense countries," including South Vietnam, Thailand, and Laos, and consisting of about 80 percent of the total category "Support for Other Nations," is already meshed into the Defense Budget. This legislative ploy has not yet been applied to Korea or Taiwan, though the reduction of our troops in Korea and the insurance of Taiwan against Communist pressure depend, in the judgment of this administration, on the freedom to substitute U.S. matériel for manpower.

To merge military assistance entirely into the regular functional appropriation categories of the Defense Budget would be to institutionalize the dual rationale for military assistance that has become traditional in debate within the Department of Defense. The first element in this rationale is the argument from "trade-off"—a calculus that compares the costs of equal units of effectiveness of U.S. and foreign troops. This is essentially an assertion of "absolute advantage" and is the basic and obvious sense of Secretary Laird's statement: "A MAP dollar is of far greater value than a dollar spent directly on U.S. forces."

The second element is the argument from "comparative advantage," borrowed from the economic theory of international trade: "Each nation must do its share and contribute what it can appropriately provide—manpower from many of our allies; technology, material, and specialized skills from the United States." The proponents of military comparative advantage assert, by analogy, that the cooperating and specializing defense community can "consume" security at a higher level. It may be, however, that they can only consume more of the tangible intermediate trappings of security; *i.e.*, the forces and arms. The essence of security, especially for the United States as the senior partner, might depend more on certain qualitative factors. In fact, there are several difficulties in the administration's ostensibly neutral and technical arguments for military assistance.

First, both trade-off and comparative advantage assume and confirm the inevitability and relevance of the shared mission—that is, the forward defense of the ally's territory. But only if we cannot avoid this mission is it proper to confine the debate to the optimal distribution of roles and costs.

Second, the argument from comparative advantage, like the economic theory at its origin, stresses specialization. But the concomitant of specialization is interdependence. Thus a policy of selective reliance on allies, in order to be effective, implies automatic involvement from the earliest moments of a conflict.

Third, early experience indicates that U.S. ground forces cannot simply be traded off with precisely calculated increments of military assistance. They must be politically ransomed by disproportionate grants, more conspicuous deployments and more fervent and explicit confirmations of our commitment.

Fourth, from the diplomatic standpoint the substitution of massive infusions of modern arms for U.S. troops is anything but neutral. To the North Koreans and their sponsors, for example, the $1,500,000,000 of support and new equipment we now intend to give South Korea might look very provocative and destabilizing. A new phase of the peninsular arms race could be the result, with a net loss to regional and U.S. security.

Finally, the legislative tactic of integrating the Military Assistance Program into the Defense Budget would remove military assistance as an object of the broader concerns of foreign policy and assign it to the jurisdiction of more narrowly defense-oriented congressional committees. The debate would be less political and more technical. The focus would shift from the question of involvement to the question of relative costs. Thus Asianization, which is the keystone of the Nixon Doctrine, would substitute some Asian forces and resources, but along the same perimeter of interest. It affords a pretext for reducing expense, but it does not enhance our security or relieve us from involvement.

III

The basic question is whether the Nixon Doctrine is an honest policy that will fully fund the worldwide and Asian commitments it proposes to maintain, or whether it conceals a drift toward nuclear defense or an acceptance of greater risk of local defeat. The most obvious change in our military posture is that the new formula provides conventional forces to counter a major Communist thrust in Asia or Europe, but not simultaneously. As the President has explained:

The stated basis of our conventional posture in the 1960's was the so-called "two and a half war" principle. According to it, U.S. forces would be maintained for a three-month conventional forward defense of NATO, a defense of Korea or Southeast Asia against a full-scale Chinese attack, and a minor contingency—all simultaneously. These force levels were never reached.

In the effort to harmonize doctrine and capability, we chose what is best described as the "one and a half war" strategy. Under it we will maintain in peacetime general purpose forces adequate for simultaneously meeting a major Communist attack in either Europe or Asia, assisting allies against non-Chinese threats in Asia, and contending with a contingency elsewhere.

What will be the ultimate force levels associated with the new one-and-a-half war strategy, and how can we assess their implications for Asian defense? Peacetime forces are obviously entailed by the extent of our commitments, but in no precisely determined way. A most important intermediate term—which could account for wide differences in strategy and forces—is the probable simultaneity of contingencies. The Nixon strategy of one and a half wars is explicitly founded on the improbability of two simultaneous major contingencies. Thus demands on the planned general purpose forces are to be considered alternative rather than additive.

Can we then expect a force reduction equivalent to the requirement for defending against the lesser of the major contingencies? To support the previous strategy of two and a half wars, the Baseline (or peacetime) Force Structure was thought to provide seven active divisions for Southeast Asia, two for Korea, eight for NATO, and two and one-third for a minor contingency and a strategic reserve—a total of nineteen and one-third. Since the present one-and-a-half-war doctrine includes only one major contingency, in NATO *or* Asia, one might derive an active ground force as low as ten and one-third divisions.

Such a literal expectation, however, is confused by the President's desire to insure "against greater than expected threats by maintaining more than the forces required to meet conventional threats in one theater—such as NATO Europe;" the fact that certain types of divisions are inherently specialized for certain geographical contingencies, so that all eight of our armored and mechanized divisions will probably remain oriented to NATO and inapplicable to Asian defense; and finally, the judgments of both the President and Secretary Laird that the force levels necessary to implement the previous two-and-a-half-war policy "were never reached."

But it seems clear that the ultimate Baseline Force Structure under the Nixon Doctrine will contain even fewer divisions for the Asian requirement than the minimal proposals for a conventional defense. The reduced conventional force is most significant as a reflection of the altered concept of Asian defense embodied in the Nixon Doctrine. The constituent propositions of this concept are: (1) the most likely threats to our Asian allies do not involve Chinese invasion, and (2) with greatly expanded military assistance our allies can largely provide the ground forces to counter such threats.

There is a third proposition, strongly implied by the logic of the problem and markedly signaled in the President's foreign policy statement: in a future Asian conflict, particularly if it does involve China, United States intervention is likely to carry with it the use of tactical nuclear weapons.

—The nuclear capability of our strategic and theater nuclear forces serves as a deterrent to full-scale Soviet attack on NATO Europe or Chinese attack on our Asian allies;

—The prospects for a coordinated two-front attack on our allies by Russia and China are low both because of the risks of nuclear war and the improbability of Sino-Soviet cooperation. In any event, we do not believe that such a coordinated attack should be met primarily by U.S. conventional forces.

Though the "coordinated" attack described by the President is improbable, it should be noted that "theater nuclear forces" are prescribed as deterrents against the *single* contingency of a "Chinese attack on our Asian allies." Also, there are more plausible scenarios that would, in terms of their potential to immobilize U.S. forces, be the functional equivalent of a major attack: a Soviet military buildup and political pressure in central or southern Europe; or China's rendering massive logistical support to one of her Asian allies to the point where that ally could release overwhelming forces against a neighboring country; or the imminent entry of China into a war where we or one of our allies might have provided the provocation. It is conceivable that two such lesser contingencies could arise, in Europe and Asia, and that one of them could develop to the point of a conflict. In that event we would be reluctant to consider our conventional forces for either theater available for the other. Motivated by illusions of decisive action and immunity from retaliation, we might be tempted to dispose of the Asian conflict by technological escalation.

Therefore, if we remain committed to the defense of interests in both theaters, but maintain conventional forces for only one large contingency, our strategy is biased toward the earlier use of nuclear weapons. Of course, there is no necessary continuum of escalation from conventional war to tactical nuclear war. But the one-and-a-half-war strategy provides the President with fewer alternatives and renders the resort to nuclear weapons a more compelling choice, as well as making nuclear threat a more obvious residual feature of our diplomacy.

And so the "balance" promised in the new security policy is achieved—but not by adjusting our commitments, restricting our objectives, or modifying our conception of the interests of the United States. Rather, budgetary stringencies inspire a reduction in force levels; a "one-and-a-half-war strategy" is tailored to fit the intractable realities; and a series of rationalizations is constructed to validate the new strategy—rationalizations that simply stipulate a reduced threat, count heavily on subsidized and coerced allied efforts at self-defense, and suggest an early nuclear reaction if our calculations prove insufficiently conservative.

Thus the Nixon Doctrine reveals an apparent contradiction between objectives and strategy. Are we seeing the beginning of a return to the defense posture of the 1950's, with unabated commitments to a collection of front-line client-states, but with limited options and a renewed flirtation with the fantasy of tactical nuclear warfare?

IV

The new security policy not only shifts substantively down to a one-and-a-half-war strategy but also changes the model for determining defense requirements. Instead of the classic progression from the definition of foreign policy interests to the formulation of objectives, to the prescription of strategies, to the calculation of forces and their costs, we now see a constrained calculus that proceeds in reverse from limited budgets to trimmed forces to arbitrary strategies. The implications are not transmitted through the system to include a revision of objectives and interests. At best the system is balanced back from resources through strategies; the imbalance is shifted to a point between strategies and objectives.

But even the strategies and the forces may be out of balance. For the budget-constrained strategy revision is complemented by a fundamental change in the defense planning process. The previous system was requirements-oriented: there was, in theory, no prior budgetary restriction. Rather, planning began with the stated worldwide defense objective and resulted in forces and a budget which were recommended to the President and the Congress as systematically entailed by our defense objectives. Of course, the ideal system foundered on the institutional realities of weapons-systems and force creation. Indeed, the philosophy of unconstrained implementation of security objectives—"buy what you need" —encouraged inflated requirements within the framework of two-and-a-half wars. And the attempts of the Secretary to limit forces only led the military to attempts to goldplate those prescribed forces, while keeping a ledger on the "shortfall" between the imposed strategy and the imposed force structure. But at least the direction and scope of the planning process compelled attention to the relevance and adequacy of the forces, and allowed the possibility of reasoning back from the rejection of excessive requirements to the questioning of overambitious strategies, extensive commitments and artificial interests.

By contrast, the new defense planning process begins simultaneously with "strategic guidance" and "fiscal guidance," established by the President and the National Security Council. The new procedure has attained certain efficiencies in managing the Pentagon budget cycle. But from the policy standpoint it is another matter: within the fiscal ceilings we will get the forces and weapons systems that the organization tends to produce—not the ones we might need. Of the two kinds of guidance, the fiscal is quantitative and unarguable; the strategic is verbal and elastic. If there is a coincidence of those forces and systems tailored to the fiscal guidance and those derived from the strategic guidance, it will be either accidental or contrived.

More likely, the services will interpret the new guidance as a set of parameters within which they can promote self-serving programs. Under conditions of budgetary stringency they will skimp on manpower, supplies, war reserve stocks, maintenance and transport, while preserving headquarters, cadres of units, research and development of large new systems, and sophisticated technological overhead. In effect they will tend, as in the 1950's, to sacrifice those items that maintain balance, readiness, and sustainability of effort, and to insist on those items that insure morale, careers and the competitive position of each Service.

Thus the administration's defense planning procedure

allows a second contradiction: between strategy and forces. This country may well end the 1970's with the worst of both worlds: on the one hand, a full panoply of commitments and a strategy that continues to serve an ambitious policy of containment; on the other, a worldwide sprinkling of token deployments and a force structure that is still expensive, but unbalanced, unready and irrelevant to our security.

V

The disabilities of the Nixon Doctrine follow from its insistence on the containment of China in face of budgetary pressures that arise not out of absolute scarcity of resources, but out of the nation's unwillingness to make large sacrifices for objectives that cannot be credibly invoked by its leadership. If the administration is to be consistent in revising our defense posture and limiting defense budgets, it must consider a commensurate curtailment of our foreign policy objectives in Asia. Adjusting the intermediate-term strategies will not effect the reconciliation and will permit an honest implementation of the force and budget cuts.

But the Nixon Doctrine does not resolve the Asian defense problem in this fundamental way: rather, it appears as another formula for permanent confrontation with China. What are the issues that elude the perennial expressions of interest, by several administrations, in accommodating China? During the Johnson administration the policy of containment ceded to a variant characterized as "containment without isolation." The shift, however, was accompanied by no tangible initiatives and induced no reciprocity from China. President Nixon entered office with a mandate—which he had created largely himself through his campaign emphasis—to bring about a reconciliation with China. His administration has relaxed certain restrictions on trade and travel and revived the Warsaw ambassadorial talks. But such moves, though impressive as indications of enlightenment, do not touch on the essential concerns of China. However we ultimately conceive our interests, we might as well be realistic about the eventual price of a real accommodation with China.

This price would include three kinds of consideration: (1) diplomatic recognition and admission without qualification to the United Nations and the permanent Security Council seat; (2) affirmation of a one-China policy, even allowing the eventual accession of Taiwan to the mainland; (3) removal of the U.S. military presence on the mainland of Asia, without substituting a naval cordon, a ring of nearby island bases, a host of Asian mercenary armies, or a nuclear tripwire. The components of such a withdrawal would be: liquidation of the Vietnam war and removal of all U.S. forces there; retraction of all U.S. troops from other mainland Asian countries and Taiwan and closure of all bases; termination of military assistance to mainland states and cessation of efforts to create proxy forces to continue our mission; and dissolution of our security alliances with the "forward-defense" countries of Thailand, Taiwan, and Korea.

Such a program would amount to a major diplomatic revolution. It might take a quarter of a century to implement, even with the most sophisticated public and political support within the United States. It would alienate client régimes, unsettle for long intervals our relations with the Soviets, and tax the understanding of major allies such as Japan and Australia. It would signify the renunciation of our efforts to control events in Asia; henceforth we would control only our responses to events.

But it is fair to ask whether we will not arrive at this disposition of affairs in Asia at some point, whether we will it or not. Should this occur after a quarter of a century of tension and devastation, or political maneuver and diplomatic search? It is also fair to speculate that a more neutral, or even positive, relationship with China might give us a new scope of advantages. We might benefit eventually from a commercial relationship with China, rather than conceding the economic penetration of the mainland by Japan and Western Europe while we remain frozen in our historic impasse. We might also, simply through the dissolution of predictable enmity with China, make it more difficult for the Soviets to challenge us in other areas of the world. And we might find it useful to have a counterpoise to Japan, which is still our principal Pacific competitor, economic and potentially military, and a possible future partner of the U.S.S.R. in such common interests as counterbalancing China and developing eastern Siberia.

The tangible expression of containment is our security alliances and the other strong, though less formal, military commitments around the periphery of China. These commitments, it can be argued, create the threat to us by transforming otherwise neutral events into situations of relevance to our interests; perpetuate the confrontation with China that gives substance to the threat, by frustrating the essential motives of China; lock us into a posture of forward defense on the mainland of Asia; and dictate the requirement for large general purpose forces or equivalent means of deterrence and defense.

Our alliances in Asia do not form a coherent and comprehensive system such as NATO. Rather they are a collection of bilateral agreements, plus the multilateral SEATO pact, contracted separately from 1951 through 1962. Even the purposes served by these alliances, as seen at the time of their negotiation, were diverse. Containment of China might have been a concurrent motive, but it did not uniformly inspire the creation of the pacts.

Quite apart from containing our enemies, several of the treaties exhibit motives of containing our allies as well.

The ANZUS and Philippine treaties of 1951, though signed against the backdrop of the Korean War, related more to the fear of Japan which these allies derived from World War II. The 1953 agreement with the Republic of Korea was, among other things, a price for Syngman Rhee's restraint from attempting to reunify the peninsula by force. Similarly the treaty with the Republic of China in 1955 was in part a quid pro quo for Chiang's acceptance of "re-leashing" during the Straits crisis of that year. The SEATO alliance of 1954, which extended protection to South Vietnam, Laos, and Cambodia, arose less from the vision of true collective defense than the desire of the United States to have a legal basis for discretionary intervention under the nominal coloration of "united action." The bilateral U.S.–Thai adjunct to SEATO, negotiated by Rusk and Thanat in 1962, reassured the Thais, during the events that led to the Laos neutralization accords, that the U.S. would respond to a threat to Thai security, regardless of the reaction of other SEATO signatories; this agreement, too, was a price to secure the acquiescence of an ally in an arrangement that suited the interest of the United States. The 1960 Security Treaty with Japan, revising the original treaty of 1951, reaffirmed U.S. administration of Okinawa and perpetuated our use of bases in the Japanese home islands, subject to prior consultation for nuclear or direct combat deployments. (The Nixon-Sato communiqué of October, 1969, pledged reversion of Okinawa to Japan by 1972, a status that implies removal of nuclear weapons and submission to the "homeland formula" for consultation on the use of bases.)

Though deterrence has always been the primary function of our alliances, their military content has changed profoundly from the time they were contracted. The

Dulles policy, in the pacts of 1953–55, did not emphasize the actual defense of allied territory or contemplate the dispatch of U.S. ground forces to any point where the Communist powers chose to apply military force. Rather, it aimed at nuclear deterrence of overt aggression. In this concept the alliances served to establish a territorial definition. The implied countermeasure was the discretionary application of American nuclear force against Communist airfields, supply centers, ports and perhaps industries and cities. The concept was not clearly resolved: it was semi-strategic and semi-tactical, partially punitive and partially for direct military effect. Also, cases short of obvious aggression, such as subversion and support for internal revolutionary struggles, were acknowledged to be imprecise and difficult. In Indochina in 1954 the Eisenhower administration could not identify an appropriate enemy or target to fit the massive nuclear response and narrowly declined to intervene. Of course, it also sensed the lack of formal alliance protection over Southeast Asia as an impediment to intervention and moved to create SEATO within two months of the partition of Vietnam.

The refinement of tactical battlefield nuclear weapons in the middle and later 1950's made conceivable the notion of actual nuclear defense confined to the theater of conflict. The Kennedy-McNamara policy of flexible response, including counterinsurgency techniques and large balanced conventional forces, provided the practical means of containing a wider spectrum of Chinese or Chinese-supported initiatives. Thus the policy of close-in containment of China—involving the actual forward defense of allied territory—acquired its content.

There is a set of propositions that qualifies military deterrence: the more explicit and obvious our commitment, the more effective in preventing war, but the less effective in preventing our involvement in war; conversely, the more attenuated our commitment, the less certain our involvement, but the more probable a hostile initiative.

An administration with a more relaxed view of Asia might take the risk of the second proposition and look more neutrally on a Communist probe. But this administration appears likely to maintain its deterrent stance and take its chances on involvement in conflict. This would mean that it will not overtly diminish any commitment; indeed it is likely to reaffirm and reinforce any commitment that is beset by doubt. But to maintain the deterrent effect of our commitments in the face of reductions in budgets, forces and deployments, the administration must replace deleted capabilities with some equivalent, such as increased rapid deployment ability or nuclear threat. This administration could not count entirely on the mobility of our forces, which can be evidenced only by massive exercises and adequate lift resources, which are far from certain to be appropriated. Residually, it is forced to rely on nuclear deterrence, which need only be hinted. The point is that our mode of deterrence and our provisions for defense will now progressively diverge from the preferences of our treaty partners. Our proposed substitution of technology and threat for our manpower and presence might be equivalent from our point of view, but not from that of our allies.

None of our Asian defense arrangements is specific about the tangible support that might be evoked by an act of aggression. No joint defense force with agreed war plans and command structures exists. Our military concept could become, rather than the forward defense of all territory, a mobile defense, an enclave strategy, or even a nuclear tripwire. In another dimension, our commitment might be satisfied by various types of support, such as logistical, tactical air or nuclear fire. U.S. contingency plans are essentially unilateral and subject to uncommunicated change. And implementation of all treaties refers to our constitutional procedures, which are themselves in a phase of more stringent interpretation. Because of this scope for maneuver or evasion, our Asian allies will be correspondingly more sensitive to interpretive commentary by U.S. officials and to shifts in our military posture. Already they sense that the substantive content of our alliances is affected by the President's choice of worldwide strategy. The selected strategy is described as defending both Europe and Asia—though alternatively. But it is clear that Europe holds priority and claims virtually as many resources as previously; the major war case associated with the reduction in active forces is Asia. Although no alliances are formally disturbed, our Asian allies, as they count our divisions and analyze our posture statements and policy declarations, have cause for concern that behind the façade of ritualistic reiteration we might have altered our capability and specific intent to fulfill our treaty commitments.

Thus we can devalue the diplomatic and deterrent effect of our alliances without even gaining immunity from involvement, simply by shifting strategies, debating criteria for intervention and making arbitrary adjustments in force levels. In view of the liabilities of this course—which is the course of the present Administration—we might as well face the problem more directly and begin to consider the broader alternatives to containment, with their full implications for our alliances in Asia.

VI

As long as we assert interests in Asia that (1) entail defending territory, (2) could plausibly be threatened by hostile actions, and (3) are evidenced by alliances that dispose us to a military response, we are exposed to the contingency of involvement. If we maintain this exposure through insistence on our present Asian commitments, while adopting budget-constrained strategies, we risk a future defeat or stalemate, or we allow ourselves to be moved toward reliance on nuclear weapons.

To avoid these alternatives, two courses are available. One is heavy dependence on allied forces to fulfill defense requirements. This is the hope of Asianization, offered prominently by the Nixon Doctrine. But this policy binds us closely to the fate of our Asian clients and diminishes our control over our involvement; and there is still the liability that U.S. forces might be required to rescue the efforts of our allies.

The other course is a process of military readjustment and political accommodation that would make it far less likely that we would become involved every time there is some slippage in the extensive diplomatic "fault" that runs along the rim of Asia. This course is arduous and complex, and as little under our unilateral and absolute control as a course of military deterrence. But the consequences of not budging from our present set of ambitions and illusions—or of trifling with the unalterable purposes of China by limiting ourselves to insubstantial diplomatic initiatives—are far bleaker.

The situation calls not for a symbolic shift in strategy —such as the one-and-a-half-war doctrine—which is founded on the hope that the contingencies that would test it, to which we are still liable, might not occur. The situation is not amenable to purely instrumental solutions, such as the calculated equippage of allied armies or the reliance on technological escalation. The situation requires a fundamental questioning and revision of the containment of China.

The confusion that surrounds the Nixon Doctrine is appropriate to its conflicting message and incomplete intent. While pledging to honor all of our existing commitments, the President has placed them all in considerable doubt. While offering promise of avoiding involvement in future Asian conflicts, he has biased the nature of our participation. Thus, in the attempt to perpetuate our control of the destiny of Asia, the Nixon Doctrine may forfeit control of our own destiny in Asia.

January, 1971

AND THE WAR GOES ON AND ON AND ON

BUSINESS WEEK'S REPORT ON ASIAN ECONOMIC DEVELOPMENTS PUTS THE DISCUSSION INTO A LARGER FRAMEWORK.

"ANYBODY SEE PATTON?"
BY HUGH SIDEY

On April 4, roughly a month before American troops invaded Cambodia, Richard Nixon, with his family, saw the movie *Patton,* which is based on the life of General George Patton, the rambunctious commander of the United States Third Army in Europe during World War II.

On April 25, just five days before the incursion, he saw *Patton* again. This time Henry Kissinger joined him; the two of them were in the Saturday emptiness of the White House, pondering the Cambodia decision and the speech with which the President would tell the nation what he was doing and why.

Three weeks later *Patton* came up again. In the aftermath of the campus riots and at the depths of the stock market plunge Nixon summoned forty-five business and financial leaders to the White House to reassure them about his outlook for both the war and the economy, to reassure them, in short, about his leadership.

The evening had gone well. The President was at ease, talking lucidly and sincerely. The economy was sound, he said, but needed cooling. For a time the slowdown would hurt. The troops would come out of Cambodia as promised. They were racing the rainy season and he hoped the monsoons would arrive on schedule as soon as the sanctuaries were cleaned out, preventing the Communists from easy reoccupation and supply. Suddenly a thought struck him. The situation was like *Patton.*

"Anybody see the movie *Patton?*" he asked. Several hands went up, including that of Arthur Burns, the head of the Federal Reserve. Anyone who saw it, Nixon joked, must have learned some four-letter words not even the college kids know (which caused at least one guest to muse that Nixon was clearly out of touch with today's college kids). But the real point of bringing up the movie was that George Patton had accomplished the impossible in rescuing the men trapped by the Battle of the Bulge. "Perhaps," Nixon said, "it was the greatest movement of forces in the whole history of warfare in a short time— 1,000,000 men about 100 miles in three days." Other generals said it couldn't be done, Nixon explained. One of the best parts of the movie, he continued, was when Patton said they needed good weather so that they could use their air power. The general sent for the chaplain. A prayer was written asking for good weather. Patton prayed bareheaded in the snow. When the weather cleared next day, the general sent for the chaplain and decorated him. Now, said Nixon, "We have every chaplain in Vietnam praying for early rain. You have to have the will and determination to go out and to do what is right for America." His audience burst into applause.

The President's fascination with Patton has been passing through the peculiar national grapevine that deals with men of power. In the process it has grown and been twisted, but it is still worth pondering.

It was noted that when Nixon flew to San Clemente only a few days after talking to the businessmen, the celluloid *Patton,* a special 16-mm. film requested by the President, was with him. This time he did not view it, but it may have been on hand for a reason. Presidential Assistant H. Robert Haldeman has counseled young White House staff members to see the movie for a better understanding of Nixon at this critical time. Secretary of State William Rogers ran into Darryl Zanuck, chairman of 20th Century–Fox and told him that Nixon was a walking ad for the movie. "It comes up in every conversation," said Rogers. The staff had talked about it in the back corridors of the White House. Why would Nixon find Patton so intriguing? Maybe because Patton had lived through criticism, endured rejection as Nixon had, and in the end was still willing to try what seemed impossible, to take the bold stroke. Patton had faith in God. Patton was a complex man, just as Nixon is. The speculation went beyond the White House to crop up in Hollywood where the movie had been conceived. Actor Peter Ustinov got his timing a little mixed up and said he heard that the night before the Cambodian invasion Nixon saw the film and was much moved, "impressed by the pressures of power and how they make a hero of a man."

In New York, Ladislas Farago, the author of the book *Patton* (1963) on which the movie was based, lunched with Dr. Margaret Mead, the anthropologist. Why, Farago wondered, was Nixon so taken with Patton? "The President thrives on opposition," Dr. Mead explained. "It is a form of stimulation for him. His enemies should take heed. Any figure who has had to make decisions in the face of opposition as he has done will seem appealing to him." Dr. Mead noted that the mementos of the President's career were relics from his fights, his victories. His book speaks of challenges and crises.

Nixon read Farago's biography soon after taking office last year. It apparently helped stimulate in him a broader interest in recent wars. The books of Dwight Eisenhower and Winston Churchill were already on his study shelves. He went through a volume on the reasons for the collapse of France in 1940. He probed Adviser Kissinger's well-stocked mind for further facts about those decades of men's miscalculations. Then came the Patton film.

Nixon is hardly the first President to scout history for examples of military wisdom and daring. John Kennedy was fascinated by General Douglas MacArthur and used to recall his meeting with the old man in the Waldorf Towers. MacArthur warned against a land war in Asia and told Kennedy that the "chickens are coming home to roost" in that part of the world. Lyndon Johnson held up Eisenhower as his military hero, night after night praising Ike's humanity and wisdom in war.

Dr. Mead suggests that there may be real danger in Presidents looking for guidance to heroes who fought wars and battles neither conceived nor structured like anything we face today. Indochina is not World War II. Nixon's White House troops disagree. In sum, they believe that the emergence of Patton as a major figure in the Nixon pantheon is a good sign, meaning that he will continue to hang tough in the crunches.

June 19, 1970

PRESIDENT NIXON DISCUSSES FOREIGN POLICY DURING TEXAS VISIT
APRIL 30, 1972

Q. Mr. President, do you anticipate any developments in Vietnam, other than those courageous statements we heard on the television the other night, that you might tell us here?

The President: Briefly, I would respond by saying that the evaluation of the situation in Vietnam today is the same that I gave then.

As General Abrams [Gen. Creighton W. Abrams, Commander, U.S. Military Assistance Command, Vietnam] reported then, and as he has updated his report as of today, the South Vietnamese on the ground are resisting very bravely a massive Communist North Vietnamese invasion of South Vietnam. That invasion will continue. The offensive will continue in its intensity, and we can expect over the next four to five weeks that there will be some battles lost by the South Vietnamese and some will be won, but it is his professional judgment—General Abrams' professional judgment—that the South Vietnamese will be able to hold and deny to the North Vietnamese their goal, which of course is to impose on the people of South Vietnam a Communist government.

Now, to keep it all in perspective, let us understand that when we hear about this town or that one that is under attack, we must remember that as of this time the North Vietnamese have utterly failed in their ability to rally the South Vietnamese people to their cause.

We also must remember that despite their moving in on certain territory and in certain towns, that over 90 percent of the people of South Vietnam are still under the Government of South Vietnam and not under control of the Communists.

So keeping it in perspective, while we can expect, and should expect—as is always the case in a war of any kind, and particularly a war of this type—we can expect some days when the news may be a South Vietnamese setback and other days when it will be otherwise. It is the view, the professional view of the man on the spot, best able to judge, that the South Vietnamese will be able to hold, provided—and this comes to what we do—provided the United States continues to furnish the air and naval support that we have been furnishing to stop this invasion.

Now, without repeating what I said last Wednesday night but simply to underline it, I would like to make just two or three points quickly, frankly, to this group of friends here in Texas.

Questions have been raised about the decision that I have made, which is to the effect that as long as the North Vietnamese were conducting an invasion and an offensive in South Vietnam and were killing South Vietnamese and Americans in South Vietnam, that I would, as Commander in Chief of our Armed Forces, order air and naval strikes on military targets in North Vietnam.

I realize that that decision has caused considerable controversy in this country. I understand why that would be the case. There are many people who believe that the United States has done enough in South Vietnam, that what we should do is to find a way to get out as quickly as we can and let whatever the consequences are flow from that which would mean, of course, a Communist takeover.

Let me tell you the reasons why I feel that it is vitally important that the United States continue to use its air and naval power against targets in North Vietnam, as well as in South Vietnam, to prevent a Communist takeover and a Communist victory over the people of South Vietnam.

First, because there are 69,000 Americans still in Vietnam—that will be reduced to 49,000 by the first of July—and I, as Commander in Chief, have a responsibility to see to it that their lives are adequately protected, and I, of course, will meet that responsibility.

Second, because as we consider the situation in Vietnam, we must remember that if the North Vietnamese were to take over in South Vietnam as a result of our stopping our support in the air and on the sea—we have no ground support whatever; there are no American ground forces in action in South Vietnam, and none will be—but when we consider that situation, if there were such a takeover, we must consider the consequences.

There is first the consequence to the people of South Vietnam. We look back to what happened historically. In 1954, when the North Vietnamese took over in North Vietnam, the Catholic Bishop of Da Nang estimated that at least 500,000 people in North Vietnam who had opposed the Communist takeover in the North were either murdered or starved to death in slave labor camps.

I saw something of that when Mrs. Nixon and I were in there in 1956, when we visited refugee camps where over a million North Vietnamese fled from the Communist tyranny to come to the South. If, at this particular point, the Communists were to take over in South Vietnam, you can imagine what would happen to the hundreds of thousands of South Vietnamese who sided with their own government and with the United States against the Communists. It would be a bloodbath that would stain the hands of the United States for time immemorial.

That is bad enough. I know there are some who say we have done enough, what happens to the South Vietnamese at this particular time is something that should not be our concern. We have sacrificed enough for them. So let's put it in terms of the United States alone, and then we really see why the only decision that any man in the position of President of the United States can make is to authorize the necessary air and naval strikes that will prevent a Communist takeover.

In the event that one country like North Vietnam, massively assisted with the most modern technical weapons by two Communist superpowers—in the event that that country is able to invade another country and conquer it, you can see how that pattern would be repeated in other countries throughout the world: in the Mideast, in Europe, and in others as well.

If, on the other hand, that kind of aggression is stopped in Vietnam and fails there, then it will be discouraged in other parts of the world. Putting it quite directly then, what is on the line in Vietnam is not just peace for Vietnam, but peace in the Mideast, peace in Europe, and peace not just for the five or six or seven years immediately ahead of us, but possibly for a long time in the future.

As I put it last Wednesday night, I want and all America wants to end the war in Vietnam. I want and all Americans want to bring our men home from Vietnam. But I want, and I believe all Americans want, to bring our men home and to end this war in a way that the younger brothers and the sons of the men who have fought and died in Vietnam won't be fighting in another Vietnam five or ten years from now. That is what this is all about.

Q. May we raise our glasses and pay tribute to the courage of the President of the United States.

The President: I am most grateful for that toast. Incidentally, I hope the champagne holds out for the evening.

But I do want to say that in the final analysis, what is

really on the line here, of course, is the position of the United States of America as the strongest free-world power, as a constructive force for peace in the world.

Let us imagine for a moment what the world would be like if the United States were not respected in the world. What would the world be like if friends of the United States throughout the non-Communist world lost confidence in the United States? It would be a world that would be much less safe. It would be a world that would be much more dangerous, not only in terms of war but in terms of the denial of freedom, because when we talk about the United States of America and all of our faults, let us remember in this country we have never used our power to break the peace, only to restore it or keep it, and we have never used our power to destroy freedom, only to defend it.

Now, I think that is a precious asset for the world. I also feel one other thing, and I will close this rather long answer on this point: John Connally has referred to the office of the presidency of the United States. Earlier this evening I talked to President Johnson on the phone. We are of different parties. We both served in this office. While I had my political differences with him, and he with me, I am sure he would agree that each of us in his way tries to leave that office with as much respect and with as much strength in the world as he possibly can—that is his responsibility—and to do it the best way that he possibly can.

Let me say in this respect I have noted that when we have traveled abroad to 18 countries, particularly even when we went to the People's Republic of China, the office of President, not the man but the office of President of the United States is respected in every country we visited. I think we will find that same respect in Moscow. But if the United States at this time leaves Vietnam and allows a

Communist takeover, the office of President of the United States will lose respect; and I am not going to let that happen.

Q. Mr. President, may I ask you about strategic targets in North Vietnam? I have been told for years by the pilots that there are dams up there that would be very much defeating to the North Vietnamese, who have defied what you have tried to prove in the way of peace. Is this true or false? Has this crossed your mind?

The President: The question is with regard to the targets in North Vietnam, and particularly with regard to the dams and the dikes, which many of the pilots believe would be very effective strategic targets.

I would say on that score that we have, as you know, authorized strikes, and we have made them over the past four weeks, since the Communist offensive began, in the Hanoi-Haiphong area.

I have also indicated, as this offensive continues, if it does continue, that we will continue to make strikes on military targets throughout North Vietnam.

Now, the problem that is raised with regard to dams or dikes is that while it is a strategic target, and indirectly a military target, it would result in an enormous number of civilian casualties. That is something that we want to avoid. It is also something we believe is not needed.

Just let me say that as far as the targets in North Vietnam are concerned, that we are prepared to use our military and naval strength against military targets throughout North Vietnam, and we believe that the North Vietnamese are taking a very great risk if they continue their offensive in the South.

I will just leave it there, and they can make their own choice.

In other words, I believe that we can limit our strikes to military targets without going to targets that involve civilian casualties. That is what we have done, and we can do that in the future and do the job.

Q. Mr. President, turning to domestic America. You know there are great misgivings in the press about how America feels about itself and where we are going. I don't think there is anyone better equipped to tell us how you feel about where America is going, not today but for its future, and about its own confidence in itself, and I would like to hear your remarks.

The President: The question relates to domestic America, the feeling that many Americans have that possibly we in America are losing confidence in ourselves. The question asks me to evaluate how I see the mood of America, as I understand it, and what the future for America is in terms of confidence in itself.

That, of course, would allow a rather extended reply. Let me see if I can get at the heart of it. First, let me relate it to the last question.

I know there are those who say that the trouble with America's confidence, most of it, is due to the fact that we are involved in Vietnam, and that once the war in Vietnam is over that then the trouble on the campus will go away, the division in the country, the polarization, and all the rest. That is just nonsense.

Let me say the American people do not want war. We did not start this war. Let me say also that when I see people carrying signs saying "Stop the War," I am tempted to say, "Tell it to Hanoi; they are the ones that have started the war, not the United States of America."

Nevertheless, while peace is our goal and peace will be achieved—not just peace in our time, but we hope peace that will live for a generation or longer—that is why we went to Peking. That is why we are going to Moscow. That is why we are trying to end the war responsibly—in a way that would discourage those who would start war, rather than encourage them.

Let us well understand that if the United States, as a great nation, fails in Vietnam as we come to the end of this long road and as we see the end and as we know that it is not necessary to fail, I can think of nothing that would destroy the confidence of the American people more than that. So I would begin with that proposition, answering it on the negative side.

Q. Mr. President, I would like to ask you this question: Mr. Moncrief spoke my sentiments, and I think most of the people in Texas, or at least 99 percent of them, are in favor of what you are doing in Vietnam, but why is it in the East you get newspapers, the students, and members of the Congress and the Senate are complaining about what you are doing, but they never mention what the Communists and North Vietnamese are doing by invading South Vietnam, and they are killing thousands of people. They seem to think that is right and what we are doing is wrong. But why don't they ever mention that?

The President: I think that would be a very excellent editorial for somebody to write. [Applause]

Let me in all fairness say this: I do not question the patriotism of any critics of this war. Reasonable and honest and decent Americans can disagree about whether we should have gotten into Vietnam. They can disagree about how the war has been conducted, disagree about who is at fault now, and so forth, but let's just look at the record as it is at the present time.

Since I have come into office we have withdrawn half a million men from Vietnam. We have offered everything that could be offered except to impose a Communist government on the people of South Vietnam, and their answer has been a massive invasion of South Vietnam by the North.

Now, under these circumstances, instead of the critics criticizing brave Americans flying dangerous air missions, hitting military targets in North Vietnam—and military targets only—instead of criticizing them trying to prevent a Communist takeover, I think they ought to direct a little criticism to the Communists that are trying to keep this war going. That is what they ought to be doing.

Q. What are the posibilities of trade with China and Russia, as you now see it?

The President: Looking at both of these countries, we must realize—and I know that there are many here who have traveled certainly to Russia and to other Communist countries, although very few perhaps have been to China, at least in recent years—and looking at both of these countries realistically, as far as China is concerned, while we have now opened the door for a new relationship insofar as trade is involved, realistically the amount of trade that the United States will have with the People's Republic of China will be considerably limited over a period of time.

The Japanese, for example, have found that out. They, of course, are much closer to mainland China, and they have been trying to trade with them over a period of years, and yet they find that the amount of trade that they are able to have with the People's Republic of China is, frankly, much less than they expected when they began to open trade up.

We should not expect too much in the short range. We could expect a considerable amount further down the road.

Now, with the Soviet Union, this of course will be a major subject that will be discussed at the summit meeting. There will be considerable opportunities for trade with the Soviet Union.

The Secretary of Agriculture, Mr. Butz, was there discussing the possibilities of trade insofar as agricultural products are concerned—the selling of some of our grain to the Soviet Union.

We have also had some discussions between the Secretary of Commerce, Mr. Stans, and Mr. Peterson, now the new Secretary of Commerce, is discussing this with the Russian delegation, and we expect more trade opportunities to develop with the Soviet Union.

Realistically, however, we must recognize that where you have a Communist country dealing with a capitalist country or non-Communist country, the possibilities of trade are seriously limited because of an inability to have a method for financing it.

I know I have heard some American businessmen say, "Wouldn't it be great if we could just sell just a few consumer items to 800,000,000 Chinese?" That is fine, but what are they going to sell us and how are we going to finance it?

That is a problem, to a lesser extent, with the Soviet Union, but also a problem with them.

I would say then these new relationships we have developed and are developing with the People's Republic of China and with the Soviet Union will certainly lead to more trade in the years ahead—trade in nonstrategic items, of course, so long as those countries are engaged in supporting activities such as those in Vietnam.

Q. Mr. President, one thing that is bothering me is what is the basis for the criticism of our bombing Haiphong and Hanoi? Were the United States in war, do you not think that they would immediately bomb Washington and San Francisco and New York, and isn't the quickest way to stop this war to stop the supplies that are going to North Vietnam from their friends?

The President: The United States has shown restraint such as a great power has never shown in history in its handling of the war in Vietnam. At the present time, however, now that we have gone the extra mile in offering a peace settlement and peace terms, a cease-fire, an exchange of prisoners of war—and Mr. Ross Perot can tell you about some of the things we have gone through there and the barbarism with which our prisoners of war are treated. We have offered a total withdrawal of all our forces within six months. President Thieu has offered to resign a month before a new election that would be internationally supervised in which the Communists would participate in the election, participate in the supervisory body.

Having offered all that and then faced with this invasion, certainly the least the United States can do—and that is all that I have ordered—is to use our air and sea power to hit military targets in North Vietnam. That is what we have done, and that is what we are going to continue to do until they stop their invasion of South Vietnam.

ASIA'S EMERGING INDUSTRIAL REVOLUTION

PACIFIC NATIONS ARE ON THE VERGE OF A GREAT ECONOMIC LEAP FORWARD

Like a sputtering fuse, industry is moving southward along the Pacific rim of Asia and firing rapid economic growth.

In the past decade, Taiwan and South Korea have launched themselves on a trajectory of rapid industrial expansion. A pall of dirty smog over Hong Kong testifies to its success in attracting industry, and in the process creating an air pollution problem as well as a labor shortage.

Farther south, Singapore is converting itself into an industrial city-state, while Thailand is developing a more balanced pattern of factories and farms. Giant Indonesia, rich in resources and with a market of 120,000,000 people, seems set for a big-scale effort to develop its industrial potential along with its agriculture, forests, oil, and minerals.

Even South Vietnam should be ready for a rapid expansion of agriculture and light industry soon after the war's end, according to a study by New York's Development & Resources Corp., headed by David E. Lilienthal, former chairman of the Atomic Energy Commission.

Potential. *Among the world's developing regions, Southeast Asia with its 260,000,000 people and its natural wealth probably holds the greatest promise for fast growth. American businessmen are becoming aware of the area's potential and are moving in to sell and invest, to tap expanding markets, utilize pools of low-cost labor for manufacturing, develop tourism, cut timber, search for oil, and dig for metals.*

Ford Motor Co., among others, intends to concentrate in coming years on making and selling autos in the region. "In South Korea, Taiwan, and Indonesia we see promising markets and we see an attractive supply of cheap labor," Henry Ford II said last week.

The attitude of many U.S. businessmen toward the area is explained by Charles F. Davis, Jr., manager of the Djakarta branch of First National City Bank of New York: "While you are frequently frustrated, there is a lot of satisfaction working here. You feel you are on the ground floor of a country taking off."

Pouring in. The rising interest is reflected in trade and investment figures. During the past decade, U.S. exports to Southeast Asia (plus Korea) rose from $2,200,000,000 to $3,600,000,000 annually, and trade both ways should continue to climb rapidly in the years ahead. Oil companies will invest at least $500,000,000 in Indonesia. Throughout the area, U.S. companies are putting money into everything from timber and mining to electronics plants and hotels.

The U.S. is not the only industrial nation with a big and growing stake in Southeast Asia. For Japan, the region is even more vital as its second-biggest market (after the U.S.) and a prime source of raw materials. The area is also strategically important to Japan, because its oil lifeline from the Middle East runs through the Strait of Malacca.

Japanese manufacturers are putting plants in Southeast Asia mainly to protect their shares in local markets. But because of rising labor costs in Japan, they eventually will probably follow the lead of U.S. companies in setting up factories using cheap labor to make products for export back to Japan and to third countries. Mitsui, Matsushita, and others have already started doing this.

In pursuit of such objectives and with government support, Japanese businessmen are all over Southeast Asia

*peddling their wares, signing long-term contracts to buy
copper and other minerals, searching for oil, developing
agriculture and fisheries, putting up factories. Farm machinery maker Kubota is even licensing a plant near
Saigon to assemble power tillers for rice planters, and
another Japanese company plans a second plant there.*

Groundwork. *"South Asian countries are all important for
Japan," says T. Kambe, deputy general manager of Mitsui
& Co.'s administrative department. "But we put first em-
phasis on Indonesia."*

*Accordingly, Mitsui is raising improved corn in Suma-
tra, teaching surrounding farmers how to grow it, and
guaranteeing to buy their crop for export to Japan. The
company is also involved in oil exploration, lumbering,
hotel building, and a proposed fertilizer plant. Another
Japanese concern with big plans for Indonesia is Toyo
Rayon, with proposals for six textile and fiber factories.*

*Backing up the Japanese business push in Southeast
Asia will be an enormously expanded government aid
program, financed out of Japan's widening balance of
payments surplus. Last year, Japanese foreign aid totaled $1,000,000,000. By 1975 it is expected to rise to
around $4,000,000,000.*

Aggressive. *Inevitably, the growing Japanese presence
in Southeast Asia stirs some old fears and resentments in
countries that were invaded by Japan during World War
II. A wry joke throughout the region is that Japan is creating by trade, aid, and investment the Greater East Asia
Co-prosperity Sphere that it failed to achieve by military
conquest. Of course, it is doing no such thing. Despite its
foot-dragging on such things as import quotas and rules
on foreign investment in Japan, Tokyo has committed itself, together with the U.S. and Europe, to building a*

*worldwide system of multilateral trade and financial flows
—a far cry from its old exclusive colonial scheme for
Southeast Asia.*

*Still, Japanese businessmen are aggressive traders
and tough bargainers, and they raise hackles in some
Southeast Asian countries. The Philippines, for one,
keeps a rein on Japanese investment with a regulation requiring a Board of Investments license for any venture
with more than 30% foreign ownership.*

*"It is hard not to do business with the Japanese," says
a Philippine businessman. "They hold the key to financing capital equipment for these capital-short countries.
They have the financing and they make it easy to get."*

New ties. *Southeast Asians welcome alternative sources
of capital and equipment as one way of avoiding excessive dependence on Japan. Australia is rapidly emerging
as a third important factor in the area, along with the U.S.
and Japan. The Australians have gone through a crisis of
identity, as their old Commonwealth ties to Britain with-
ered, and have determined to seek their future as an
Asian and Pacific power. They intend to station troops
and aircraft in Singapore and Malaysia after Britain with-
draws from its bases there, as a contribution to regional
security. The Australians are stepping up their aid to
Southeast Asian countries. And Australian businessmen
are investing in the area.*

*The Australian Produce Board, for example, has milk
plants in Singapore, Bangkok, and Manila, and has just
opened a fourth in Djakarta to turn out condensed milk
made from Australian dried milk. Even more active in
Southeast Asia is Broken Hill Proprietary, Australia's big
iron and steel maker. BHP has a tie-in with Singapore's
National Iron & Steel Co. in a reinforcing bar mill, and will
probably participate in a blast furnace there.*

"The Japanese have never quite forgiven us for hooking up with BHP," says a Singapore official. "They think they should be the big brother of iron and steel in Asia."

Now BHP is setting up a wire and wire rope plant in a joint venture at Kuala Lumpur in Malaysia, and a wholly owned plant in Taiwan to make tungsten carbide and related products. It is expected to join with National Iron & Steel of Singapore in a $9,000,000 rolling mill in Indonesia.

U.S. BUSINESSMEN ARE MOVING IN TO SELL AND INVEST IN MARKET RICH WITH POTENTIAL

There are other sources of investment for Southeast Asia. One is the Asian Development Bank, headquartered in Manila, with $1,100,000,000 in commitments from the U.S., Japan, and other contributors. The ADB is trying to use its financial leverage to promote regional economic integration. One such project is for complementary fertilizer plants to be built in Taiwan and Korea.

A group of more than 100 leading Japanese, U.S., European, Australian, and Canadian companies this year set up the Private Investment Company for Asia (PICA), with $40,000,000 initial authorized capital, modeled on ADELA, a similar investment group operating in Latin America. Chairman Yoshizane Iwasa, who also heads Tokyo's Fuji Bank, says PICA will try to strengthen private enterprise in Asia by helping to finance private ventures. "This is essential both for economic development and to strengthen political stability," he says.

__Tensions.__ Actually, there is already a strong sense of private entrepreneurship in Southeast Asia, and that is one reason that the region is growing fast. Much of the busi-

ness drive and the local capital is concentrated in the overseas Chinese communities that control a big share of the wholesale and retail trade, banking, and light industry in most Southeast Asian countries. They move their money to where the opportunities are—lately, capital has been flowing out of Hong Kong to Singapore and Indonesia.

But the Chinese, who migrated to Southeast Asia during the colonial period, have been a factor in the political instability of some countries. In Thailand and the Philippines, the Chinese have assimilated fairly well. But Malaysia is currently split by political tensions between Malays who control the government and Chinese who dominate business. In Indonesia, many Chinese businessmen fled from persecution and took what capital they could salvage after the overthrow of Sukarno in 1965.

Now the Djakarta government is encouraging Chinese money to return, and promises that no questions will be asked about its origin.

"Here pragmatism has won," says Ambassador Soedjatmoko, Indonesian envoy to the U.S. "The government is aware that the bulk of investment is going to come from the Chinese community."

Open door. *Such a pragmatic approach to the job of economic development is being adopted increasingly by other governments in the area. The first generation of post-colonial leaders, like Sukarno, was often obsessed with resentments against foreigners and convinced that ideology offered a shortcut to solution of national problems. The new leaders have few such illusions and they welcome foreign investment if it will help speed development.*

Hedged bets. *The big unknown in Southeast Asia, of course, is how U.S. withdrawal from Vietnam will affect* the region. Among most businessmen and politicians, there is a lot of confidence that other countries will be able to weather the economic and political shocks— though Thailand in particular will feel the strain of cutbacks in U.S. spending.

Despite the debate in the U.S. about whether the American strength and commitments are over-extended, it is hard to find anyone in Southeast Asia who believes the U.S. will relinquish a major role in the area.

Nobody is betting any long-term money in South Vietnam, but there are quite a few businessmen who think it is worth a short-term gamble. One company that plans to set up an office in Saigon is Manila's SyCip, Gorres & Velayo, the Far East's biggest accounting and management consulting firm.

Explains Robert V. Ongpin, a partner in the firm: "There certainly is going to be free enterprise in South Vietnam and there certainly is going to be a need for our services."

December 13, 1969

 SECTION

THE NIXON PLOY: A WORLD TURNED UPSIDE DOWN

NIXON'S AUGUST 19, 1971, SPEECH TO THE VETERANS OF FOREIGN WARS IS PERHAPS THE CLEAREST EXPRESSION WE HAVE OF THE PRESIDENT'S POST-COLD WAR VISION, ESPECIALLY THE INTERRELATIONSHIP OF POLITICS AND ECONOMICS. JAMES BURNHAM COMMENTS FROM THE RIGHT ON THIS VISION. PRESIDENTIAL AIDE WILLIAM SAFIRE ADDS TO THE PICTURE IN HIS ARTICLE ON THE *MOSCOW* SUMMIT CONFERENCE OF 1972. WASHINGTON POST WRITERS MURREY MARDER AND MARILYN BERGER DELVED INTO THE FIRST BIG U.S.—SOVIET GRAIN DEAL, AND CAME UP WITH A FIRST-RATE STORY ON THE TRIUMPH OF POLITICAL ECONOMY OVER IDEOLOGY. THE CONCLUDING SELECTIONS OFFER TWO EVALUATIONS OF NIXON'S "FIVE-POWER WORLD" POLICY.

A STRONG ECONOMY AND A STRONG NATIONAL DEFENSE: ADDRESS BY PRESIDENT NIXON TO THE VETERANS OF FOREIGN WARS, DALLAS, TEXAS AUGUST 19, 1971

Now, today I want to address my remarks to a subject that is usually not presented to an organization like a veterans' organization. It is one, however, which is deeply related to our national defense, and as you can see, I shall relate it to the problems with which you have been concerned over this past week.

On Sunday evening, I outlined to the nation a bold economic policy which was designed to build a new prosperity for America, a prosperity in which we are going to have full employment with freedom, with opportunity, without inflation, without war. That is a great goal. It's one that we can, it's one that we must, achieve.

It is most appropriate that as I traveled across the country these past three days, that I should end my travels, as far as speaking is concerned, here in Dallas before this organization, because here in your hearts, in your minds, are the qualities that America needs in the stirring days ahead, the stirring days ahead in which we have to meet the challenges of peace: your patriotism, your self-sacrifice, your courage, your proven ability to deliver when the chips are down and serve this country superbly in war.

Now we come into a time when we need the same patriotism, the same self-sacrifice, and the same courage as we meet the challenges of peace.

Now, how much does America need her veterans? General Patton had an answer for that. You may recall it. He said, "It takes very little yeast to leaven a lump of dough," and then he went on to say, "It takes a very few veterans to leaven a division of doughboys."

My answer is much the same. We need the very best of your soldiers' spirit, your veterans' spirit, to inspire the rest of the nation in the great battle for a lasting peace and a new prosperity in America. That is what we need.

Now, it isn't going to be easy. As a matter of fact, nothing worthwhile in life is easy. War is not easy. Building a lasting peace is not easy. It won't be easy with the distractions and temptations of the coming years to make America remember this truth:

The strength that commands respect is the only foundation on which peace among nations can ever be built. I am glad that Secretary [of Defense Melvin R.] Laird and Senator [Henry M.] Jackson and others who have addressed you have emphasized the need to maintain America's strength. I associate myself with their remarks here today.

The argument for weakness, weakness whether it is military or economic or in any other field, wears two masks. Let's look at them for a moment, look right through those masks.

There are those who attack the necessity of strength with the claim that armaments cause conflict—the very fact that a nation is armed, that causes war. Well, the reverse is true: it is conflicts of vital interest which cause nations to build armaments.

Nothing but patient, firm, hardheaded negotiations such as we are now conducting on several very important areas in the world can adjust those fundamental differences and so pave the way for a safe reduction of armaments.

To those who attack the morality of strength with claims that our defense establishment is "militarist" and evil, we must reply it is war that is evil and the vigilance and the strength which prevents war is honorable and good. Let's say that, and let's stand for it.

Let's understand some propositions: We should devote as large a proportion of our natural resources as we can to the works of peace. All of us want to do that. We shall take vigorous steps to correct the occasional abuses which are bound to occur in the military as in any other human organization, and we are doing that.

But on one point let no American, and particularly let no member of the VFW, ever yield an inch; and that point is our deep pride in the armed forces of the United States and our enduring tribute of gratitude to the men who comprise them, professionals and citizen-soldiers alike.

It won't be easy to follow through on the measures that I announced Sunday night and in what seems to be unrelated but is closely related to the field that I have just talked about: to generate 20,000,000 new jobs over the next ten years, that is how many we are going to need for the younger generation coming along; to stop the rise in the cost of living; to protect our dollar against attacks of international speculation.

This hits very close to home. I know what it means for some of you to forgo a pay raise that you deserve, for a time, for others to wait a little longer for dividends that your invested dollar has earned. And yet the willingness to make short-term sacrifices in the drive toward a long-term goal is the very essence of a disciplined fighting force and is second nature to veterans like yourselves.

In other words, if delaying a pay raise, if not getting a rise in dividends which you expected for some of the people is going to result in stopping the rise in the cost of living for all the people, then that is good. Let's do it. Let's make that kind of sacrifice. And consequently, I ask for your support, above party, crossing all economic lines, for this program of revitalizing America's economy, rekindling her competitive spirit.

It is essential that these two goals be mentioned together, for they are inseparable. The new prosperity we seek is in no sense a cushion of a self-indulgent old age in this republic; rather, it will serve as a launching pad for new greatness in America's third century, which will be arriving in five years.

The steps we have taken with regard to import charges and protection of the dollar do not amount to the building of a permanent protective wall around this country, in which we can relax and afford to be inefficient and noncompetitive. They are aimed at simply preparing us to participate and compete more vigorously than ever in world affairs and with any other economy on the globe. It was our competitive spirit that made us a great nation, a strong nation, a rich nation, in the first place. We need a rebirth of that spirit today.

This is the challenge of peace. Nearly seventy years ago, when the organization that later became the VFW was a brandnew group of young Spanish-American War veterans, an American philosopher wrestled with the meaning of war and the problems of peace. The great need, William James wrote, was to find what he called "the moral equivalent of war: something heroic that will speak to men as universally as war does and yet will be as compatible with their spiritual selves as war (is) incompatible."

Four times since he wrote those words Americans have gone to war but, to our great credit, never for conquest, never to gain territory, but because other leaders in the world were attempting to gain territory, were embarked on conquest. It is to the credit of the United States of America that we do maintain strength, the greatest strength in the world, but that that strength will never be used to break the peace, only to keep it, never used to destroy freedom, only to defend it. This we can be proud of as a nation.

And now at last we find grounds to hope that the potential aggressors of this world will turn away from war, which costs so much and buys so little. We are realistic. We are pragmatic. We take nothing for granted. We maintain our strength until we can negotiate the reductions which will be mutual in their character.

And yet peace itself, as William James discovered, brings new challenges of its own. If we simply think of peace as the absence of war and that everything is just fine, that is not true. It poses the deep question of whether a nation, without some external threat to unite and motivate it, can find a higher inspiration to lift us all above the mire of softness and stagnation and division and decay. When people don't have a challenge, they do not become a great people.

Throughout the turmoil of the 1960's, America struggled for the answer to that question. And now, in the seventies an answer begins to come closer.

James' heroic and universal ideal does exist in a form both rich with age and new with promise. It goes by many names—the American dream, some call it, the spirit of '76. But essentially it is a unique mixture: liberty and order, we stand for that; justice and opportunity, that is an American ideal; competition and teamwork, knowledge and faith, which our forefathers envisioned two centuries ago and which, though not perfectly realized even today in America, has ennobled millions of Americans who have striven for it down the years.

The great challenge of peace is for each of us individually, and for all of us as "one nation, under God," to rededicate ourselves to this magnificent American dream. With this as our moral equivalent of war we can move into a generation of peace. We can blaze a trail toward a new prosperity, with freedom, with justice, with opportunity —without war.

With this new spirit of '76 in our hearts we can make the third American century the greatest century of all.

Over the past three days I have had a very great privilege, both as the President of this country but just as an American citizen, to see great parts of America very quickly and to see hundreds of thousands of American people in various states.

I was in New York Tuesday night. The next day I flew to Illinois, to the Illinois State Fair, where there were 125,000 Americans joined there in the great tradition of state fairs that we have all over the country. The next day, on to Idaho, to Idaho Falls, where tens of thousands of people were out there at an airport. And then to Wyoming, to the Grand Tetons, where there were people from all over the United States having a holiday there at one of the most beautiful places I have ever seen.

And finally, today, down to Dallas, seeing that magnificent skyline which seems to grow every day—the progress here is fantastic—and finally before you. All of America I see out here. I feel all of America among you.

Let me tell you how someone feels who holds the office I do, after he travels over America, as I have, and sees thousands of Americans in the space of three days.

First, this is a beautiful country. It is a beautiful country. Don't let anybody tell you anything else.

And second, it took a great people to make this country. When you think of those thirteen states, with 3,000,000 people on the Atlantic seaboard, when you think of what they did across those prairies and then across those huge mountains into Idaho and then on to California, down into

Texas and the rest—what kind of people did this? They were strong. They were competitive. They had a sense of purpose. They were a great people. Let's be worthy of the great pioneers of the past in America today.

Also at a time like this I think of the problems America faces, the problems of ending a war and ending it in an honorable way, winning a peace, which we are doing, the problems of building a new peace and a new prosperity, the problems of inspiring a people—and that is the problem that all of us have—and the responsibility that all of us have, whether we are Republicans or Democrats or whatever we may be; to go back into our communities and see that young America understands what a beautiful country this is, what a great history we have, and what a great future we have, provided that they have a sense of mission, a sense of destiny, and a sense of purpose.

What is it? What should it be? What can we settle for? There is an insidious line of propaganda, insidious in my view—some believe it is not—that runs through some public commentaries today. And that is this: it doesn't matter whether America is number one. We are number one in terms of our military strength today. We are number one in terms of our productivity economically today. We are rather proud of that—not in a jingoistic sense— because of what it has meant to us and what it has meant to the world.

Well, let me tell you something: It matters very much for America to continue to be the leader of the world and to be number one. First in the field of foreign policy—look at the free world. There is no other nation in the world that has the strength, potentially, to defend freedom around the world and negotiate for peace; so the United States must maintain that strength if we want a generation of peace, and we shall.

Our purpose in being number one is not simply to have

somebody else feel that he is inferior. It goes much deeper than that, and that brings me to the other side of the coin.

Why should America care whether we are the most productive nation in the world? Not simply because we want the highest standard of living, which we have, but for something far more important: because once any people resign themselves to being second or third or fourth best, they will cease to be a great people.

My comrades of the Veterans of Foreign Wars, the history of civilization is strewn with the wreckage of nations that were rich and that fell before people that were less rich and considered to be inferior to them intellectually and in every other way, because the rich nations, in their maturity, lost their drive, lost their desire, lost their dynamism, lost their vitality.

In the world today, let's face something: Other nations —some built up, and it was right to do so, as the result of our assistance after World War II—are now our strong competitors economically. Others are competing in other ways. We should not complain about that, because competition is what we believe in. Competition is what has made this country.

But let it not be said of this generation of Americans that we were the ones that, when America was the strongest nation in the world, when America was the most productive nation in the world, and the richest nation in the world, that we were the ones that said it really didn't matter and we became inefficient, we lost our willingness to sacrifice, to drive, to work hard, to continue to maintain that position of leadership in the world.

That is what is on the line today, and that is what America needs to hear from those who are its veterans, who have risked their lives to see that America lived, and who now must live their lives in such a way that we can set an example. You can set an example for other Americans so that this nation will have a new birth, as I am sure it can and will have, a new birth of vitality, a new birth of faith in itself, a new desire to be just as good, to be just as efficient, to be just as strong as we need to be and as we can be.

President de Gaulle once said, toward the end of his life, that France was "her true self only when she was engaged in a great enterprise." That is true of America. Americans are engaged in a great enterprise, to build— and without us it cannot be done—but to build a generation of peace, something that Americans have not enjoyed in this century. That is a great goal and a great enterprise.

And in order to build that, it means that Americans must continue to be competitive in the world and to have the strong economy without which we cannot have the strong national defense which is essential if we are to build that peace.

And so, to the Veterans of Foreign Wars I leave this challenge today: here we are, 25 years after World War II, we have been through Korea, we are finishing Vietnam. We are looking toward the time when we will have peace.

And the question for America is far more serious than the challenge that we confronted even in the dark days of Pearl Harbor. The question is our spirit. Do we have the spirit? Do we still have the drive? Do we still have the competitive urge to try to make this the best country in the world, to keep it the best country in the world? I think we have, and I think you are going out and tell the world that.

RICHARD DE NIXON, GAULLIST?
BY JAMES BURNHAM

THE THIRD WORLD WAR

Most commentators discounted President Nixon's Parisian apostrophe to President de Gaulle as diplomatic bombast. Some found it fulsome almost to the point of caricature. But it may be he really meant it. At any rate, he is behaving lately rather like an admiring pupil of *le grand professeur.*

Take the four-power conference on the Mideast that got discreetly off the ground April 3. This was de Gaulle's idea, proclaimed in January. Accepting it represented a big turn in U.S. policy, and—as Tel Aviv did not hide—a direct affront to Israel. The diplomatic implications are of more than casual moment. By thus sitting down with Soviet representatives to discuss, in that small circle, the destiny of the Mideast, we are recognizing the legitimacy of the Soviet Union's drive to establish itself as a Mideast power. We complete the process of erasing Moscow's aggression against Czechoslovakia from the record. We appease de Gaulle's ego by giving him a seat at a sort of rerun of Yalta!

It is likely, however, that in both the Paris and the Washington lessons Professor de Gaulle spent most time on Vietnam. We can be sure that in this private tutoring as in his public lectures, he urged on his pupil the example of the Algerian affair. France, too, had become entangled in a sordid, seemingly endless—and terribly unpopular— war, from which the incumbent regime was unable to extricate her. He, de Gaulle, coming fresh into office in the midst of domestic discord, took the ax in his hands, cut the anchor chain, and pulled away. France survived and prospered; he, de Gaulle, swept public opinion with him —and was still in office eight years later.

A wonderfully tempting prospect, all in all. And all the more so to Richard Nixon because the handling of the Korean affair by his first and primary mentor doubtless seemed a reconfirming example. In Korea, too, was not the nation stuck in a sordid, seemingly endless, and growingly unpopular war from which the incumbent regime had not been able to extract it? And did not Dwight Eisenhower, freshly come into office, take the ax in his hands, cut the anchor chain, and pull away? Did not Eisenhower, too, sweep public opinion with him—and himself triumphantly back into office?

Historical analogy is many-sided, as we all know. It is certainly true that a leader who puts an end to an unpopular war is likely to get a boost in his Gallup rating—for a while at least. But presumably that is not the only issue at stake in wars.

There is at least one fundamental difference between the Korean example and the Vietnam war. In the Korean war we did not win a general victory in the classic sense, but we won a limited victory within the local theater. We defeated the enemy—Chinese regulars, North Korean regulars, and guerrillas—in South Korea. The military reality did not permit us to achieve the positive goal of freeing all Korea from Communist rule, but it was sufficient foundation for a political solution that fulfilled our minimum commitment: to prevent a Communist takeover of South Korea.

We have not defeated the enemy in South Vietnam. Therefore, we are not in a political position to fulfill our minimum commitment. No political solution on the given military foundation will guarantee South Vietnam against Communist takeover. The possible political solutions will only express variant routes and timing for that takeover.

The relevance of the Algerian model is also circumscribed. A pullout by the No. 1 power is not the same thing as a pullout by a junior power, just as the monarch's heart attack is not the same thing, in public significance, as a commoner's. France could not abandon Algeria without adverse consequences in the West, but these consequences were relatively minor because the United States, not France, manned the basic strategic defenses of the West. De Gaulle could get away with the withdrawal because he was sheltered by the American strategic shield.

It is not a junior but No. 1 who is entangled in Vietnam. It is the strength and will of No. 1—therefore, of the non-Communist world quite generally—that is being tested by Vietnam. There is no escaping the *Economist's* conclusion: "It is an illusion to imagine that the United States can agree to a compromise peace that would amount to a sellout, and retain any credibility in Asia. Nor in Asia alone; for in this shrunken world credibility is indivisible." We must add: and if the United States has lost strategic credibility, where in the non-Communist world is credibility to be found?

Within the past few weeks the signs have multiplied that President Nixon's decision, as of now, is to take the Gaullist course to pull out of ("disengage from") South Vietnam. To pull out on the best available terms but to pull out in any event. (It is hard to see how terms can be expected to be much good when you have decided in advance to settle anyway.) This is the only possible interpretation of the whole series of hints and leaks: the cut in B-52 missions, Thieu's expressed willingness to talk to the NLF and Vietcong and to accept their presence in an election, the public talk about secret talks, the rumors of early troop withdrawals, the Wall Street flurries, the planted stories. It may be that the realities of the domestic situation—including the realities of Mr. Nixon's own character and potential—rule out any sterner alternative.

However that may be, let us at least hope that Mr. Nixon is not going to try to fool us about what a pullout signifies, which means he will first have to make sure not to fool himself. A defeat is a defeat is a defeat.

April 22, 1969

THE MOSCOW SUMMIT
BY WILLIAM SAFIRE

At 4:29 A.M. on Tuesday, May 23—the first morning that an American President awoke in Moscow—a United States Secret Service agent was startled to see Richard Nixon, dressed casually in a maroon sports jacket, pass the agent's post on the way to a Kremlin stroll.

Two other American agents were promptly alerted by radio; joined by three KGB men, they took their flanking and following positions as the President walked downstairs and out into Moscow's strong early morning sunlight. He walked past the great, cracked iron bell, ignored the black czar's cannon, and crossed a wide street leading to a monument with fresh flowers at its base. There the thirty-seventh President of the United States stopped and took a long look at the statue of Lenin, the first Chairman of the Council of People's Commissars.

On the way back, using one of the KGB guards as an interpreter, he stopped to chat with a Soviet soldier. "How old are you?"

"Twenty-five."

"You have a long life ahead of you." At 4:53, the President retired to his quarters, made some notes, and by 5:30 was back to sleep.

Soldiers like the one Nixon stopped to talk with will have a better chance at a long life if the United States and the Soviet Union can work out a way of competing without colliding—a possibility, with its curious admixture of realism and hope, of caution and daring, that brought Richard Nixon back to Moscow in 1972. The city of Moscow offers a useful prism through which to study the changing nature of the only man in American history to be a major party's candidate for national office in five out of six Presidential elections.

It was in Moscow in 1959 that he capped his reputation

222

as a man who would "stand up to the Communists" in the "Kitchen Conference" with Khrushchev; it was in Moscow in 1965, and again in 1967, that the outcast character of his role as a private citizen was underscored; it was in Moscow in 1972 that his talents as peacemaker and world leader were tested.

How was the Nixon who came to Moscow in 1972 different from the man who visited that capital in the mid-1960's and in the late 1950's? What was there about him that changed, and what apparent changes were only in the eye of the perceiver?

Psychohistory is not my game. I do not profess to know whether the President glared balefully or gazed beneficently at that statue of Lenin, or what was going through his mind at the time. But as one of his Moscow aides in 1972 who also happened to be in the kitchen with him in 1959, I could see some differences with an insider's myopia. He changed, as did the world and his adversaries, and the change in each accelerated the change in the others.

Conventional wisdom has it that Vice-President Nixon traveled to Moscow in 1959 as an ardent Cold Warrior, determined to beard the Russian bear in its den—and thirteen years later returned as one who had seen the light to become the instrument of détente. A sharp contrast makes a good story, but that is not the way it was.

I am convinced that Nixon came to Moscow in 1959 with no confrontation in mind; on the contrary, he was determined to be courteous and friendly as "host" of the American Exhibition in Moscow. His opening statements were conciliatory and would have remained so, but for the fact that he was given a sustained verbal shove by Nikita Khrushchev.

Millions of Americans think they witnessed the Kitchen Conference on television. They did not: what they saw was a video-tape of an earlier conversation in a television studio, with the American Vice-President trying to be Mr. Nice Guy and the Soviet Premier jumping all over him. In my reading of the incident, as they left the studio, Nixon knew he had been handled roughly—that unless he countered the assault quickly, the world would see an American leader on the defensive, gently trying to turn aside the thrusts of a truculent Soviet leader. He redressed the imbalance in the kitchen of the "typical American house." As the press agent for that house, it was my job to get the two leaders inside and keep them there long enough for a story and pictures to blossom. An authoritative-sounding "Next stop, the typical American house!" enticed them into our exhibit, trailed by a crowd of newsmen; on cue, a crowd of spectators spilled into the house from the only exit, trapping Nixon and Khrushchev inside. The Vice-President spotted the kitchen and seized his opportunity to continue the debate.

Nixon held his own in the kitchen, making telling debating points, but a study of the notes of the kitchen conference shows the American introducing all the restraining notes with the Soviet leader skillfully losing, and using, his temper. The worldwide impression of Nixon talking tough was left not by what was said, but by two photographs of the debate: one, taken by Elliot Erwitt of Magnum shooting for *Life* magazine, with Nixon poking his finger in a nonplussed Khrushchev's chest, and another —also showing Nixon doing the talking—shot for the Associated Press when their photographer could not get into the kitchen and, in desperation, lobbed his camera in to me. (I tried to compose that picture with three elements: Nixon, Khrushchev, and the washing machine they were talking about at the time; but another man's face was in the middle, and I couldn't shoot the picture without him. (Recently, the anonymous party functionary whose face appeared in so many newspapers the next day has been identified as Leonid Brezhnev.)

The impression of a no-nonsense Nixon putting the Soviet leader in his place was first made in the newspapers which used the A.P. shot the following day, in *Time* and *Life* the following week, and was heavily reinforced by advertising used during the presidential campaign in 1960.

Pictures, which do not lie, do not necessarily tell the whole truth; a more accurate impression of Nixon in 1959, I think, was that of a man who—although badgered by Khrushchev, as well as by a series of questions planted in the mouths of the people he met— was keeping his cool and maintaining his balance.

Those of us who exploited those photographs in 1960 as evidence of tough-mindedness cannot now complain that they failed to convey the sense of conciliation and restraint that was present. No complaints—but the "cold warrior" impression was simplistic.

Just as the perception of the 1959 Nixon is somewhat distorted, the 1972 perception of him as the dauntless devotee of détente is somewhat exaggerated. A recurrent theme before, during, and after the 1972 visit was in derogation of "spirits." Nixon told newsmen on the eve of departure, "There was the 'Spirit of Vienna,' the 'Spirit of Geneva,' and the 'Spirit of Glassboro,' and the 'Spirit of Camp David.' What they all added up to . . . was all froth and very little substance."

In his first toast to the Soviet leaders in the Kremlin, he reminded them: "Summit meetings of the past have been remembered for their 'spirit'; we must strive to make the Moscow Summit memorable for its substance." (Immediately to the President's left as he spoke in Granovit Hall of the Grand Kremlin Palace was a large painting of a saint rejecting temptation, an apt subject at that moment.) He repeated this idea in his speech to the joint session of the Congress, exorcising summit spirits with bell, book, and candle.

All this spirit-baiting had a point: that atmospherics were not the name of the game, that goodwill was fine but not enough. The summit was a marriage of mutual convenience, not a love match. Central to the Nixon mode of dealing with the Soviets is the idea that a realistic respect for each other's power and interests is far more reliable a basis for a permanent relationship than ringing protestations of friendship.

Both the final approach to the summit itself, and the subsequent handling of the SALT negotiations, illustrate how this cool-eyed assessment determined events. In his speech announcing the mining of Haiphong Harbor two weeks before the summit, Nixon made it plain that while he was looking forward to the meeting, the prospect did not have him salivating. I think that one important reason a successful summit took place was the clear impression Nixon left that he did not consider a summit indispensable.

In the same way, when negotiations on SALT reached an impasse Thursday night, May 25, the President did not appear in the least anguished. Earlier, Soviet spokesmen had passed the word to the press that the agreement would be signed the next day, providing a fitting climax to the week's package of accords.

Two points, however, could not be resolved, both of which Nixon considered important to United States security. The President gave Henry Kissinger firm instructions to be followed even if it meant that no agreement would be signed that week. The President's national security adviser went to bed Thursday night convinced there was no final deal; before he went to an 11 A.M. meeting the next day with Andrei Gromyko, Kissinger told Ron Ziegler to pass the word to the press not to expect a signing that day.

At that point, it must have become clear that the United States was not bluffing; that Nixon was quite prepared to let Friday come and go without a SALT signing ceremony, in the hope that something could be worked out the following week or month. Then, and only then, did the pressure shift direction, and what the diplomats call "movement" took place on the Soviet side. I think it is clear that because Nixon did not appear to be anxious, an agreement considered fair to both sides was reached that morning and signed that night. I ran into a State Department official in an elevator at 3 P.M. that afternoon and told him I had heard a new treaty would be signed that evening. He smiled and explained why it would be impossible; due to the time needed to match translations, to transcribe to parchment ("One doesn't sign treaties on typing paper, you know") and to bind the pages into an impressive couple of books. Soon afterward, he got the word that the signing was scheduled for 11 P.M. He made it under the wire, but they had to sign the treaty looseleaf; a corrected version was quietly re-signed by the two leaders the next day.

Another change reflected in Nixon is the change in adversary (a word now used in place of "enemy" or "other side," soon to be replaced by "competitor," preferable to "coexistee"). Khrushchev used exuberant bombast like a locomotive's cowcatcher, pushing aside obstructions with colorful turns of phrase like "not until shrimps whistle," and a handy stock of proverbs: "You are my guest, but truth is my mother" was one used to impress Nixon, who did not learn until later that many Russian "old sayings" are made up on the spot.

The personalities faced by Nixon in the Moscow of 1972

were considerably different, as was his reaction to them. The word journalists used to describe Kosygin is "dour"; Kosygin is as closely tied to dour as inextricably is to linked. He does not smile often. Only when Nixon told the first plenary session, "I have a reputation as a hard-line anti-Communist," did the first grin spread across Kosygin's face, as he said, "We know, we know." His humor is used to make a political or negotiating point. At the dinner given by the President at the American Embassy, no bread was served; when Kosygin looked around for his favorite dark bread, the President shrugged and passed along a plate of nuts. Kosygin, who had been negotiating about grain purchases all day, observed to Mrs. Nixon, "No wonder you Americans have so much grain—you don't eat bread."

Brezhnev, too, uses humor for political purposes. Henry Kissinger had a series of meetings with him in early May, preparatory to the summit. At the final meeting, Kissinger brought along all the members of the National Security Council staff who had traveled with him to Moscow. Brezhnev, noting the increased size of the United States delegation, slipped in a gentle barb: "For people who talk so much about your withdrawals, you bring your reinforcements up very quietly."

Nixon, seated next to Brezhnev at two state dinners, let the Soviet leader do more of the talking, responding to conversation rather than leading it. When Brezhnev walks, he strides with an unmistakable command presence, stately and studied; but when he sits down to dinner, he becomes animated and expressive. His right hand helped to conduct the conversation; cigarette between index and middle finger, elbow on the table, he used his hand to shape arguments and indicate nuances. In this kind of lively conversation, he seemed reluctant to put up with the interpreter's delay; Nixon, on the other hand, consciously used the interpreter, never getting too far ahead, working with him to make his points. Six years younger than Brezhnev, Nixon has had more experience communicating across a language gulf; he speaks slowly, using a simple construction and plain words wherever possible. In such circumstances, facial expressions become important; both Nixon and Brezhnev have pronounced, expressive eyebrows and use them to advantage. Nixon has a good "Is that so?" look, reminiscent of the famed photo of Eisenhower when informed of MacArthur's resignation; Brezhnev is adept at an eye-widened "So that's it," briskly nodding, projecting an air of welcome discovery.

The contrast between Nixon '59 and Nixon '72 was striking in the way he dealt semipublicly with Soviet leaders. In the old days, Nixon would be leaning in, pressing his points home, aware of cameras, careful not to appear to be missing a thing; a junior determined not to be put down for fear his country would be put down. Now he is more relaxed, less concerned with the scoring of individual points, taking a longer view. He is more deliberate in movement and speech; he seems to know who he is and what he wants.

Another contrast with 1959 was in the attitude of the American party toward electronic eavesdropping. Bugs, tapes, and hidden cameras were subjects of considerable worry on that first visit, as if some decisive advantage could be wrested from the United States if discussions about a cultural exhibit were overheard. American travelers in Moscow liked to tell of a cake of soap missing from the bathroom, a loud complaint made in the general direction of the chandelier, and the subsequent replacing of the soap, suggesting that unseen monitors handled room service as well as espionage.

On his 1965 visit—a hastily arranged one-day trip from Finland, where he went as a lawyer to help the Premier of Newfoundland and oilman John Shaheen arrange a pulp and paper development—Nixon showed a more relaxed attitude about real or imagined snooping. He left an open briefcase in his hotel room containing his personal income tax return, which he had been working on; his client, a former OSS operative, noticed the open briefcase and warned him about a surreptitious search. Nixon started to go back to close it, then smiled and said that if the Russians wanted to know how much he was making in private life, it didn't bother him.

A decent respect for the requirements of security was paid in 1972; United States agents swept the quarters for evidence of surveillance (and were not surprised to find none). Certain conversations and messages traveled by totally secure means, but the American party—duly briefed about the ease with which conversations could be overheard and classified material photographed—did not act uptight about unseen ears and eyes. When the SALT negotiations reached the point that required some quick Xerox copying, Henry Kissinger held a document up toward the chandelier and said to an imaginary lens, "Could I have half a dozen of these in a hurry?" Andrei Gromyko shook his head and deadpanned that the hidden cameras in that Kremlin palace had been installed in the time of Ivan the Terrible and were not sensitive enough to copy documents. Such a colloquy would not have taken place in 1959.

At the least significant meetings, of course, the greatest precautions were taken. When Ron Ziegler asked a few of us to consult with him in his Intourist suite, he tuned his TV set's volume up to the loudest; Herb Klein played his transistor radio; John Scali banged a highball glass steadily on the coffee table, and I hummed a series of Al Jolson favorites. It is to be hoped that this brouhaha caused some difficulty for any eavesdropper, because it certainly made it impossible for any of us to hear each other.

Nixon's 1965 visit should not be so lightly passed over
in this piece, since it reveals a man less constrained and
self-analytical than in 1959, and more impulsive than in
1972. I was not on that trip, but my source is good. Nixon in
1965 was a political has-been. With little to lose, he could
afford to be daring; besides, a little publicity could do
some good. Soon after his arrival, his Intourist guides
took him to Moscow State University, where he was
promptly engaged in debate by the deputy rector in front
of a classful of students; reporters were there as well, and
Nixon the New York attorney sparred politely. But his eye
was on a bigger event. With the aid of a Canadian newsman, he obtained Nikita Khrushchev's address; both
were private citizens then, and a renewal of the old ac-
quaintance could not have been considered a diplomatic
embarrassment and could have made an interesting
story.

Nixon excused himself from the dinner table, leaving
his wary Intourist guides in the company of two of his com-
panions, and slipped out of the hotel, taking a cab to the
Canadian Embassy, which was in the neighborhood of
Khrushchev's apartment. With a friend, he walked to the
house, to be met by two stone-faced, burly women who
said Mr. Khrushchev was not there. Nixon pressed, but
was rebuffed; frustrated, he wrote and left a letter ex-
pressing the hope they could meet and talk again. In all
probability, that handwritten note from an American non-
candidate to a Soviet nonperson is the most interesting
document in the Kremlin's file on Richard Nixon. It was
probably not delivered; historians can hope it was not destroyed.

What brought about the change in Nixon—from the
self-conscious figure in the kitchen in 1959 to the self-
confident figure in the Kremlin in 1972? Part of the answer
may be that Nixon's effectiveness as a leader increased
when he applied the policy of containment to himself; the

self-justification so labored in *Six Crises,* with each detail sifted and each motive painfully scrutinized, cannot be found in the prose of his speeches and toasts in the Soviet Union this year. No rationalizations, recriminations, or apologies were offered.

Hyperbole, too, was set aside for the Moscow trip. Nixon admitted turning over a new leaf to reporters before he left: "So my remarks deliberately are not made with the overblown rhetoric [for] which you have properly criticized me in the past." That was a startling thing for a President to say, especially one not noted for his sensitivity to criticism; it caused his aides to look at each other with a wild surmise.

Compare the two speeches he made to the Soviet people in 1959 and 1972. Although the themes were essentially the same—while our philosophical differences are profound, we can cooperate in bringing peace to the world—the styles were poles apart. The 1959 speech is used in public-speaking texts as a classic in refutational rhetoric, setting up and knocking down a series of beliefs held by the audience, a rational and almost legalistic presentation of an argument that had to be fresh to the minds of listeners. It was a well-reasoned, well-written speech, achieving its limited aims.

The 1972 speech, however, was an effort to reach and stir the emotions of millions of Soviet citizens. Like a diamond cutter permitted one crucial tap, he studied his approach with great care, structuring his television talk on three images rooted in the Russian character. The first was reference to the "mushroom rain," a sun-shower that greeted him on arrival in Moscow, considered a good omen by Russians who think of mushroom-gathering in the woods the way American suburbanites think of backyard barbecues. The second was the story of the traveler who wanted to know how far he was from town, and was

only answered by a woodsman when he had established
the length of his stride; and the third and most powerful
reference was to Tanya, a young Leningrad heroine
whose story moves Russians in the way that Anne Frank's
moves us, with its evocation of innocence and hope
amidst hatred and war.

The President was alerted to the "mushroom rain" idea
by Harriet Klosson, wife of the Deputy Chief of Mission at
the United States Embassy, who passed it to me to pass
along to fellow-writer Ray Price; he was told the woodsman story by Henry Kissinger, who got it from Leonid
Brezhnev a couple of weeks before; and he researched
the reference to Tanya by himself, reading a display on
his visit to Leningrad. One United States correspondent
dismissed the speech as a tearjerking waste of time; another, who speaks Russian and watched it on television
with a Russian family, reported a misty-eyed reaction by
deeply moved human beings. (An interesting footnote:
during Nixon's 1959 speech, an American capably interpreted for Vice-President Nixon; this year he chose Viktor
Sukhodrev, the top Soviet interpreter, to handle the
agreed-upon simultaneous interpretation. Soviet viewers
who saw Nixon heard Sukhodrev, the best in the business
at the top of his form—not dryly translating, but dramatically driving home Nixon's mood and message. Obviously, no one told him *not* to do his professional best.)

Another example of the change from self-conscious to
self-confident: a willingness to ad-lib. Of course, necessity has a way of encouraging ad-lib performances—for
example, at one dinner on the trip, the lighting was such
that the President could not see the words on his papers,
and an extemporaneous toast was necessary. However,
there has been a change in Nixon's conscious use of the
ab-lib. On his first visit in 1959, he relied heavily on words
he had written; the Kitchen Debate could not be prepared,

but other remarks and speeches were honed and cleared beforehand. And this year, at every occasion in the Soviet Union, at airports, dinners, or any occasion that required a verbal message, Soviet leaders read from a piece of paper, a technique especially suited to collective leadership. But Nixon varied his style. His opening toast on the evening of his arrival was carefully scripted, with each word studied for diplomatic shading, and he never departed from the text ("The only way to enter Moscow is to enter it in peace" was especially well received). In Kiev, however, he set aside a toast prepared in advance, seizing on a note the writer had added as an afterthought about Kiev's eleventh-century "Golden Gate." He built his remarks around the similarity of the experience of two cities of the golden gate—Kiev and San Francisco —one ravaged by war, the other by earthquake and fire, both with citizens spirited enough to rise and rebuild their cities greater than before. Appropriate; illustrative of historic sweep; well-phrased.

That, I think he believes, is the way Churchill or de Gaulle might have done it. Such extemporizing is statecraft in the grand manner, and Nixon has a lot of respect for the grand manner. His reading for relaxation in the past month has been *Jennie,* the biography of Churchill's mother. And the passage in de Gaulle's memoirs about the need for aloofness and mystery in leadership is quite familiar to him. It may be contradictory to identify with Churchill and de Gaulle—giants who disliked each other —but it is something Nixon does, and a man could have two worse heroes than men with a sense of history and a pride in country.

The scope of the change in Nixon, in Moscow and in the whole situation was best expressed to me by an exasperated Soviet editor toward the end of the visit:

"Here we are, welcoming as members of your party the

representative of the Voice of America, not to mention Victor Lasky, author of *The Ugly Russian.* And here we are listening to somebody shout political slogans in the Bolshoi theater—it's strange enough to hear shouts at political leaders, but at the Bolshoi it is inconceivable. And here we are, listening to Richard Nixon, of all people, reminding the Soviet peoples of Tanya and the siege of Leningrad and our wartime comradeship. That is not a matter of change. That's the world turned upside down."

July 2, 1972

U.S.—SOVIET GRAIN DEAL: CASE HISTORY OF A GAMBLE

BY MURREY MARDER AND MARILYN BERGER

A week ago the 35,000-ton cargo ship *World Neighbor,* loaded with corn, sailed from the United States for the Soviet Union to help meet domestic political problems of both countries.

The Soviet Union needs the grain as much as the United States needs to get rid of it.

With a massive grain harvest of about 260,000,000 tons this year, there is too much for 207,000,000 Americans to consume, export, or store. Corn is piled high on the streets of several Iowa towns, forcing the government to provide some price relief to farmers staggered by the surplus.

The problem is exactly the opposite in the Soviet Union. It is in the midst of a dietary revolution to supply more meat for its 240,000,000 people. The Soviet Union has promised its people that the Russian grain harvest will be raised to 220,000,000 tons by 1975.

On the face of it, the United States has the resources to help fill the feed grain gap for the growing Soviet livestock and poultry industries. This could relieve the perennial problem of American food surpluses. In theory, at least, such shipments could also assist the ailing American merchant marine, which is desperate for cargo.

This is the logic on which the Nixon administration, in a major switch of policy, is banking its hopes for achieving a major breakthrough in East-West industrial and agricultural trade.

What was denounced only a few years ago as "trading with the enemy" is now championed in the White House as "crossing the trans-ideological barrier."

To critics in and out of the government, the administration's expectations are alternating [sic] totally unrealistic, or appalling if they do materialize.

The United States, they warn, will be drained of its industrial and agricultural know-how, will gain only limited Soviet sales, and will risk distorting its own economy by reaching for such Soviet state trading practices as barter in place of cash sales.

The sailing of the *World Neighbor* from New Orleans, headed for the Black Sea under a Liberian flag, represented the Nixon administration's decision to make the gamble. The policy is now being pursued in many other forms.

This is the story of that first complex exercise by the Nixon administration in clearing the sale of from $135,-000,000 to possibly $190,000,000 worth of American grain to the Soviet Union. The agreement, announced November 5, required bargaining that spanned several months and two continents.

In Paris, last July, the Russians dropped word that they would be interested in purchasing American feed grain later in the year. Negotiations began in New York in early October. The bargaining reached through the offices of two $2,000,000,000-a-year agricultural marketing firms, one in a skyscraper overlooking the Statue of Liberty and the other in the replica of a French chateau on Lake Minnetonka, near Minneapolis; negotiations then passed repeatedly through the White House and other government offices; circled through the headquarters of the American maritime unions, and officially ended at an outsized motel at Cherry Hill, New Jersey, on November 4.

Statesmanship purportedly breached the union barrier, winning the agreement of American longshoremen to load ships bound for the Soviet Union with grain. "Statesmanship in this case is spelled G-R-E-E-D," grumbled one Midwestern grain merchant. Two House subcommittees have scheduled hearings beginning Wednesday to examine the grain sale portion of the deal. U.S. officials claim confidence over the outcome.

From interviews in Washington, Minneapolis, New York, and Cherry Hill, New Jersey, *The Washington Post* pieced together the complex grain-sale shipping story, which is still unfolding.

Long before the plunging deficit in the American balance of payments led to Mr. Nixon's August 15 shock treatment to curtail imports and expand exports, the administration had its sights fixed on eliminating obstacles to East-West trade.

On June 10, the administration slipped into its packet of overtures toward China a presidential decision canceling a 1963 order by President Kennedy. That order required half of all exports of wheat and feed grains to Communist countries to be carried in American ships. The 50–50 rule cut an intended sale of $250,000,000 in grain to the Soviet Union almost in half and became a virtual epitaph for all such transactions because of high American shipping costs.

On June 9, the day before the ill-fated 1963 order was rescinded, Thomas W. ("Teddy") Gleason, president of the International Longshoremen's Association, was invited to the White House to see Presidential Security Adviser Henry A. Kissinger.

Also invited with Gleason was AFL-CIO International Affairs Chief Jay Lovestone, whose name has been synonymous for a generation in the labor movement with intractable anti-Communism.

At a 1964 Maritime Administration hearing, when Continental Grain had sought a waiver from the requirement to ship half of the American wheat sale to Russia on U.S.

ships, the record shows, Gleason rebelled, shouting, "Let the Russians go to hell. Let 'em starve."

It was a considerably milder-mannered Gleason who called at the White House last June 9 and who now describes the new grain shipment to the Soviet Union, after his own negotiations with the Nixon administration, as "humane." By then the administration had labeled him a "statesman."

As Gleason describes his meeting with Kissinger: "There was just myself and Lovestone. Kissinger was there by himself. He told us of the announcement and asked me what my intentions were. I said we wouldn't load the ships. We had an agreement with the maritime unions. If there was to be any changes I'd have to know what the hell the situation was."

MEETING CALLED

Gleason added his own assessment of Kissinger. "He's a very solid citizen," Gleason said. The ILA leader went directly to AFL-CIO headquarters in Washington for a meeting of the SOS (Save Our Ships) Committee. Gathered in President George Meany's office were Gleason; Jesse M. Calhoon, president of the National Marine Engineers' Beneficial Association; Paul Hall, president of the Seafarers International Union; Joseph Curran, president of the National Maritime Union; Captain Thomas F. O'Callaghan, president of the International Organization of Masters, Mates and Pilots.

The only major maritime group absent that day was Harry Bridges' West Coast International Longshoremen's and Warehousemen's Union. Under Bridges, the 65,000-member union has continually supported efforts to expand trade and had long ago adopted a resolution in support of "free and expanded trade with China and other socialist countries." Soviet ships have called at West Coast ports while the East has been closed to them and have taken on and unloaded cargo.

But the AFL-CIO unions were sticking to their traditional position.

"We were going to fight the waiver," Gleason says now; "It meant jobs for American seamen. We drafted a letter that day."

The joint protest letter, signed by Meany, was dated June 15. The union leaders say they received no reply. Gleason said the leaders did nothing more because "nothing happened"—no shipments were going out.

But sources inside the government have a different version. They said the Kissinger-Gleason-Lovestone meeting produced "no fuss." Said one official referring to the union men, "They said they'd keep their mouths shut and they did."

He evidently meant that the union leaders were expected to limit themselves to pro forma objections. In the letter to the President, Meany wrote, "The representatives of these workers who are daily being deprived of their job opportunities most earnestly protest your decision of June 10." The letter urged the President "to reconsider your action."

On June 16 Meany publicly used stronger language. He attacked the revocation of the special U.S. shipping requirement as "a breach of faith and an unwarranted blow at the livelihood of American seafaring men."

WARNING ISSUED

But everyone waited to see what would actually happen. Calhoon said he was warning everybody he saw in government that if they wanted cooperation on future shipments to the Soviet Union, they had better start talking with the maritime unions and not simply rely on President Nixon's decision to produce results.

One person who apparently listened was Charles W. Colson, special counsel to the President, who maintained contact with the unions, before and since the June 10 announcement. There were pressure points on both sides, the decline of the American merchant marine, for example.

By the end of October, 1971, the number of shipboard jobs for American seamen had dropped to a 20-year low. According to the Transportation Association there were 93,163 seagoing jobs in 1951. By October 31, 1971, that figure had dropped to 31,988.

The size of the U.S. flag fleet of 1,000 gross tons or more had dropped from 1,262 active vessels in 1951 to 604 in October 1971. In 1951 U.S. vessels carried 42.9 percent of U.S. oceanborne trade. By 1970 these vessels accounted for 5.6 percent of the trade.

American seamen, when they worked, were paid two to three times as much as a foreign sailor. But work was disappearing, and as even union men now said, "50 percent of nothing is nothing."

Other pressures were building in Paris. In July, according to private sources, Nikolai Belousov, a top official of the Soviet Union's Export Khleb (*khleb* means "bread" in Russian), which handles all imports and exports of grain, spoke with several grain traders. One was Michel Fribourg, principal owner of Continental Grain Co. of New York.

Belousov and his Soviet associates were well aware of President Nixon's June 10 order. They indicated that later in the year, they would want to talk about purchasing American feed grains to further the "dietary revolution."

International agricultural specialists had been intently observing the quickening trend toward meat consumption in Communist Europe. "Over the last four years," said

Clarence D. Palmby, assistant secretary of agriculture for international affairs and commodity programs, "we have noted that the U.S.S.R. has come into Western Europe and bought sizeable numbers of pork carcasses and frozen broilers [chickens]".

"That indicated that the U.S.S.R. was prepared to put out more hard foreign exchange to grow swine and broilers."

POSSIBILITIES NOTED

The largest American grain processors and dealers operate their own private worldwide intelligence services which they boast are better than the government's in these areas. They are intrigued by the possibilities for large-scale business with the Soviet Union and, one day, China. These firms are fiercely competitive, and because most of them are privately owned, maintain unusual secrecy. Continental's Fribourg, who is credited with launching the 1963 sale to the Soviet Union, is described in the trade as the American with the best sources in the Soviet Union.

Fribourg, 58, is Belgian-born, became president of Continental when he was discharged from the Army in 1944, and took over a family business which traces back to 1813 and moved its headquarters from France to the United States after World War I.

He is suave, soft-spoken, and has developed Continental's international business to a $2,000,000,000 sales volume in recent years.

His strongest rival is Cargill, Inc., which claims $2,-000,000,000-plus in annual sales and which describes itself as the world's largest processor and marketer of agricultural products. Its pastoral base of operations is in a post–World War I replica of a French chateau on the shores of Lake Minnetonka, 15 miles west of downtown Minneapolis.

Continental gained a strong lead on the current grain sales to the Soviet Union. Export Khleb's Belousov arrived in New York quietly about October 4 and began secret negotiations with Fribourg, Harold Vogel, executive vice-president, and other Continental officials.

The bargaining was well along when Cargill's top command arrived in Moscow about October 18, reportedly after its Geneva office learned that the Russians were already negotiating with Continental.

The bargaining was well along when Cargill's top command arrived [sic] for initial negotiations in Moscow—Erwin E. Kelm, chairman of the board; Walter B. Saunders and M. D. McVay, vice-presidents; and other officials.

According to the Agriculture Department's Palmby, who is constantly in communication with U.S. grain exporters, "The story came back that the Russians wanted some barley and oats" which the Commodity Credit Corporation can sell for export from U.S.-owned stocks at prices below the market price in the United States. Palmby said the Nixon administration offered to sell barley and oats only to exporters who could sell an equivalent amount of American corn for Soviet destination.

ACCORD REACHED

Continental ended up with an agreement to sell the Soviet Union 2,000,000 tons of corn, 600,000 tons of barley and 300,000 tons of oats, which is said to be worth about $135,000,000 to $140,000,000 exclusive of shipping, which may add about $20,000,000 to the delivered cost at Soviet ports. Continental is free to supply 1,000,000 tons of corn from sources anywhere in the world, but said it will try to funish as much of the entire sale from U.S. stocks as circumstances and profit margins permit.

Cargill's more closely guarded sales reportedly include agreements to ship the Russians 500,000 tons of barley from any world origin, plus 300,000 tons of oats and barley from U.S.-owned stocks and an offsetting tonnage of corn, plus, it is said, some additional sales.

U.S. officials say the assured sale of American grain to the Russians therefore will be a minimum of $135,000,000. It could go to $180,000,000 to $190,000,000.

Continental's sale of corn alone would be the equivalent of 15 percent of total U.S. corn exports last year, the barley 36 percent of last year's exports, and the oats 117 percent.

While Continental's president Fribourg was in the midst of his negotiations with the Russians, he began exploring whether the American maritime unions would permit American grain to be loaded for shipment to the Soviet Union.

SOUNDINGS MADE

Fribourg and two associates came to the Battery Place office of the International Longshoremen's Gleason, just a few blocks from Continental's headquarters to ask if the dockworkers would handle the grain.

Gleason, who speaks in the full accent of the New York docks, controls his 116,000 members from an office desk displaying three small American flags, a full-size one behind him on a standard, and a "Like It or Leave It— AMERICA" sticker on the wall. Gleason said he told Fribourg that although the longshoremen get the work no matter what kind of ship carries the cargo, he wouldn't load the grain unless there was a 50–50 split for American shipping.

That would have scuttled the transaction. The Russians do not care what kinds of ships are used as long as they pay only world shipping prices, not the higher U.S. costs. The next day Fribourg met with a larger group of maritime union leaders and got the same negative answer.

On October 18, Fribourg and several associates brought their dilemma to the White House, to the office of Richard V. Allen, deputy to Peter G. Peterson, assistant to the President and executive director of the Council on International Economic Policy. Peterson sat in on the meeting for a while, along with Richard F. Schubert, executive assistant to Labor Secretary James D. Hodgson.

The expansion of export trade, especially agricultural exports which Peterson and others regard as holding great prospects because of American cost advantage over foreign competition, already held a Nixon administration priority. By presidential order, the 50–50 shipping requirement was dead. But U.S. officials do not load ships.

Allen told Fribourg he would see what could be done. But Fribourg and his colleagues left Allen's office with little hope. A legal adviser for Fribourg, Frederick R. Livingston, met that same day with George P. Schultz, director of the Office of Management and Budget.

OTHER PRIORITY

That night, the Fribourg group had dinner with Labor Secretary Hodgson, who reportedly told them the administration was obliged to give priority to its other labor problems. At that time, dock strikes blanketed East Coast and Gulf ports, one crisis with the nation's top labor leadership over Phase II wage-control policy had just been narrowly averted, and more tension was ahead.

But the opportunity to export 3,000,000 or more tons of American grain, with corn surpluses flooding the Midwest and depressing prices, strongly tempted the administration. Cargill at that point also had registered its own export interests with the White House while it negotiated with the Russians.

With no shipping breakthrough in prospect, White House officials said the President himself started holding meetings the week of October 25. Officials said the President met with Agriculture Secretary Clifford M. Hardin, Commerce Secretary Stans, and Presidential Assistants Peter M. Flanigan and Colson.

White House sources said the President told Colson to negotiate with the recalcitrant unions and to reaffirm his commitment to the Maritime Act of 1970. It provides for greater federal assistance and subsidization of the shipping industry. In other words, more potential money and jobs. But the maritime unions rarely gamble on shifting policy in return for hopes of distant dividends.

Colson, according to White House sources, called Calhoon on October 29, told him things were "moving fast," union cooperation would be needed, and invited him to come to Washington November 3 "with whoever else he wanted to bring with him."

FORMULA PONDERED

Meanwhile, Peterson, Colson, Assistant Secretary of Commerce Harold B. Scott, Undersecretary of Labor Laurence H. Silberman, and Flanigan put their heads together to try to figure out some formula that might appeal to the unions. One official said they rejected at this time a bold concept of reserving a portion of U.S. oil imports for

American ships as too impractical and too difficult to sell to the oil companies.

Instead, one official said, they settled on proposing to both the unions and the Russians the equally and not universally admired unprecedented concept of bilateralism —a scheme for carrying the cargo of U.S.–Soviet trade exclusively in Soviet-American vessels. There was no assurance the Russians would buy it but it was something the unions would go for.

"This was a breakthrough," SIU President Hall said later. "This is the first time it is being discussed by the government."

Andrew E. Gibson, head of the Maritime Administration, was selected to put this new East-West trade idea to the maritime unions to win their support.

"Andy," as he is known to union man and shipper alike, emerges from conversations with leaders on both sides as something of a superhero and seagoing Horatio Alger who came up through the shipping industry as a seaman, pier superintendent, graduate of a merchant marine academy, executive vice-president of the Grace Line, consultant. Both shippers and union leaders praise him as a trustworthy negotiator, and more than that, a friend.

Most U.S. officials involved in the negotiations, all the union leaders and a number of shipping executives are inclined to credit Gibson with bringing the unions around —if only for the one-shot grain sale, for that is all that has been pinned down so far, union leaders insist.

Gibson, however, publicly stated on November 5, and other U.S. officials also say, that they have "an open-ended commitment" from the unions. Despite the apparent disagreement, union officials still laud Gibson, suggesting that both sides regard future shipping arrangements to be fluid.

Gibson and Presidential Adviser Colson were persuasive at that November 3 meeting, according to the labor leaders. Marine Engineer President Calhoon had asked Hall of the Seafarers International to come along, and after two hours of talks they seemed to think it made sense for the maritime unions to allow the grain to move. They hoped it would become the first in a series of big transactions in which they would get their "fair share." But all the unions were in this together.

"IMPORTANT MATTER"

Gleason, who was then meeting in New Jersey with representatives of the shipping industry on the 34-day-old longshoremen's strike recalled: "They called me in Cherry Hill . . . I sent out a telegram for a meeting (the next day) of all the maritime unions. . . . They said it was an 'Important matter' but I was in the dark about it."

Cherry Hill (population 65,000), lies midway between Philadelphia and Camden. Suburban houses coexist with smoke-free industry, but the community appears to be best known as the site of the Garden State Race Track. The clerk calls the town's two motels, the Cherry Hill Inn and Lodge, "ritzy places," visited by thoroughbred fans. They have also been the site of other labor negotiations. The Lodge, the Inn, and the raceway are all owned by one man, Eugene Mori.

The leaders of all the major maritime unions, or their representatives, responded to Gleason's summons to meet November 4. "We met . . . from 10 to 3 without breaking for lunch," said Hall, a big man with an apparent zest for both life—and lunch. "And we all stayed sober."

Gibson, according to those who were there, urged the unions to allow the grain to move so that there would be a chance to negotiate future sales and to develop a thriving trade. Preconditions imposed now could undermine this chance, he told them. There was talk about bilateralism and what it would mean for the American merchant fleet.

According to Hall, Gibson told the unions he "would try to do what he could. We didn't get any written guarantee . . . and we didn't ask for any. . . . This was a guy talking to us who had kept the faith. . . . He wanted a commitment to move the grain; we gave it."

Gleason said he agreed to go along with the seagoing unions, but for the grain sale only. "I said we had only been helping them."

THE EXPLANATION

His dilemma was clear as he explained that he was taking a wait-and-see attitude toward future arrangements. "It's the union position," he said, "a long-time policy with us—over 20 years. . . . We're not going to unilaterally change this. . . . Mr. Meany is involved in this. You just don't overnight change your policy."

Even with this reservation, though, there is considerable consternation in the industry that the unions would have gone along on little but hope for future gain instead of making their usual demands for immediate reward. But the leaders explain it this way:

Calhoon: It's simple mathematics. We could have held to our position on the grain and made it stick but the total it could have meant for the United States was twenty to twenty-five shipments. And then it would probably be over for the next ten years. . . . If there's going to be a continuing trade some participation in it was more important than a one-shot grain deal.

Hall: The main reason I voted for it . . . was that it was very evident to us that this meant a lot to Gibson. Measured against how hard he's worked . . . on the basis of his track record alone, I felt he deserved this opportunity. . . . All I know is we've got a strong horse running for us and he's running. . . .

But even Gibson's strongest supporters are keeping a skeptical eye open for future arrangements, and the unions are still in a strong position to throw a monkey wrench into any deal they do not like. What would happen, for example, if a big shipment were prepared for April, a month before Mr. Nixon's scheduled trip to Moscow? Calhoon's verdict, his blue-green eyes sparkling: "That's when we get our 50 percent."

U.S. officials are not so sure. Once trade gets going, many of them seem to think, it will be difficult for the maritime unions to stand in the way of an exchange that helps the American balance of payments and American labor in general.

On November 5, with the unions in line, the Nixon administration made the grain sale announcement with extravagant praise for union "statesmanship."

ALL SMILES

The union leaders were wreathed in smiles. The administration evidently had accomplished something other than a grain deal; it had helped widen labor's division on East-West issues.

AFL-CIO President Meany, with whom President Nixon long shared an unyielding posture on anti-Communism, was dismayed over the President's multiple defections. On August 10 in San Francisco, Meany scoffed at the President's planned trip to China as "the No. 1 stunt of the No. 1 stunt man of our time."

But many maritime union chiefs had only warm words

251 The Nixon Ploy: A World Turned Upside Down

for the administration. Marine Engineers' president Calhoon said in an interview last week on the grain transaction: "Labor agreed because of the treatment it has received from this administration. No matter what anyone says the Nixon administration has been good to the maritime industry. It's the first time since the Eisenhower administration that there is any program but drift."

For East-West trade, administration officials expect continuing expansion of most-favored-nation treatment for Communist nations, plus the extension of U.S. export-import credits. The Soviet Union's agriculture minister, Vladimir V. Matskevich, is due to visit the United States from December 8 to 19, with American agricultural exporters awaiting him anxiously.

Soviet Premier Alexei Kosygin last month held out new but unspecified opportunities provided there is removal of "artificial restrictions in trade with the Soviet Union, created by the United States."

Skeptics in this country caution against American "pie-in-the-sky talk" of "billions of dollars" in foreseeable U.S.–Soviet trade. There are also deep private misgivings among many economists and diplomats inside the Nixon administration about resorting to bilateral trade agreements with Communist nations for engaging in any form of barter trade. But the Nixon administration's command post is in the White House. There the spirit of economic adventure is running strong.

December 7, 1971

IN SUPPORT OF NIXONOMICS
BY PIERRE A. RINFRET

For about a year now we have been telling our clients that the United States may be on the verge of one of the most dynamic expansion periods in our postwar history. We say "maybe." The position is hedged because we believe that the election of Senator George McGovern would materially damage the long-term growth prospects of the American economy. Given the re-election of President Nixon, we believe that our growth from 1972 to 1976 will be dynamic, vigorous and different from what has gone before.

My purpose here is not to criticize, knock, or denigrate the economic programs of Senator McGovern. My purpose is to lay out the broad outlines of our economic development under President Nixon as I see it.

There are many things I could talk about, but I have delineated five areas. I have chosen these five areas because I believe they are of particular interest and value to the business and financial community. The order of discussion is not an order of priority. Only the President can set his order of economic priorities.

I believe that there is now a new growth industry in the United States: that growth industry is agriculture and the products related to it. It seems to me that the President's trips to China and Russia have not yet been fully understood or appreciated for the revolution in trade which they represent.

Look at it this way: the United States has an asset that has been suppressed for about 40 years. We have the most prolific and productive agricultural system in the world. We have the ability to feed our entire population and then some, with only 3.75 million people employed in agriculture.

Yet we have had to suppress agricultural production because our system is too prolific. Russia and China combined have about 1 billion people and they cannot feed themselves. It is said that Nikita Khrushchev was ousted because his costly efforts to expand agricultural production were a dismal failure.

President Nixon has reopened trade with China and Russia. This trade will depend heavily on agriculture and the capital equipment that produces food.

We are witnessing the rebirth of agriculture and the daring utilization of a dormant asset by employing the most basic ability of all: the ability to fill empty bellies. The trade agreements with China and Russia are good politics and even better economics.

The importance of trade and barter with China and Russia transcends agriculture and has important bearing upon our world trade position.

Twenty-five years ago the United States set out to reconstruct and rebuild the world economy. It created, among other things, the Marshall Plan which did so much to rebuild Europe.

When the Common Market concept came along, the United States endorsed and supported it in word and deed. Today the United States finds itself increasingly shut out of world markets.

The French preach "Europe for the Europeans." The Japanese will yield to no one in their drive for even larger balance-of-payments surpluses. The Canadians are intractable in their increasingly anti-American stance.

The United States has no desire to disrupt the smooth economic progress of the world. It cannot go back on the trade agreements it has signed. But it can seek new trading partners.

The Russians, for example, are now considering bartering liquefied natural gas for a variety of United States products. China used to buy 25 percent of her imports from the United States and ship 18 percent of her exports to the United States.

I believe that we are witnessing a new alignment in world trade. The willingness to sell food and nonstrategic goods to Russia and China puts us in competition with the rest of the world, which has had a monopoly on trade with China and Russia for a little too long.

We have, in my judgment, dealt ourselves a new hand in world trade and done it with a trump card.

It is obvious to anyone who reads and thinks that the vigor and vitality of the American economic system are critical to the foreign policy objectives of the United States.

Would the United States be able to start the long walk to peace with China and Russia if the American economy were in trouble? I doubt it.

It is truer than most people realize that our position of leadership in the world is based on our economic superiority.

Recently, many people on Wall Street have been espousing a singularly silly theory, to wit, that President Nixon will produce a recession in 1973 in order to solve inflation. That silly idea ignores some basic facts.

The first basic fact is that the recession of 1970 did not solve the inflation problem.

The second basic fact is that the President started the drive for economic expansion in May, 1970, intensified it with the full-employment budget of the fall of 1970, and pulled out all the stops with the announcements of August, 1971.

The third basic fact is that we now have wage and price controls.

In short, I do not believe there is any compromise with full employment. This Administration is dedicated to the work ethic and the work ethic requires the ability to find work.

Full employment is the goal of the Employment Act of
1946, the desire of the American people, and the objective
of President Nixon. His objective is a meaningful job for
every man and woman who is able to work. That requires
driving for maximum production and purchasing power.

This brings me to the inflation battle. Ever since I have
known President Nixon, I have seen him deeply concerned about inflation. Inflation was an issue in 1966 and
again in 1968.

Since his election to the presidency, he has fought the
battle to slow down inflation. The methods and techniques used to win that battle have changed, but the goal
has been inviolate: inflation must be stopped, the inflation
psychology must be destroyed.

Four long years have been spent in waging that battle,
and it has not yet been totally won. The battle will not be
abandoned and it will be continued as long as necessary.

The Administration—unlike Senator McGovern—has
been unwilling to set a specific date for the end of wage
and price controls because it is (1) not willing to make idle
or dishonest promises it cannot keep and (2) not willing to
spark a new inflation psychology based upon the near-
term ending of controls.

On the contrary, it is impossible to precisely date or define the termination or direction these controls will take.
Both depend on time, circumstances, and the degree of
success that has been achieved. Controls will end, I
believe, when the inflation psychology has been destroyed.

This brings me to interest rates. The banks are falling
over each other to raise interest rates. They have forgotten that the President has the authority to control interest
rates.

I ask the reader one question: If you were the President
who had labored long and hard to produce an economic
upturn and had used wage and price controls to contain

inflation, would you permit a rise in interest rates that's severe enough to abort the economic expansion?

You know the answer: No.

This economic expansion cannot be curtailed until it reaches full employment. Neither inflation nor rising interest rates can stand in the way of a fully employed economy.

As the President has indicated clearly since August, 1971, he prefers a fully employed economy with controls to a less than fully employed economy without controls. And if I read the latest profit and wage figures correctly, American industry as well as American labor are thriving on the former combination.

The fifth point I want to discuss is the most interesting of all, namely, tax policy.

The longer I am in the economic, investment, and financial counseling business, the more I realize that people's memories tend to be both short and warped.

The great economic debate about taxation was started by the Brookings Institution not too long ago, when they came to the conclusion that no matter who was elected in November, federal taxes had to go up. Their study analyzed the outlook for spending for some of the very programs which Brookings economists had fathered while advising the previous Administration. That's like the author of a stage play writing his own reviews.

In any event, the theory is that taxes must go up. But President Nixon's record has been forgotten. The record of Richard Nixon is one of tax cuts—not tax increases.

In 1969 and 1970 the President permitted the removal of the income tax surcharge. In 1969 the Administration sponsored the Tax Reform Act of 1969, which placed a 50 percent ceiling on federal taxes as a percentage of personal income. In 1971 there were corporate and personal income tax cuts and in 1972 there are additional personal income tax cuts.

The President has both the record and the authority for holding the spending line.

In 1968, 1969, and 1970, federal spending in terms of the gross national product remained around $98,000,000,000. In fiscal 1969 (July 1, 1968, to June 30, 1969), the President ran a small surplus—compared with a $25,000,000,000 deficit for fiscal 1968 under President Johnson. In fiscal 1970, the President ran a small deficit.

The key is that President Nixon has made a spending ceiling work in the past. And here's a critical point: under the authority of the Anti-Deficiency Act of 1950, the President can impound money authorized by Congress and can, in fact, switch money from one legislative area to another. In short, even though Congress foolishly refused to give the President the spending ceiling he desired, he can, in fact, impose such a ceiling.

Again, the best taxpayer is an expanding economy. I don't believe there is going to be a federal tax increase in 1973. On the contrary, the President's record would suggest additional tax relief.

In my judgment, the next four years will be totally unlike the past four years. I look for a vigorous, renewed expansion of our free-enterprise system under Richard Nixon. Nixonomics are good economics.

THE FIVE-POWER WORLD OF RICHARD NIXON
BY JAMES CHACE

"All you need is a competent cabinet to run the country at home. . . . You need a President for foreign policy."—
Richard Nixon, 1967

The flag of the People's Republic of China has been flying from a pole at the Roosevelt Hotel. The United States prepares for a visit of its President to Peking on George Washington's birthday. Agreements are being prepared in Vienna to limit the deployment of weapons of mass destruction by the United States and the Soviet Union. Washington has virtually declared that the dollar can no longer be used as the currency for financing world trade. In broad terms, the President is proceeding not only to establish a rapprochement with Peking but to work out specific accords with China's main adversary, the Soviet Union, and to encourage new trade with the restive Communist nations of Eastern Europe, all the while trying to stabilize a non-Communist Government in South Vietnam. Without repudiating U.S. commitments, he hopes to avoid new ones. He keeps out of disputes whenever he can, wary of U.S. intervention in such explosive situations as the India-Pakistan conflict and the Middle East. In short, postwar U.S. foreign policy has been turned upside down. Rarely has there been a more dramatic, more ironic, and more seemingly paradoxical series of moves on the global chessboard. And the man most responsible for moving the United States into the uncharted area of the post-postwar world is the allegedly conservative Richard Nixon.

The Richard Nixon whose early crusade against Communism was unstinting and often merciless, and who said

258

in 1968, "I do not believe that the United States can afford to accept a concept of parity with the Soviet Union," is now promoting mere sufficiency of nuclear forces vis-à-vis Russia. Not only has Nixon reversed policy on China, but he is about to fulfill the dire consequences of which he once warned. Now, as he readies himself for his appointment in Peking this week, after supporting the admission of Communist China to the United Nations, one can turn back to the debates with John F. Kennedy in 1960 when Nixon warned that admitting China "would give respectability to the Communist regime, which could immensely increase its power and prestige in Asia, and probably irreparably weaken the non-Communist governments in the area." This is a roughly accurate statement of what is likely to occur.

But few politicians have been consistent. John F. Kennedy, after all, was the only Democratic senator who did not vote to censure Joe McCarthy in 1954, and later ran for the presidency as a man who incarnated the liberal tradition of his party. Nor should it be forgotten that the then Senator Lyndon Johnson, also in 1954, refused to support any plan to send American troops to Indochina. In both Kennedy's and Johnson's cases their apparent changes of heart evolved out of the premises which they later felt their party and their country were committed to. But what of Richard Nixon? How do we explain his reversals of posture and policy? Is he a man who has no world view, but merely seizes opportunity whenever it presents itself? Are his preachments of earnest moralism mere lip service to a world which has no relevance to a nation that questions its own values, that confuses hero and villain, that has found itself in a dark wood where the straight way has been lost?

For those who view him most critically, as Garry Wills has put it, "There is one Nixon only, though there seem to be new ones all the time—he will try to be what people want." A more sympathetic observer, such as French political analyst Pierre Hassner, will deem him a "pragmatic conservative." Whatever it is called, the President's course reveals a man who has begun to formulate an overall foreign policy sharply at variance with the dominant U.S. postwar vision of the world, a vision which he himself had shared.

In part, Nixon has learned from his years as a protégé of Dwight Eisenhower to be skeptical of purely military solutions, and he has certainly embraced the concepts of Henry Kissinger, once the foreign policy adviser of the man who was his arch rival, Nelson Rockefeller. But a major key to Nixon's philosophy in foreign affairs is his link with General de Gaulle. It is this which best helps us understand a man whose response to the highest office of this land is not unlike that of the towering figure from another age who befriended him when his political career was at its nadir and provided him with a model of greatness.

In asking for support for his New Economic Policy last September, the President concluded his appeal to the Congress by citing and then paraphrasing General de Gaulle: "America can be her true self only when she is engaged in a great enterprise." The echo of de Gaulle's memoirs was deliberate, for in his mature years Nixon had become an avid admirer of the General. And when, on occasion, the President startles the nation with a sudden reversal of policy, the General's admonition that "once action starts, criticism disappears" seems particularly apt. Both the tactic and the rationale are Gaullist. Ruse, cunning, surprise—de Gaulle used all these in order to advance the vision of restoring France to the first rank. Unexpected tactics were necessary for the Machiavel, so that Saint Joan might conquer.

It is of fundamental importance to realize that Nixon is often consciously trying to imitate de Gaulle and that he wants history to view him the way history will view de Gaulle. De Gaulle wrote of "the contrast between inner power and outward control from which ascendancy is gained, just as style in a gambler consists in his ability to show greater coolness than usual when he has raised his stake." In a similar vein, Nixon has written: "The ability to be cool, confident, and decisive in crisis is not an inherited characteristic, but is the direct result of how well the individual has prepared himself for battle." It is amusing that General de Gaulle, the theorist of modern tank warfare, took his example from the game of poker, while Richard Nixon, an enthusiastic and successful poker player, chose the battlefield metaphor.

Nixon, like de Gaulle, was a man whose career seemed to be finished. In 1953, when de Gaulle was brooding alone at his country estate at Colombey, who would have predicted his return to power five years later? Who in 1962, when Nixon lost the governorship of California to Pat Brown, would have predicted his election as President of the United States only six years later?

Yet, when Nixon was out of office, de Gaulle treated him courteously; he spoke of Nixon as someone who should not be counted out, and seemed to agree that Nixon might, in some respect, be able to pattern himself after de Gaulle. Upon Nixon's election, almost the first order of business of the new President was to pay a visit to the French leader; moreover, Nixon's foreign policy adviser, Kissinger, shared in his admiration for de Gaulle, and in Nixon's desire to repair the fabric of U.S.–French relations. It was on the 1969 visit to de Gaulle, according to C. L. Sulzberger, that the General told Nixon that "it was easier for the United States to leave Vietnam than it had been for France to leave Algeria with its large French population." Nixon agreed and said that had he been in de Gaulle's position during the Algerian crisis, he would "probably have done the same thing."

They make a curious pair, Charles de Gaulle and Richard Nixon, both of them profoundly shy human beings, the Frenchman cloaking himself in cynicism and elegance, the American in earnest moralism. Both have employed a rhetoric of the past. In de Gaulle's case, his cynical tactical methods, combined with his vision of France's global role, enabled him to achieve a new reality by asserting France's independence from the two superpowers. Will Nixon be able to emulate him? And, finally, in the service of what vision will Nixon's tactics and moralism be employed?

There have always been two dominant strands among those seeking an international order in the postwar world. They are most easily defined in European terms and can be roughly divided into the Gaullist and the Monnetist camps. The Gaullist view, stressing what Stanley Hoffmann, Harvard professor of government, has called "the new legitimacy of the nation-state," believes in the viability of the nation as a major actor on the world's stage. Big powers such as the United States and the Soviet Union thus take their places as matinee idols, upon whose leading roles in shaping the future the peace of the world depends. Another group of policymakers believes that the day of the nation-state is drawing to a close; transnational forces will combine to create a more centralized international system. They derive much of their inspiration from de Gaulle's great opponent, Jean Monnet, who saw economics and technology as leading to a political federation of Western Europe. Their version of the Monnetist dream is that of a community of advanced, industrialized, non-Communist nations. As one of their most articulate spokesmen, Zbigniew Brzezinski of Columbia, has put it:

"The emergence of a community of the developed nations must still remain the central goal of U.S. policy."

Such a community would presumably stretch from Japan to Scandinavia, with the United States as its centerpiece, and would be a kind of model of the Atlanticist "grand design" of the Eisenhower-Kennedy eras. Moreover, in this federalist view, the community could be the beginning of a new international system that would be better able to cope with such problems as monetary stability, trade barriers, pollution, population control— problems that would seem to transcend the ability of the nation-state, no matter what its size, to solve. This community would presumably develop joint policies toward the poorer countries of the globe, and hold open the possibility of membership for Communist nations.

The world which President Nixon perceives conforms much more closely to the Gaullist model than to the Monnetist. His approach to world politics is to see a pattern of relationships involving five major power centers: the United States, Russia, China, Japan, and, eventually, Western Europe (including Britain). In this pentagonal world each power center will be constrained by the others. The President first made this vision explicit last summer in Kansas City, when he explained the passing of the Cold War. "Twenty-five years ago," he said, "we were No. 1 in the world militarily, with no one who even challenged us, because we have a monopoly of atomic weapons. . . . Now, 25 years having passed . . . we see five great economic superpowers: the United States, Western Europe, the Soviet Union, China, and, of course, Japan."

Though it is palpably untrue that all five are "economic superpowers," the President's words do reveal his consciousness of the pentagonal world that he now believes will be the next stage after the end of the Cold War and the confrontation politics of the two superpowers which characterized that period. Were he to have taken the older view—that the balance of power was really a nuclear balance of terror between the U.S. and the U.S.S.R.—his rapprochement with China would not be perceived in Moscow as a possible counterweight to Russia's global engagement.

More recently, Nixon has articulated a concert of great powers that resembles in some respects the balance of power in Europe during much of the nineteenth century. "We must remember," he has said, "the only time in the history of the world that we have had any extended periods of peace is when there has been a balance of power. . . . I think it will be a safer world and a better world if we have a strong, healthy United States, Europe, Soviet Union, China, Japan—each balancing the other, not playing one against the other, an even balance."

In the search for a global balance of power, however, there are risks. For the nations that came together in Vienna after the generation of war that ended in Waterloo generally agreed on the desirability of such a balance among the five great powers in order to maintain the peace. Those who gathered at the Congress of Vienna in 1815—and, in particular, Metternich, Talleyrand, and Castlereagh—understood the need to prevent any one power from becoming too dominant in Europe and thereby threatening the continent with another war. Metternich, the great Austrian statesman who, in Henry Kissinger's words, became for the next generation the virtual "Prime Minister of Europe," laid down as an axiom of policy "the application of the principle of solidarity and equilibrium . . . and of the united efforts of states against the supremacy of one power." Russia, Prussia, Austria, France, and England—these were the five great powers of the post-Napoleonic world, and their achievement was to bring about a balance of power that was to give the world a century without a major war.

As Harold Nicolson has pointed out in his study of the Congress of Vienna: "It is thus a mistake to regard the balance of power as some iniquitous plotting of forces; it was rather the achievement of such a distribution of strength as would render aggression by any single country a policy of the greatest uncertainty and danger." The five European powers disagreed, however, about the extent to which they would act in concert to impose their will upon nations that were infected by the revolutionary virus that could destroy the established order. It was a static world, based upon the sacred principle of legitimacy, that they sought.

In writing of U.S. foreign policy prior to the election of 1968, Henry Kissinger, author of a book on Metternich and a study of Bismarck, echoed principles Metternich would have endorsed: "Part of the reason for our difficulties," Kissinger once wrote, "is our reluctance to think in terms of power and equilibrium." He went on to criticize the American tendency to feel that "while other nations have interests, we have responsibilities; while other nations are concerned with equilibrium, we are concerned with the legal requirements of peace." As Talleyrand would have urged in the last century, and as de Gaulle advised in turn, Nixon and Kissinger pursue a quest for equilibrium in a world in which the nation-state persists as the most important force to be reckoned with.

There is, of course, a crucial difference between the balance of power sought in the early nineteenth century and such an order in the contemporary world. For the five major power centers today do not agree that such a global balance is even a desideratum. Unlike the European nations which tried to implement a Concert of Europe to maintain equilibrium, the global great powers that Nixon is dealing with cannot operate together; a balance of power will exist only insofar as the powers act to constrain the overweening aspirations of any one power. And there is no guarantee that this will always occur.

Nor should it be supposed that a five-power world and the balance of power necessarily imply a policy of "spheres of influence." Though the great powers will always try to insure that the countries bordering them are not hostile—and to this extent certainly seek spheres of influence, as in Eastern Europe and the Caribbean—the competition among them in other parts of the world is more likely to be for access and influence than for hegemony.

If the great powers, in concert or individually, constrain one another, they are likely to find themselves increasingly excluded from spheres of influence. Indeed, even in Eastern Europe, Romania enjoys a large measure of independence; Cuba, moreover, has successfully resisted the United States. And one purpose of the new American rapprochement with China was to deny the Russians a sphere in South Asia.

George Canning, the British foreign secretary, when he supported the independence of the South American republics in 1826, declared that he had "called the New World into existence to redress the balance of the Old." Nixon might be said to have recognized the status of China as a great power in order to counteract the growing power of the Soviet Union.

The difficulty of playing great-power politics to contain conflict and establish a balance of power was demonstrated most graphically by the interplay of Russia, America, and China in the conflict over Bangladesh. As did de Gaulle in his assessment of France's role in the Israeli-Arab conflict, so, too, did Nixon mistake the situation in South Asia, and with the same result. Both countries would have preferred that such a conflict not take place. Both countries would have been wiser to remain completely neutral in the event of an attack. Neither really did so. Both lost influence to the Soviet Union.

By aligning itself with China, the United States tried to create a situation in which India, despite its alliance with the Soviet Union, would be so intimidated as to not initiate military operations against Pakistan. But neither Peking nor Washington was prepared to make its threats effective. For the United States, domestic constraints against American involvement in Asia prevented any substantial U.S. engagement, either of men or matériel. China, though free from domestic limitations, was constrained by her own strategic problems. Fearful of Russian advances along her own border, her military leadership weakened after the recent purge, China was wary of putting any direct military pressure on India; thus, Peking was left to fulminate in the United Nations against Russian ambitions. Only Russia had neither domestic constraints nor shortage of weaponry.

Once it became clear that India had indeed attacked, and that Russia would fully support India's course, Washington let it be known that such behavior would jeopardize the scheduled visit of President Nixon to the Soviet Union this spring. But the threat lacked credibility; Nixon would have had to sacrifice, at least temporarily, a major objective—closer U.S.–U.S.S.R. relations—for a relatively minor one: supporting a weak regional power. The effectiveness of the Indian attack, the weakness of Pakistan in the west—both also made ineffectual the administration's efforts to show its authority by sending warships into the Bay of Bengal.

From Pakistan's vantage point, relying on the great powers to balance off one another may have been the only choice she had. But it proved a poor one. Pakistan erred in evaluating the ability of either America or China to deliver the goods. The balance of power that had existed in some tentative form in South Asia prior to the Bangladesh upheaval and the Indo-Pak war was finally shattered. Russian preponderance is now evident to all. Misperceptions on the part of two of the great powers involved— America and China—resulted not in the success but the failure of the two powers to constrain the third.

Nor does cooperation between the U.S. and China have a much better chance of resolving that enduring world dilemma: the war in Indochina. The condition of success of Nixon's foreign policy lies in ending that war, just as de Gaulle's depended on getting out of Algeria. Until the U.S. successfully disengages from the conflict, Nixon can never be totally free to play out the great game of world politics. In this case, the ability of a small power like North Vietnam to manipulate the big powers points up the problem of working within the balance of power.

In a sense, the three great powers involved are all hostages to Hanoi. Neither Communist power wants to jeopardize possible agreement between it and the United States on other issues; yet neither Russia nor China can abandon North Vietnam. Washington, in turn, wants to better relations with both Peking and Moscow; but to do this, it must be wary of any massive reescalation of the war. Despite his great-power diplomacy, the price of Nixon's reelection could well be an accommodation with Hanoi. The ultimate power to end the war lies with the North Vietnamese, as Henry Kissinger has pointed out: "We expect to settle this war with Hanoi, not with Moscow and not with Peking."

The situations in South and Southeast Asia also illustrate both the global and the regional nature of the pentagonal world. Only America and Russia are truly global powers. Only these two great antagonists can meet to contest or compromise in almost any area of the world. The other three powers, at least in the near future, will remain regional powers. Though a balance of power in Southeast Asia and the Pacific—after a settlement of the Indochina War—might well involve the United States, the Soviet Union, China, and Japan, it is hard to envisage Europe playing a major role. In Africa and Latin America, on the other hand, China would certainly be limited by her economic and military resources. And in Europe itself, neither China nor Japan would be likely to have a voice in any overall settlements.

Despite its limitations, however, a five-power world, with shifting coalitions, with few entangling alliances and reduced spheres of influence, may be inescapable. It may also be a more chaotic, though not necessarily a more dangerous, world than most of us have known. But as one can see by examining Nixon's approach to some major foreign policy problems, it is in the understanding of just such a configuration that U.S. foreign policy is being conceived. For Nixon believes that such a balance may yet help to fulfill his promise of providing, as did Metternich, "a generation of peace."

It is, of course, Nixon's visit to China that has revealed most clearly the lineaments of this policy. In planning the China trip the old tie to de Gaulle is again evident. According to Professor Ross Terrill in a recent issue of the *Atlantic,* Nixon first let it be known that he would like to "normalize relations with China" when he saw de Gaulle in 1969. The General passed this on to the Chinese leaders who were avowed de Gaulle admirers. That initial contact, combined with the continued withdrawal of the U.S. troops from Southeast Asia, apparently convinced Peking that Nixon meant what he said.

The roots of his China policy, however, are certainly not evident during his years as Vice-President when he seized on the so-called loss of China to the Communists by Truman and Acheson as a potent campaign issue with which to belabor the Democrats. On the other hand, it cannot be said to date solely from his post-election relationship with Henry Kissinger. A full year prior to the election in 1968, Nixon was writing in *Foreign Affairs:* "Taking the long view, we simply cannot afford to leave China forever outside the family of nations, there to nurture its fantasies, cherish its hates, and threaten its neighbors. There is no place on this small planet for 1,000,000,000 of its potentially most able people to live in angry isolation." He went on to warn that "if our long-range aim is to pull China back into the family of nations, we must avoid the impression that the great powers or the European powers are 'ganging up.' " This theme was repeated after the election in early December, 1968, in a conversation with a British journalist. After repeating some of the points he had made in *Foreign Affairs,* Nixon concluded: "Thus our aim should be to persuade China . . . that its own national interest requires a turning away from foreign adventures and a turning inward toward the solution of its own domestic problems. Then, I believe, Communist China will begin to come to the conclusions the Soviet leaders came to several years ago. Then the dialogue with China can and should be opened."

The China policy is also a good illustration of the difficulty of knowing where Nixon begins and Kissinger leaves off. Or maybe it is just the marriage of true minds, for Kissinger himself was saying in 1966 that "policy could probably be altered much more dramatically in Communist China than in the more institutionalized Communist countries." Certainly Nixon's belief that a conservative President has more freedom to pursue a radical policy toward the Communists than a liberal one is something the young Nixon might have learned from Eisenhower, who ultimately settled for terms ending the Korean War that Truman had been unable to accept. And since the China visit is taking place during the closing days of the New Hampshire primary campaign, the President can be both opportunistic and statesmanlike, a practice not unknown to incumbents of the White House.

Despite this not entirely fortuitous timing, something more substantial than an increase in his political capital may come out of his appointment in Peking. In his State of the World message, issued just prior to his China trip, the President suggested that Taipei and Peking negotiate their differences. "The ultimate relationship between Taiwan and the mainland," he said, "is not a matter for the United States to decide. A peaceful resolution of this problem by the parties would do much to reduce tensions in the Far East." Such a remark has been unprecedented since 1949 when President Truman declared that Taiwan was "China's internal affair." If this is any indication of further moves by the President to develop a new China policy, then matters of substance rather than a mere exchange of views may result, even if the effects are not immediately apparent.

Convinced that the five-power world is both inevitable and desirable, believing like de Gaulle—or Eisenhower —that it takes a conservative to negotiate liberal positions, Nixon carefully prepares for his voyage to the East realizing that this is a not unimportant facet of his presentation of himself as a "peace president" in the fall of 1972.

February 20, 1972

WEIGHING THE BALANCE OF POWER
BY STANLEY HOFFMANN

"The end of the bipolar post-war world" has been acknowledged by the latest presidential State of the World message. Although it is elliptic in describing the new design for a lasting and stable "structure of peace," there is little doubt that the blueprint for the future is inspired by the past. It is the model of the balance of power which moderated, if not the aspirations at least the accomplishments, of rulers in the eighteenth and nineteenth centuries. It restrained violence (without curtailing wars). It provided enough flexibility to ensure a century of global peace after the Congress of Vienna, despite drastic changes in the relative strengths and fortunes of the main actors.

If, in the quest for international stability, this model is in favor again, it is not only because of the preferences of that student of nineteenth-century diplomacy, Henry Kissinger. It is also because the Yalta system is coming to an end. For many years, the world has ceased to resemble the confrontation of Athens and Sparta. Nuclear weapons have muted the rivalry. The universal drive for independence has made each rival's hegemony over, or interventions outside, his camp costly and delicate (on the Communist side, it has led to the Sino-Soviet break). The very heterogeneity of a world filled with stubborn crises which do not let themselves be absorbed by the East-West conflict has made the Cold War irrelevant for some areas and has dampened it in others, given the superpowers' reluctance to allow themselves to be dragged into partly alien causes and to let confrontations by proxies turn into direct clashes.

In such circumstances, the balance-of-power model is

tempting. As long as the world remains a contest of actors without any supranational force, the ambitions of troublemakers have to be contained by the power of the other states; but equilibrium would be assured in a more shifting, subtle, and supple way than in the recent past of fixed blocs. In a world of several main actors, the need for a superpower to be not merely the architect but chief mason of global containment would fade away. Restraining a troublemaker would be either the joint affair of several major states, or even of merely some of them, on whom the United States could rely, just as Britain could often rely on the Continental powers stalemating one another. The small nations would find security, not in submission to a leader, or in a neutralist shelter, but in the balance of power itself, which would allow them to pursue more actively their interests within its less constraining limits.

Thus, mobility would return to the scene. A new age of diplomacy (and perhaps of its traditional concomitant, international law) would begin. Muted bipolarity has subjected the United States to maximum exertions and minimum results, or at least maximum constraints. The new system would provide two remedies for frustration: the political corrective of self-restraint, and the psychological compensation of openly pursuing one's national interest without having either to subordinate it to the solidarity, or to wrap it in the priorities, of one's camp. The United States would again be able to choose when, where, and whether to intervene at all. Therefore it could concentrate on the long-range, instead of rushing from the pressing to the urgent.

The President's reports and statements point to a pentagonal system in which the United States, the Soviet Union, China, Japan, and Western Europe would be the main actors. This vision raises three sets of questions. Is the United States, as a society and as a state, willing and able to pursue such a policy? Does the world of the last third of the twentieth century lend itself to a system based on the model of European cabinet diplomacy? If the answer to these questions should be no, what ought to be the alternative? I have dealt elsewhere with the first question. This article addresses itself to the second question and only inferentially to the third. Since it is a critical exercise, two preliminary caveats are in order. First, this essay does not state that the new policy is a simple resurrection of the European balance of power. It examines the features of the present world that do not lend themselves to any direct transposition. It also asks whether recent U.S. tactics contribute to the advent of that moderate structure called for by its leaders. Secondly, it does not deny that the ends of international moderation and American self-restraint are highly desirable. It wonders whether they are likely to be delivered through the means of the balance. Indeed, are these ends themselves entirely compatible?

II

To use Raymond Aron's terms, the balance of power is a model of "strategic-diplomatic behavior." The essence of international relations is seen as a contest of states on a chessboard on which the players try to maximize their power at each other's expense, and on which the possibility of war makes military potential and might the chief criteria of power. This view still fits much of the "game of nations," for it follows from the logic of a decentralized milieu, whatever the specific nature of the units or the social and economic systems which they embody.

For such a game to be played according to the rules of the balance, various conditions had, in the past, to be met. First, there had to be a number of major actors superior to two—it usually was around five or six—of comparable if not equal power. Today's distribution of power among the top actors is quite different. Only two states are actual world powers, involved in most of the globe, indispensable for all important settlements. China is still mainly a regional power, more concerned with breaking out of encirclement than with active involvement outside. While Chinese leaders assert that China will never want to become a superpower, there is no way of predicting that this will indeed be the case. Even if both dogma and growing power should push Peking toward a global role, given its internal problems the transition will be long, and China is bound to remain in the meantime a potential superpower; *i.e.,* a major player presently limited in scope but exerting considerable attraction globally.

As for the other two "poles," they do not exist at all. Both Japan and Western Europe are military dependents of the United States. Neither, despite huge economic power, behaves on the strategic-diplomatic chessboard as if it intended to play a world role under the American nuclear umbrella. Japan, so far, does not have even a clear regional policy. Western Europe, so far, is a promise, not a real political entity. The current *relance* of her integration was made possible by a kind of tacit agreement to reverse the Gaullist order of priorities and to put the economic, monetary, and institutional tasks of enlarged community-building ahead of the painful and divisive ones of foreign policy and defense coordination. In the traditional arena of world politics, pentagonal polycentrism does not yet exist. It would have to be created. Can it be?

A second condition for the functioning of the balance-of-power system in the past was the presence of a central balancing mechanism: the ability of several of the main actors to coalesce in order to deter or to blunt the expansion of one or more powers. This corresponds to two fundamental realities. One was the inability of any one power to annihilate any other, the other was the usefulness of force. Aggressively, force was a productive instrument of expansion; preventively or repressively, the call to arms against a troublemaker served as the moment of truth. The invention of nuclear weapons and their present distribution have thoroughly transformed the situation. The resort to nuclear weapons can obviously not be a balancing technique. Indeed, the central mechanism's purpose is the *avoidance* of nuclear conflict, the adjournment *sine die* of the moment of nuclear truth.

The central mechanism of deterrence is likely to remain for a long time bipolar. Only the United States and the Soviet Union have the capacity to annihilate each other—a capacity distinct from that which France, Britain, and China possess, of severely wounding a superpower but suffering either total or unbearable destruction in return. Only the superpowers can deter each other, not merely from nuclear but also from large-scale conventional war and from the nuclear blackmail of third parties. Their advance over other nuclear powers remains enormous, quantitatively and qualitatively. It is doubtful that Peking could find the indispensable shortcuts to catch up with Moscow and Washington. Nor is a nuclear Japan likely to outstrip the Americans and the Russians; political and psychological inhibitions in the Japanese polity are likely to delay, for a while at least, a decision to join the nuclear race, and to limit the scope of an eventual nuclear effort. Western Europe continues to have an internal problem not unlike that of squaring a vicious circle. Mr. Heath may prudently prod Mr. Pompidou toward nuclear cooperation. But Britain's special nuclear relationship to Washington, plus Gaullist doctrine, are obstacles even to that modest proposal. A genuine "West European" deterrent would require a central political and military process of decision, of which there are no traces; nor is there a willingness by Bonn to consecrate the Franco-British nuclear duopoly or a willingness by London and Paris to include Bonn. This problem, unresolved within NATO, risks being insoluble here too.

A pentagon of nuclear powers is not desirable, and could be dangerous. It is not necessary: the deterrence of nuclear war is not a matter of coalitions. What deters Moscow, or Peking, from nuclear war is the certainty of destruction. To add the potential nuclear strength of a Japanese or of a West European strategic force to that of the United States may theoretically complicate an aggressor's calculations, but it does not change the picture. One might, of course, object with the familiar argument according to which nuclear parity between the superpowers vitiates the U.S. guarantee: would the United States risk its own destruction for the protection of Paris or Tokyo? Granted that coalitions are not important, is not the deterrence of nuclear war, nuclear blackmail, and large-scale conventional attack likely only if the most tempting targets develop their own deterrents? To this, there are three replies.

First, there is never much point in desiring the improbable. For a long time, if not forever, the inferiority of Japan's and Western Europe's nuclear forces would be such that deterrence could not be assured by them alone. At the nuclear level, the United States could not expect to play the role of non-engaged holder of the balance which theorists have described as Britain's in the past centuries. Only the two superpowers would have the capacity—if not the will —to declare that certain positions are vital to their interests, and protected by their missiles. Other *forces de frappe,* even if invulnerable, would not have a credible protective power outside of their territories.

Secondly, the Chinese would feel threatened by a nuclear Japan, capable of dwarfing China's costly efforts, and the Soviets would react vigorously to any formula that put a West German finger near or on the trigger of a West European integrated *force de frappe.* For the United

States actually to support the nuclear development of Western Europe and Japan, in the hope of being ultimately relieved of its role as nuclear guarantor, and in the conviction that the present central balance makes any Soviet or Chinese retaliation impossible would sacrifice, if not nuclear peace, at least the chances of moderation and détente to a distant and dubious pentagonal nuclear "balance."

Thirdly, a world of five major nuclear powers would be of questionable stability and probably foster further proliferation. Maybe five strategic forces of comparable levels could be "stable": each would-be aggressor would be deterred, not by a coalition, or by a third party's guarantee of the victim, but by that potential victim's own force. However, we are talking about five very uneven forces. The balance of uncertainty which up to now has leaned toward deterrence and restraint could begin oscillating furiously. Even if it should never settle on the side of nuclear war, it would promote an arms race à cinq. It is impossible to devise a "moderate" international system under these circumstances. Moreover, the very argument which stresses the dubious nature of nuclear guarantees to others would incite more states to follow the examples of Western Europe and Japan. In such a world some would have a second-strike capacity against each other, but a first-strike capacity against others.

In this area, then, the desire for moderation and the dream of self-restraint are hardly compatible. If the United States, in order to prevent proliferation to nations which are currently its allies, acts so as to keep its nuclear guarantee credible, the tensions of over-involvement will persist, and the world will not be pentagonal. If the pursuit of a more narrowly defined national interest, if doubts about the long-run credibility of nuclear guarantees, and if the desire for "burden sharing" should lead the United States to encourage nuclear proliferation, the result would be neither very safe nor conducive to the world of the balance of power with its central multipolar mechanism. For even if global peace should remain assured by the central mechanism of bipolar deterrence, the globe would probably fragment into a series of uncertain regional nuclear balances.

What of a return to a conventional balancing mechanism comparable to that of the past? It has been asserted that the very unusability of nuclear weapons restores the conditions of traditional war. But the picture is likely to be the same. Against a nuclear power, conventional forces are simply not a sufficiently credible deterrent. Deterrence of nuclear attack, or of nuclear escalation by a "conventional" aggressor, depends on either the possession of nuclear forces, or on protection by a credible nuclear guarantor. Even if conventional war provides moments of partial truth, ultimate truth is either nuclear war or its effective, *i.e.* nuclear, deterrence. For Japan and Western Europe to concentrate on conventional forces alone would mean consecrating a division among the "great powers." They are unlikely to want to do so. But if they should, there would still be a qualitative difference in status and influence between the three nuclear powers and the other two.

Moreover, from the viewpoint of a conventional balance, a pentagonal world would not resemble the great-powers system of the past. All its members sought a world role. It is difficult to imagine either a West European entity or a conventionally rearmed Japan seeking one. Each one could become an important part of a regional balance of power—no more. This, of course, is not an argument against a conventional effort in Western Europe, which faces the Russian armies. Any such effort would have a considerable deterrent value. But this is a different problem from that of a central, worldwide balancing mechanism.

Under the nuclear stalemate, the logic of fragmentation operates here too. Would, even at this level, the United States be able to "play Britain," *i.e.* to contribute to a regional balance merely through its nuclear guarantee? In the West European case, nothing short of a disintegration of the Soviet Union—or the most drastic and unlikely mutual and balanced force reductions—is likely to make purely West European conventional forces comparable to Soviet and East European armies in the near future. Even if one believes that somewhat lower conventional forces in Western Europe *plus* the U.S. nuclear guarantee equal a credible deterrent, the plausibility of the guarantee will continue to depend on at least some U.S. presence, in the form of troops or tactical nuclear forces.

In the case of Japan, there is a difference, obviously. The main issue is not the deterrence of an invasion; a strong Japan could theoretically replace the United States as a balancer of Chinese or Soviet conventional designs in East Asia. But third parties—especially our former Asian outposts—may not want to be protected from one or another Communist plague by what they might consider the Japanese cholera. As long as there are strong defense ties between Japan and the United States, a Japanese conventional rearmament would lead to complications for us. If we should loosen those ties in order to avoid these strains and to let an East Asian balance operate without us, we would encourage nuclear proliferation, and a loss of influence. On the conventional front, in Western Europe, the desirable is not likely; in East Asia, the likely is not desirable.

On this front, in the coming international system, three phenomena will manifest themselves. First, only the two superpowers are likely to remain, for a long time, capable of sending forces and supplies to distant parts of the globe. The world conceived as a single theater of military calculations and operations is likely to remain bipolar.

Secondly, as long as the fear of a nuclear disaster obliges the superpowers to avoid military provocation and direct armed clashes, and as long as China, Western Europe, and Japan remain endowed only with modest conventional means, and largely neutralized militarily by their very connection to the central nuclear balance of deterrence, other states, equipped or protected by a superpower and in pursuit of objectives vital to them, will be able to provoke their own "moment of truth" and to build themselves up as regional centers of military power, as Israel has done in the Middle East, or North Vietnam in Southeast Asia. A coalition of states with great power but limited stakes is not enough to stop a local player with limited power but huge stakes. For the superpowers and for such local players, conventional force used outside their borders still has considerable productivity (although, paradoxically, the superpowers can use such force only in small doses or in limited spheres). For the other "poles" of the pentagon, however, the greatest utility of conventional force is likely to be negative: its contribution to deterrence.

Thirdly, the fragmentation which results both from the impact of nuclear weapons on world politics and from the regional nature of two, if not three, of the points of the pentagon, suggests that a future conventional balance of power will have to be regionalized some more. A strong Japan and a strong Western Europe are unlikely to ensure a sufficient balance in the Middle East or in South Asia, or even in Southeast Asia and the Western Pacific.

Nuclear weapons have not abolished war, they have displaced it. The central mechanism of the past was aimed at the problem of large military interventions by a main actor. Now, whether they succeed depends less on a global mechanism than on a local one. No amount of coalition-building would have saved Czechoslovakia. No adversary coalition could have prevented the United

States from moving into the Vietman quagmire. Moreover, due to the fear of escalation, much of international politics on the diplomatic-strategic chessboard becomes a game of influence—less violent but more intense. There is an art of knowing how to deploy force rather than to use it, how to exploit internal circumstances in order to dislodge a rival. The traditional balancing mechanism may perhaps still function where the stakes are influence, not conquest; for military strength in an area can deter or restrict the subtle access which influence requires. A strong Western Europe associated with the United States would be guaranteed against "Finlandization," for instance. However, there are complications even here. A coalition aimed at stopping a great power may actually goad it into "leaping" over the coalition, and leaning on local parties determined to preserve their own freedom of maneuver (a U.S.–Chinese coalition in Asia is not sure to stop Soviet influence). Also, if much depends on the internal circumstances in the area, neither military buildups nor coalitions may compensate for local weakness. Anyhow, moderation at a global or even at regional levels is compatible with occasional setbacks.

The traditional mechanism is too gross for the modern variety of the old game. Also, its logic is a logic of arms races, nuclear or conventional. A game of influence partly played out with weapons supplies, in a world in which many statesmen continue to see in force the only effective way of reaching vital goals, risks leading to multiple wars. In past centuries, global moderation was compatible with such explosions; in a nuclear world, are they certain to be as limited as, and more localized than, before? Does the need for moderation not point both toward the preservation of the superpowers' nuclear stalemate and toward more arms-control agreements to prevent unilateral breakthroughs and competitive escalations into the absurd; toward both a multiplication of regional balances of power and regional arms-control systems?

III

A third requirement for an effective balance of power used to be the existence of a common language and code of behavior among the major actors. This did not mean identical régimes, or the complete insulation of foreign policy from domestic politics, or a code of cooperation. But the existence of a diplomatic *Internationale* reduced misperceptions, if not miscalculations. In the nineteenth century, it provided for congresses and conferences that proved the existence of a European Concert, however dissonant.

Today, summits too are fragmentary. To be sure, the imperative of avoiding destruction, and the need to meet internal demands inject into the major powers such a dose of "pragmatism" that the purely ideological ingredient of their diplomacy, or of their rhetoric, or both, has spectacularly declined. But we are still very far from a common language. Even a tacit code prescribing how to handle conflicts, how to avoid or resolve crises, how to climb down from high horses, and how to save one another's face remains problematic for several reasons.

First, there is one important residue of ideology: the Sino-Soviet conflict, based largely on conflicts of interest but deepened and embittered by mutual charges of heresy. The United States can enjoy friendlier relations with either Communist state than Moscow can have with Peking, and our détente with one may help to improve our relations with the other. But this does not suffice to bring about a moderate balance of power. To manipulate that animosity so as to benefit from it while avoiding getting entangled in it may require diplomatic skills far in excess of ours. Moreover, however much their mutual hatred softens their tone toward us, each one is likely to try to manipulate us against the other, and neither can reduce his hostility toward us too much—especially in so far as support of third parties against us is concerned—out of fear of opening the field to his rival.

Next, however much we may congratulate ourselves on having kept great-power conflicts under control and on negotiating with Moscow and Peking without ideological blinders, neither capital subscribes to a code of general self-restraint. An effective balance of power requires either agreements on spheres of influence and dividing lines, or hands-off arrangements neutralizing or internationalizing certain areas. Today, some spheres of influence are being respected: the Soviets' in Eastern Europe, ours in Latin America. Black Africa appears to be, in effect, neutralized. But Moscow and Peking both apply to the world a conceptual framework that dictates the exploitation of capitalist weaknesses and contradictions. Regimes in which the state not only controls but molds the society are better at granting priority to foreign affairs than regimes in which the impulses of the society actually control the state's freedom of action. The heterogeneity of many nations split along ethnic, class, or ideological lines, which would make it impossible even for an angelic diplomacy dedicated to the principle of nonintervention to carry out its intentions, offers irresistible opportunities for diplomacies tied to a strategic (which does not mean necessarily warlike) vision of politics and to a dynamic reading of history. Khrushchev's proclamation of the "non-inevitability of war" was a landmark, but the less likely the use of overt force, the more subtly can influence be sought.

Those who, for years, feared a monolithic Soviet design for world subjugation were wrong, but so today are those who see in the Soviet Union merely a traditional power, or one interested mainly in the conservation of its sphere of influence. Prudence, yes, the simple preservation of the status quo, no. The very delicacy of the status quo in the one area where Moscow most assuredly tries to perpetuate it—Eastern Europe—the Soviet Union's inability, for domestic and external reasons, to separate security from domination there, the fact that the West cannot easily accept an equation which enslaves half of Europe, all this is likely to oblige the Soviet Union to keep trying to weaken the West in Europe, or at least to prevent it from strengthening itself. In the Middle East, in South Asia, on the world's oceans, the Soviets, without encouraging violence where it would backfire, and while supporting it where it works, behave as if any retreat, voluntary or not, of the United States and its allies, or any weak spot constitutes an invitation. This is not the code of behavior we would like Moscow to observe. But multipolarity is not Moscow's game, or interest.

Such tactics, if skillfully used, do not destroy moderation. But they test self-restraint. Of course, Moscow should be constrained to adjust its behavior to *our* code (and so could Peking if necessary), should we encourage other powers to fill the vacuum and to strengthen the weak spots. But we are caught between our own desire for détente and the fear that it would be compromised if we built up those of our allies whom our adversaries most suspect. Our rivals' game is to improve their relations with us in so far as we tend toward disengagement without substitution—in which case, our self-restraint could benefit them.

Two requirements for a new balance of power—relaxed relations with ex-enemies, and greater power for ex-dependents—are in conflict. Such will be America's dilemma as long as our interest in "flexible alignments" is matched by our rivals' search for clients; as long as their revolutionary ideology (not to be ignored just because their vision, is, literally, millennial, and their tactics flexible), as well as their great-power fears or drives, result in a demand for security tantamount to a claim for either permanent domination where it already exists, or regional hegemony to exclude any rival. Whether or not Western Europe and Japan become major actors, Eastern Europe and East or Southeast Asia will remain potential sources of instability.

Multiple asymmetries are at work, therefore, in so far as a common code is concerned. There is the asymmetry between the ideologies of the Communists, and our conceptions, which envisage order as a self-perpetuating status quo, as a web of procedures and norms rather than as the ever-changing outcome of social struggles. There is an asymmetry between the active policies of the superpowers and the still nebulous ones of Western Europe and Japan—not so much poles of power as stakes in the contest between the United States, the Soviet Union, and China. There is an asymmetry between the untenable global involvement of the United States, and a Soviet (and, potentially, Chinese) strategy that has to do little more than move into the crumbling positions on our front lines, or jump across into the rotting ones in the rear. Order and moderation used to be organic attributes of the international system, corresponding to domestic conditions within the main states, as well as to the horizontal ties between their diplomatic corps and codes. Tomorrow order and moderation will be more complex and mechanical, corresponding to the necessities of survival and to the price of opportunity.

A fourth condition for an effective balance-of-power system had to do with the international hierarchy. While the world was a much wider field in days of slow communications, the international system was simple: there were few actors, and the writ of the main ones covered the whole field. In Europe, the small powers had no other recourse but to entrust their independence to the balancing mechanism. Outside Europe, the great powers carved up the world. Today, the planet has shrunk, the superpowers are omnipresent, but there are more than 130 states. The small—thanks to the nuclear stalemate, or by standing on a greater power's shoulders—have acquired greater maneuverability and often have intractable concerns. Any orderly international system needs a hierarchy. But the relations of the top to the bottom, and the size of the top, vary. In the future world order, these relations will have to be more democratic, and the oligarchy will have to be bigger.

Consequently, and given the asymmetries described above, for the United States to worry almost exclusively about the central balance among the major actors, as if improved relations among them were a panacea, is an error. There are three ways of making such a mistake. One is benign neglect; we have practiced it in the Middle East for a couple of years after Israel's victory in the Six-Day War, and again in the Indian subcontinent, during the months that followed Yahya Khan's decision to suppress East Bengal. This provides one's rivals with splendid opportunities for implantation.

So could the second kind of error: reacting to a local challenge in one's traditional sphere of interest in an axiomatically "tough" way—for instance, cutting off aid to and exerting pressures on Latin American regimes intent on expanding control over their nation's resources.

Thirdly, it is a mistake to treat issues in which third parties are embroiled as if these countries were merely pawns in a global balancing game, instead of dealing with the issues' intrinsic merits and the nations' own interests. For it is most difficult to bring a theoretical balance no longer sanctioned by the moment of truth to bear on the local situation. To be sure, some important disputes among third parties, while autonomous in their origins, have become so much a part of the great powers' contest that the balancing game makes sense, either in the direction of escalation or in that of a settlement once the risks become too high. Such have been the Middle Eastern dynamics since 1970—when first the Soviets, then the United States, displayed increasing commitments to their respective clients, but also maneuvered so as to defuse the powder keg a bit. Yet this has not been the norm.

In the India-Pakistan war of December, 1971, the United States, China, and Pakistan did not "balance" India and Russia. Neither America nor China were ready to commit forces, and a verbal "tilting" toward Pakistan, aimed at safeguarding our rapprochement with Peking and at warning Moscow, merely underlined Moscow's successful exploitation of India's desire to dismantle Pakistan and strengthened unnecessarily the bonds between Moscow and Delhi. The traditional balance-of-power mechanism, while enforcing self-restraint upon ambitions, depended on the opposite of self-restraint—the readiness of the great powers to use force. If the risks are too high or the stakes too low, the balance cannot operate.

Vietnam yields a similar lesson. We have not dared escalate the war to the point of actually cutting off all Soviet and Chinese supplies to Hanoi. As a result, our attempt to coax Moscow into "restraining" Hanoi, *i.e.* to make of Vietnam a great-power issue, was doomed. Indeed, Vietnam, turned by us first into a test of misconstrued Chinese dogmas, now into a test of Soviet assumed intentions, shows that too much emphasis on the central balance and too little on local circumstances can be, if not globally, at least regionally destabilizing and destructive.

The proliferation of nations, like the impact of nuclear weapons, suggests a fragmentation of the traditional scene. The balance-of-power system assumes that peace is ultimately indivisible—although perhaps not every minute, as pure bipolarity does; more tolerant of minor shifts, it still sees any expansion by a great power as a threat to others. Our analysis suggests a greater divisibility of peace, and the more evanescent character of influence, as long as the central nuclear equilibrium lasts. What will have to be balanced, so to speak, are that equilibrium and the regional balances. Each one of these will have its own features, its own connection with (or perhaps, as in Black Africa today—but for how long?—disconnection from) the central balance. Thus, in the traditional arena, the *model* of the balance of power provides no real prescription, however wise the *idea* of balance remains. Five powers are not the answer. What matter is, first and still, the Big Two, in pursuit of universal influence, and in possession of global military means; secondly, if not all of the others, at least many more than China, Western Europe, and Japan.

IV

Not only have the conditions of the old game drastically changed, but there are other games as well. The model of interstate competition under the threat of force accounts only for some of what goes on in world politics. Two distinctions which provided its bases are being eroded. One is the distinction between domestic politics and foreign policy. The latter is often the direct expression of domestic forces or the by-product of bureaucratic constellations (some of which involve transnational alliances of services or agencies) or the victim of equally transnational waves or contagions—constructive or destructive—carried by the new media. These waves both prove and promote the erosion of the distinction between public activities of states and private activities of citizens across borders.

In the nineteenth-century balance, the latter provided an underpinning for interstate moderation, but they were not the constant or primary object of states' concerns (whenever they became their concern, the system deteriorated). Today, state policies are often impaired or inspired by transnational forces that range from corporations to scientists. Partly because of the importance of economic and scientific factors in a world driven by the quest for material progress, partly because of the relative decline of the traditional arena due to nuclear weapons, transnational relations raise increasingly important issues for states, and provide many new chessboards on which states pursue their interests, compete for advantages, yet are not the only actors.

The model of the balance of power is doubly irrelevant to these new games. First, the logic of behavior is not the same. Although there is a competition of players for influence (as in all politics), and there is no power above them (as in all international politics), the stakes are not those of traditional diplomacy, and there are other restraints than those which on the other chessboard the "state of war" itself creates or destroys. Here, the threat of violence (however muted or diffuse) is of no utility or rationality. In the strategic-diplomatic arena, the central assumption of the contest is that ultimately my gain is your loss. My interest consists of either preventing or eliminating your gain or, should the costs prove too high, of "splitting the difference," or extracting a concession in return for my acceptance of your gain. It is not always a zero-sum game: at times, both sides can increase their power. But the perspective is still that of the final test of strength, which requires a constant calculation of force. Two powers cannot be number one simultaneously. Unless one is a seventeenth-century mercantilist lost in the twentieth, one can see that this is not an appropriate description of rational behavior on most of the economic and technological chessboards. The rules of interdependence, which condition the competition there, are not those of strategic interaction, which structure it here. The logic of the world economy, of world science and technology is, for better (growth and welfare) or worse (population explosion, pollution, and depletion) a logic of integration. The logic of traditional international state politics is that of separateness. One may, as the Communist states still partly do, refuse to play games of interdependence; but if one plays them, their logic becomes compelling.

Here, quite often, your loss risks becoming mine: there is a worldwide transmission of depression, unemployment, or inflation. Even when there is a test of wills—between, say, oil-producing countries and big oil companies—there is a joint incentive, often not merely to compromise but to "upgrade the common interest." A competition in fields where solidarity prevails because of the very nature of the factors in operation consists simply of the manipulation of interdependence. Even on the traditional chessboard, as we have seen, the old rules of strategic-diplomatic warfare are modified by nuclear interdependence, and tests of strength without the ultimate sanction of war become tests of will, at least among the major powers. Why apply the balancing model to new chessboards, when it falters on the old?

Secondly, not only does the balance of power not provide an answer, it addresses itself to the wrong problem. A world in which the autonomy of states is curtailed by transnational trends, drives, and forces which operate unevenly, unpredictably, and carry political flags and tags, a world whose states' policies reflect internal wants and bargains, is permanently threatened by "statist" reactions against global integration and outside intrusion —precisely because, however sievelike, the state remains the final unit of decision, and the more like a sieve it becomes, the more it may try to plug the holes. Hence a curse of immoderation and instability, but in an original way.

It is not the use of force which is the daily peril, it is, literally, chaos. It is not war that brings the moment of truth, it is economic or monetary or environmental disaster. It is not the failure of the balance to work and curtail excessive ambitions, or the rigidity of the balance when it splits the world into rival, frozen coalitions, it is anomie. It is not the neglect or deterioration of familiar rules. It is the failure to clarify and to understand the new rules which govern the relations between different chessboards, the transfer of power from one to the other—these have only recently become major arenas of world politics: scholars are in the dark and statesmen experiment in ignorance or by analogy. Also to be feared is the inadequacy or breakdown of those rules, not of balance but of cooperation, that were devised in the past (for instance, the law of the seas), and the absence of rules of cooperation in a variety of disruptive cases in which no state can be successful in isolation—from the environment to short-term capital movements.

To apply irrelevant concepts is dangerous for general and for historical reasons. To proclaim "the primacy of the national interest" gives a free hand to domestic forces damaged or frustrated by the way these chessboards function, and encourages an epidemic of protectionist or aggressive measures. To use the logic of separateness in fields of integration invites disintegration here and discord on the traditional chessboard. Of the five "economic blocs" among which the balancing game is supposed to go on, two—those of our strategic-diplomatic rivals—are not fully integrated into the world economy. To treat Western Europe and Japan as rivals to be contained, just as we count on them to play a growing role in balancing our adversaries on that traditional chessboard, assumes that they will draw on it no consequence from our behavior on the economic chessboards, even while we use on the latter the advantages we have on, and the strong-arm tactics appropriate to, the former. This can only be self-defeating, for while each political function of a state—defense, welfare, economic growth, etc.—has some autonomy and logic, and each corresponding international chessboard has its rules, these functions all connect again at the one level that integrates them all, *i.e.* a state's foreign policy.

Historically, what requires a new policy is not the passing of the bipolar era but the end of a unipolar one. The rules of trade and finance prescribed at Bretton Woods and by GATT were those the United States wanted; they established a dollar-exchange standard and tended toward a liberal system of trade, which other nations accepted in return for security or aid. The United States tolerated exceptions to these rules in return for immediate military advantages (American bases in Japan) or for expected political benefits (a would-be "Atlanticist" Europe, growing out of the Common Market). It is this system which collapsed with the monetary crisis of 1971 and the acrimonious trade quarrels between the United States and its allies. The problem is to avoid a fragmentation of the world economy, which would breed chaos as surely as, in the strategic-diplomatic arena, fragmentation is likely to contribute to moderation.

A single world system must still be the goal. Of course, in the new monetary order, there should be a modicum of decentralization. A West European monetary union, with its own rules governing the relations of currencies within the EEC, would be a part of such an order; a stronger and more coherent EEC would be better able than its members in the past to bargain with the United States for world rules of commerce, investment and money less geared to American specifications. But this is quite different from a breakup into independent economic blocs with fluctuating relations based on nothing but bargaining strength. The aggressive pursuit by the United States of national interest narrowly defined will inevitably be seen as a naked attempt at retrieving the dominating position we lost.

The United States, which is the lynchpin of the non-Communist world's transnational system, risks playing Samson in the temple. The flexibility which the world economy needs is not that of shifting alignments and reversible alliances. Even in cases where the United States has legitimate grievances, the solutions cannot be found in the functional equivalent of the strategic-diplomatic game of chicken: reprisals and protectionist threats. Given the stakes, the building of a moderate international system and the goal of a "world community" (utopian on the other chessboard) will have to be made increasingly close. Moderation is a negative goal: organizing the coexistence of hugely different players. It has, in the past, been compatible with a variety of woes—wars, assaults on the quality of life, arms races, internal massacres, a vast amount of domestic and internal inequality.

But it is difficult to conceive of a future international system remaining moderate if there is so much inequality between its members and turmoil in some of them as to incite permanent fishing in troubled waters, or recurrent violent exports of discontent. While, especially in the traditional arena, sovereignty would continue to manifest itself through unilateral moves or concerted diplomacy (although rather more for restraint than for self-assertion), there is a growing need for pooled sovereignty, shared powers, and effective international institutions in all the new realms. Of course, a precondition is the maintenance of the central political-military balance. But American policy has tended in the past, and tends more than ever, to concentrate far too much of its energy on the precondition. There are two kinds of essential tasks: those which, if neglected or bungled, could lead to the ultimate disaster; those which the very success in postponing the "moment of truth" and the realities of a materially interdependent planet push onto the daily agenda. In a world full of active self-fulfilling memories—states which behave as if, despite nuclear weapons and the increasing costs of conquest, military might were still the yardstick of achievements, and by behaving in this way keep the past present—there ought to be equally active self-fulfilling prophecies: states moving on the conviction, so frequently asserted in words only, that on the seas of interdependence we are all in the same boat, and should worry more about common benefits than about national gains.

Community-building raises formidable questions of its own. Should it be primarily the duty of the developed nations, as some advocate paternalistically? Can an international system as diverse as this one function effectively without the active participation of all its members, even if one grants both the wisdom of "decoupling" the great powers' contest from the internal tribulations of the developing countries, and the risks of paralysis, corruption, or waste present in more "democratic" world institutions? Can community-building proceed in such a way as not to seem a neocolonial device through which the rich and strong perpetuate their hold on the poor? Is it compatible with economic spheres of influence? If such questions are recognized as imperative, then an economically and financially more cohesive Western Europe and a dynamic Japan would appear, not as "poles" to be contained or pushed back when they become too strong, but as contributors.

Yesterday's dialectic was that of a central balance between a handful of powers and imperialism, which pushed back the limits of the diplomatic world. Tomorrow's dialectic will have to be that of a complex balance, both global and regional, allowing for a fragmentation of the strategic-diplomatic contest under the nuclear stalemate, and an emergent community in which competition will, of course, persist, but where mankind ought, perhaps, slowly to learn to substitute games against (or with) nature for the games between what Erik Erikson has called "pseudospecies."

V

Faced with a world of unprecedented complexity, it is normal that U.S. policy-makers should seek a familiar thread. But they display a basic ambivalence. They aspire to a world in which the United States could share with others the burdens of being a great power. But they understand that self-restraint would be safe only if the game were played according to rules advantageous to us, and they realize that our favorite models and concepts may not at all be those of our would-be partners. And so they fall back on another conceptual habit, derived from the more recent past: that of explaining that we must still be the leaders and teachers of others, even if the goal is now defined as the balance, and the lesson called collective moderation. Between the desire for national self-restraint, and the ambition of shaping a system in which our influence endures, there is a tug of war.

If we define, as the President does in his moments of exuberance or in his fighting moods provoked by Vietnam, our main goal as the preservation of as much influence as possible, even limited disengagement will be hard to pursue. For it increases the chance that one or the other of our main rivals will move into the void, especially in those parts of the world where our clients are weak and have depended on our military presence or on huge injections of aid. Our extrication from Vietnam has been slowed down by this fear of a loss of influence, magnified by the belief that a victory for Hanoi would encourage anti-American forces everywhere: as if we were still in the mythical world of bipolar battle to the death. Should voids be filled by one of the new centers whose emergence we call for and should these decide to play their own game, we could find ourselves as deprived of influence as if we had been evicted by our rivals (against whom it would be more easy for us to react).

Our very concern for better relations with our chief rivals argues against disengagement in Europe and East Asia: for they may well prefer a U.S. presence in their respective neighborhoods (and the strains it creates in Washington and with our allies), to the might or magnetism of their immediate neighbors. At home, within or outside the Executive, many fear that any further disengagement would open the floodgates to "neo-isolationists" or protectionists. Influence remains an incentive for worldwide commitment, a goad to presidential rhetoric about indivisible peace and domino-shaped credibility. In Western Europe, it argues for having the Europeans contribute to the costs of American troops, rather than for a West European defense organization. This "burden-sharing" formula pleases the Treasury, reassures the military, and seems a better way of deflecting Senator Mansfield.

If, on the contrary, we define our goal as devolution—the building of new centers of power in Western Europe and Japan—we are faced with a triple problem. One is their own long habit of dependence, their concentration on their internal problems or economic growth, which have insulated them from world responsibilities. De Gaulle's failure to create his "European Europe" resulted even more from the resistance of his neighbors to his global concerns than from their dislike of his style. Since last July, we have often appeared to kick our allies into rebellion deliberately. But that method of injecting pride conflicts with our ambition of having these new centers tied to us, playing our kind of game. Up to now, Western

Europe and Japan have been far more eager to develop their power where it annoys or hurts us—in the trade and monetary fields—than in the military realm.

Secondly, our policy of détente encourages the West Europeans (some of whom preceded us) and the Japanese (who didn't dare) to seek their own entente with their Communist neighbors; the goal of reconciliation interferes with that of a more dynamic diplomatic-strategic entity. The result, so far, is a postponement of the defense issue.

A third obstacle is the hostility of many of our smaller allies to a reduction of American power. South Korea, the Philippines or Taiwan clearly prefer our economic and military presence to Japan's—a distant protector is better than a close one. Even within the Europe of the Ten, some of the smaller powers may like America's military presence better than a European defense community dominated by the Bonn-London-Paris triangle. All three factors lead, incidentally, to one conclusion: if devolution is our goal, and especially if we want it safe, with partners rather than disaffected ex-allies, its forms and timetable should be negotiated between us and them, not between us and our chief rivals, as, in Western Europe, the linkage between the issue of American troops and mutual and balanced force reductions dangerously leads to, and as, in Asia, the moment and manner of Mr. Nixon's China trip inevitably suggest.

In our ambivalence, we have attempted to get the best of all possible worlds. On the traditional chessboard of world politics, this attempt has been given a name: the Nixon Doctrine. To preserve our influence, we maintain our commitments. But we expect our allies to do more for their own defense, and to count primarily on themselves if their fight is against subversion. A limited recipe for devolution and self-restraint, it raises two questions. One, will our allies continue to accept our definition of their job;

i.e., will they play, in the new game, the role we assign to them? Our reinterpretation of our commitments provides them with a choice. They may read our doctrine not as a redistribution of strength but as a retreat from the contest, feel quite unqualified to take up the assignment, and define their national interest in a more neutralist direction.

Two, granted that they'll need tools for the job, will it be our tools—as in Vietnamization—or theirs? Will we, for instance, encourage them to develop their own defense industries? We have been most reluctant to do so. Our balance-of-payments problem has been one of the reasons for not encouraging too much local competition for our arms producers. So has our belief that we could have better control if we were the providers. This may be quite wrong. For dependence on a nation whose policy is not always clear, and whose supply of the tools may fluctuate according to domestic whims or sudden external shifts, creates the kind of insecurity that may breed accommodation with our chief rivals instead of "balance."

On the chessboards of interdependence, we have devalued the dollar, and the President's State of the World message speaks of the need for a new international monetary system that will "remove the disproportionate burden of responsibility for the system from this country's shoulders." However, our current policies seem aimed at preserving or increasing our advantages, as if to compensate for limited disinvolvement elsewhere. We have not taken steps to restore even partial convertibility. The world is still submitted to a dollar standard, and it is not clear that we are willing to subject the dollar to the constraints imposed on ordinary currencies. We seek a commercial surplus that would allow us to develop our exports of capital as well as goods. Allusions to the link between our role as providers of security, our demands for trade concessions, and the dollar's dominant position (which serves our investments abroad) reveal the depth of our ambivalence about the emergence of other power blocs. Should we succeed, because of Japan's and West Germany's continuing need for American protection, or because of the penetration of the British economy by the United States, we would actually make it more difficult to extend the Nixon Doctrine to Western Europe and Japan. Japan, utterly dependent on exports to advanced countries, would face a crisis; Western Europe, whose integration barely begins to expand from trade and agriculture to currencies, would in effect become just a free trade area, and cease to be an entity.

Should they resist our attempt to get the best of all possible worlds, we might actually get the worst. American tactics could consolidate the EEC. A separate West European trade and monetary bloc could challenge the United States and destroy the chances of a single orderly world system for currencies and trade. But at the same time, the emergence of any West European diplomatic-strategic entity may be prevented by continuing divisions among EEC countries, the hostility of their public opinion to military and world responsibility, the desire of most leaders for a détente, and perhaps, if confidence in the United States declines, for some accommodation with Russia in anticipation of American force withdrawals. The United States would only have the choice between a military presence made even more unpopular at home by the EEC's economic separatism, and a disengagement that would spell a major loss of influence.

Japan has greater freedom of maneuver than Europe. She is under no threat of subjugation, however diffuse, and is part of a four-power game. American shock tactics and humiliation could breed two equally bad alternatives. One would be a rapprochement with China but in an anti-American context (by contrast with Brandt's *Ostpolitik*). Japan would move toward neutralism and pay the price China would demand for reconciliation. However, this price would be high in security terms, and the switch would not provide an answer to Japan's commercial needs. The other possibility is a gradual rapprochement with Russia, and an increasing militarization—conventional or nuclear—due to the fear of Chinese hostility and to a declining faith in the credibility of America's guarantee. Such a policy might help "contain" China, but in a highly unstable way, to Russia's benefit, and, again, with a considerable loss of influence for the United States.

The worst is never sure. But to avoid it, we must face two problems: of tactics and of goals. Tactics are particularly important in periods of transition from one system and policy to the next. There are two kinds of pitfalls. Sometimes one lets the past linger on too long, as in Vietnam. Vietnamization, aimed at facilitating military retreat, has also made the necessary political concessions more difficult. The stated fear of a disastrous impact of such concessions on America's other Asian allies sounds a bit hollow, given the shock to them of the way in which we undertook our rapprochement with Peking. The other pitfall consists of acting as if a desired future were already here in order to produce it. We have, especially in Asia, moved as if the era of horizontal great-power diplomacy had arrived; and our weaker allies are disconcerted. We have, both in Europe and in Asia, behaved as if our principal allies were already part friends, part rivals; and they are resentful.

Never have consultation, clarity, candor, and coordination (as distinct from mere ex post facto information) been more important. Henry Kissinger, ten years ago, complained that the Kennedy administration, in its overtures to Russia, failed to consult and to reassure the West Germans sufficiently. The same could now be said about the China visits and the Japanese. To be sure, the present policy aims at having the three major competing powers establish together (or rather, at having each Communist power establish with the United States) the framework within which all others would have to operate. We are trying to teach our allies to swim in the proper lanes—this may be a reaction against their past tendency to leave most of the swimming to us. But they may sink, or refuse to swim at all, or insist on choosing their own lanes.

Is this merely a contradiction between high-handed "great-power tactics" (partially explained by our concentrated policy process) and the goal of a less exposed role in world affairs? Does it not rather reflect our hope to preserve our past eminence, although at bargain prices? Does it not show that our brave talk about "breakthroughs" conceals far more continuity than change? What we seem to want bears a strong resemblance to Bismarck's system. We desire, at the same time, improved relations with the Soviet Union and with China, the continuation (in perhaps modified form) of our alliances with Western Europe and Japan, an improvement of our economic position as compared with that of our main allies-competitors. Bismarck was able to have tolerable relations with France, and defensive alliances with Austria, Russia, and Italy. But the purpose of his alliances was limited to preventing France from building a coalition for revanche against Germany. They did not impose on Berlin the burden of protecting its allies against French aggression. They existed in a world of relative equality among the main powers, and considerable disconnection between *Grosspolitik* and the economic chessboards. They occurred in a century of secret diplomacy, when alliances were known to be passing affairs, and their terms could be kept in the dark without creating panics. Moreover, even Germany soon had to choose between the Russian and the Austrian connections—a choice that marked the end of the grand Bismarckian attempt at being both master and part of the balance.

Our current equivalent amounts not to a multipolar system, but to a tripolar one, with a comparably decisive but actually far heavier role for the United States. It is the United States which, in effect, protects the weakest of the three (China) from a Soviet strike; it is the United States which tries to hold the balance between Russia and China; it is the United States which attempts to contain each of these with the help of two subordinate alliances; it is the United States that guarantees its chief allies' security; it is the United States which tries to retain preponderance in the arena of interdependence. Such a vast design may be wishful thinking. Having proclaimed the primacy of the "free world" interest for twenty-five years, the United States can hardly make its new emphasis on the national interest the sole criterion of policy, and its way of using the power it enjoys on some chessboards in order to preserve or gain influence on others appear compatible with lasting alliances.

Our policy actually entails far less self-restraint than it promises and much less multipolarity than it pretends. World moderation will have to be pursued through other means. Neither in the strategic-diplomatic realm nor in all the others does a pentagonal world make sense: there are no likely or desirable five centers of comparable power in the former; and while there may well be in the latter, the issues and needs there have little to do with a balancing of poles. As for self-restraint, given the nature of our chief rivals, the responsibilities of nuclear might and the constraining need of a nuclear umbrella over Western Europe and Japan, there will be serious limits to its scope in the traditional arena. But our tactics of influence and instruments of policy are not doomed to remain as blunt and massive as in the past. Our goal should certainly be to build up autonomous strength in the main areas of the great-power contest.

But this does not mean worrying only about the "Big

Five," nor does it necessarily mean a militarization of Western Europe and Japan. Western Europe's future offers possibilities of a conventional defense organization, which it is in our interest to encourage even by reorganizing NATO's structure. Soviet opposition could hardly be effective if these moves were linked to gradual American withdrawals in a context of increasing East-West exchanges. The failure of such an organization to emerge and to grow could breed a transatlantic conflict about American troops in Europe. But even if these should leave, and if West European military cooperation remained imperfect, economic prosperity and political self-confidence would be the keys of West European strength.

In East Asia, we have nothing to gain by encouraging Japanese rearmament, conventional or nuclear, which could revive fears of Japanese domination. But the only chance of preventing it may be to provide Japan with real productivity for the power she has—economic power. Elsewhere as well, strength need not be defined too strictly in military terms, however important military might remains as an insurance against trouble. But when no autonomous strength can be found, we should disconnect ourselves entirely—as we should have done from Vietnam or Yahya Khan's Pakistan: then, our rivals' increase in influence has a greater chance of being fleeting. In all the other arenas of world politics, self-restraint may well be a necessity, and would assuredly be a virtue. Here, we must accept, rather than resent, the shift of power that has benefited our allies, and find ways of building a community against anarchy. But here as in the traditional sphere, self-restraint, contrary to the hopes of some, will consist of a variety of involvements, not a promise of disentanglement.

Above all, let us not confuse a set of worthy goals—the establishment of a moderate international system, new relations with our adversaries, the adjustment of our alliances to the new conditions of diplomacy and economics —with a technique—a balance of five powers—that turns out to correspond neither to the world's complex needs nor to our own ambivalent desires. A "structure of peace" cannot be brought about by restoring a bygone world. Rediscovering the "habits of moderation and compromise" requires a huge effort of imagination and innovation.

July, 1972

SECTIO

POST-COLD WAR: THE END OF U.S. HEGEMONY?

THIS FINAL SECTION CONTAINS TWO REACTIONS TO THE WHYS AND WHEREFORES OF THE SO-CALLED DECLINE OF AMERICAN POWER. BUT THE NOTION OF AN AMERICAN DECLINE MUST BE JUDGED IN RELATION TO SOME FIXED POINT. IN THIS CASE THE FIXED POINT SEEMS TO BE THE COLD WAR, WHEN AMERICAN MILITARY POWER WAS UNCHALLENGED. THE DEVELOPMENT OF A SUCCESSFUL POST-COLD WAR POLICY, WHICH WILL TAKE INTO ACCOUNT THE RISING POLITICAL AND ECONOMIC POWER OF OTHER COUNTRIES, AND THE END OF AMERICAN HEGEMONY, WILL BE THE MAIN CHALLENGE FOR NIXON'S SECOND TERM AND THE TERMS OF HIS SUCCESSORS. IT MAY BE PREMATURE TO TALK ABOUT A DECLINE OF AMERICAN POWER AT ALL UNTIL WE KNOW MORE ABOUT THE FIXED POINTS OF THE POST-COLD WAR WORLD.

THE DECLINE OF AMERICAN POWER BY JOHN KENNETH GALBRAITH

**NOTES ON A STYLE WHICH,
THANKS TO GOD, THE VIETNAM WAR,
AND EVEN RICHARD
NIXON, IS FINALLY CHANGING**

The last ten years, the last five in particular, have been ones of unparalleled introspection on American foreign policy. And from much of this thought has come the conclusion that the policy is wrong. The day is coming when we will have to begin to decide what is right. One prominent cause of our trouble in the twenty years following World War II was the habit of accepting, uncritically, what the Pentagon, the State Department, and the White House said was needed and must be done. This led to the propagation, among numerous other errors, of the large fantasy that a non-Communist government in Vietnam was essential for our national survival and the pregnant detail that our right of innocent passage was being denied in the summer of 1964 in the Gulf of Tonkin. But if it is dangerous to suppose that the government is always right, it will sooner or later be awkward for public administration if most people suppose that it is always wrong. When the government does better we should be aware of it; we shouldn't assume, more or less automatically, that a new insanity is replacing the old.

I am going to argue presently that, without ever quite identifying the nature of the disorder, we have come some distance in correcting one of the more grievous faults in our foreign policy in the years following World War II. This has come about partly as a result of the Vietnam War. Partly it is the sound political reaction to men and policies which were productive of great sorrow. Some credit must also go to Richard Nixon. I am, like many others, sensitive about giving Mr. Nixon credit for anything. On a wide range of matters, from Supreme Court appointments to racial equality to the problems of the cities and the poor, his instinct seems unerringly for the regressive or divisive course. I intend, for whatever effect it may have, to oppose him in the future as in the past. And I think little of the tradition in American political comment which is relentlessly impelled to prove that it is evenhanded—which on encountering some categorically regressive, comic, or obsolete figure like John Mitchell, Spiro Agnew, or J. Edgar Hoover feels obliged to remind people of his redeeming tendencies as a husband, athlete, or onetime nemesis of Baby Face Nelson. But Mr. Nixon does respond to public opinion even when it is in conflict with his longtime preference. When this brings better results one cannot deny him the credit.

These last years have brought the disintegration, not complete but appreciable, of what I propose to call the Sub-Imperial Style in Washington. It was a dangerous thing. It was also offensive to other countries. It was also, I think, on any continued exposure, repugnant to the American people—or at least those that were not directly engaged. Although many of its exponents were Republicans, the Sub-Imperial Style flourished in Washington under the Democrats. I hope that in the next election they will make clear their determination to divorce themselves from this part of their past—that their candidate will emphasize his intention to outdo Mr. Nixon in avowing a style of administration and most notably a foreign policy that is both more republican and more democratic than our past tendency. But first and urgently a word of definition.

The Imperial Style, not surprisingly, is what comes with an emperor—with one who possesses genuine power and

exercises it on a suitably imperial scale. It is not likely to
be safe or comfortable for those who resist it and perhaps
even less so, as the experience of common soldiers from
Darius the Great to Napoleon I attests, for those who do
the dangerous and very tiring work of upholding it. But
there is an undoubted grandeur in the exercise of power
however inimical it may be to the average citizen. And this
redeems and makes something of even the smallest and
most offensive of emperors at least so long as they are
successful. So it was even with Napoleon III, Wilhelm II,
and Benito Mussolini.

In the years following World War II, or so the oratory
emphasized, the United States assumed large new responsibilities in the world. This included administration
in the recently defeated countries; organization of economic recovery in Western Europe; the construction of
military alliances notably in Western Europe but also
under Dulles with the indigent non-powers of the planet;
the provision of leadership in the strategy, tactics and
financing of the Cold War; and assistance to the economic development of the poor countries of Asia, Africa,
and Latin America all combined with a scrupulous watch
to make sure that the Communists were not getting a foot-
hold anywhere.

These were tasks of considerable complexity; unlike
past extensions of national power they could not be accomplished by putting a reasonably trustworthy general,
ambassador or relative in charge. They required a bureaucracy in the foreign country and another to supervise
it from Washington. The Sub-Imperial Style is what you
get when power is exercised not by individuals but by an
organization.

My reference, it will be observed, is to style in American
foreign policy—to the attitudes and manners that are associated with the conduct of foreign policy. Style cannot,
of course, be divorced from substance. The same factors

which led to an offensive style in our foreign policy in the years following World War II led also to grievous errors in the policy itself.

Specifically the policy in these years was unnecessarily ambitious. Especially in the Third World it set itself tasks that could not be performed, did not need to be performed, and which it was disastrous to attempt. This effort has been assumed by the sophisticates to affect some imperial interest—some need to harness these people for economic advantage to the American chariot. This I do not believe. No compelling economic interest was served by our costly and demoralizing preoccupation with Indochina; when the Japanese took it over in 1941, the dollar loss was never noticed. Had it gone at the same time as China, it would not have been missed. Like the style, the substance was a reflection, in substantial part, of policy-making by bureaucracy—including, of course, the military bureaucracy. Imperialism serves a genuinely imperial interest. Sub-Imperialism serves only a bureaucratic interest.

The word bureaucracy is pejorative. This is not accidental and has little to do with the people who comprise the bureaucracy—the subordinate expressions of classical imperial power—chamberlains, grand inquisitors, military governors, mandarins, tax farmers rarely enjoyed the same prestige and acclaim as the monarch himself. It was usually safer to blame them for the hardship, cruelty, stupidity, and extortion which, properly, should have been attributed to their principal. And similarly in the United States the bureaucracy is regularly accorded the rap for errors which are those of the President himself. But an organization, all should realize, is also an unpleasant manifestation of authority.

As with any acolytes, the members of bureaucracy enjoy power not by personal right but from association. An official of the Pentagon or the State Department is dis-

pensing authority that derives not from his personal qualities but from the majesty and power of the United States.
There is interesting proof of the point in the life style of an
ambassador or a member of the Joint Chiefs of Staff. An
American ambassador to a country of more than marginal
consequence is accorded considerable deference by
most people, including himself, until the day he retires.
Then he disappears into a Stygian and often well-merited
darkness; unless he lends his name to some offshore fund
of a peculiarly fraudulent sort he will never be heard of
until his obituary, which will be brief. Similarly the general. Unless he is so ill-advised as to join up with George
Wallace his name will again be in the papers during his
lifetime only to announce that he has joined General Dynamics. It was the United States, in each case, that made
the man important and not, unhappily, any quality of the
man himself. This fact, not surprisingly, quite a few organization men fail to grasp. In consequence, they parade
the power under the impression that it is their own. The
contrast between the biggish authority and the smallish
man is an unpleasant thing to see.

In most capitals of the world, the diplomatic representatives of the smaller countries are rather more pleasant
and popular than those who speak for the great nations,
including the United States. This is not because Swedes,
Danes, Canadians, Mexicans, or Ceylonese are intrinsically more amiable than Americans. It is because their
countries have little power; their officials, in consequence, do not have a repellent association with authority
that is not their own. I doubt that Americans exercising
such power are more unpleasant than have been Romans,
Spaniards, Englishmen, Germans, or Japanese similarly
circumstanced in the past. It is that our bureaucracies
have been much larger—we have had more people pre-
tending to power that was not their own.

Power exercised through a bureaucracy has other objectionable features which mark the Sub-Imperial Style. It is the will of the organization, not that of the individual, that is expressed. This is inevitable; were everyone associated with the State Department, the Pentagon, or (a rewarding thought) the CIA to speak his mind, or whatever passes therefor, the result would be chaotic. Organization is only possible if organization men when the decision is taken hew, more or less reliably, to the organization line. Democratic centralism is an imperative in Washington as in Moscow. It follows that those who possess power must defend its use not with their own arguments but with those of the organization. They seem to be parroting the official line for that is what they must do. A skillful bureaucrat is not a man who speaks his own mind; he is a man who gives the impression of doing so while, in fact, making the organization case. The bureaucratic tendency is intensely conformist for that is the only way a bureaucracy can function. If it is doctrine that Communism is original sin, Castro a world menace, or that the North Vietnamese, if not stopped at the Demilitarized Zone, will proceed on to Hawaii, one must have the kind of men who will go along with those thoughts. One cannot have individuals who will go before the Senate Foreign Relations Committee and admit to Fulbright that it is all a lot of balls.

The need to accept the official line does not, in principle, exclude the expression of individual opinion before the line is established. In practice, however, it does. The man who goes along in public almost invariably develops the habit of going along in private. The consequence of this is very far-reaching; it means that there are never any very strong internal pressures to change the official line. Once it is established—once something becomes policy —it remains policy.

This would seem to suggest that a bureaucratic policy would be a cautious policy. That cannot be assumed; it is what is being done already and if that is reckless the policy will be reckless. In the 1950's and 1960's it was accepted policy that the Communist countries were conspiratorial and relentlessly expansionist. Any divisions within the Communist world, as Secretary Rusk used regularly to warn, concerned only the best way of destroying the free world. This was fully accepted by the State Department; it is still military gospel. It was not a formula for caution but a sanction—in Vietnam, Laos, the Dominican Republic—for a great deal of dangerous adventure. It fostered, notably in the CIA, an American Bondism based on the thesis that Communist disregard for international law and accepted standards of behavior could only be countered by an even more sanguinary immorality on the part of the United States. Soon after I went to India in 1961 I became aware of a set of screwball adventures including (as has since become known) support to some highly theoretical rebel operations along the Nepal border against Tibet. I was impressed by their potential for embarrassment and even danger. My fears were dismissed by the bureaucracy; it was entirely sufficient that Communists were on the other side. More, I think, as a result of the Bay of Pigs humiliation than my efforts these games were eventually closed out. The people conducting them remained indignant. They were established policy.

The bureaucratic mood is also exceedingly self-centered. All organization sees outside intervention as a threat to its purposes. Accordingly it elaborates its defenses against such aggression. In foreign policy this means indifference to the feelings of other countries. It means an equal resistance to domestic interference—including such as might come from the public, the Congress or perhaps even the President himself. No other lesson emerges so clearly from the Pentagon Papers as this. The need to bend other countries, the Congress or the public to the organization view of Vietnam is a recurrent theme, as is also the need on occasion for simply ignoring inconvenient opposition. In November, 1964, Vice Admiral Lloyd M. Mustin, on behalf of the Joint Chiefs of Staff, offered the following guide on bombing North Vietnam:

We recognize quite clearly that any effective military action taken by the United States will generate a hue and cry in various quarters. The influence that this kind of "pressure" may have upon the United States acting in support of its national interests will be no more than what we choose to permit it to be. . . . There are too many current examples of countries acting in what they presumably believe to be their own [word illegible] self-interest, in utter disregard for "world opinion," for us to accept the position that the United States must at all times conduct all its affairs on the basis of a world popularity contest. In short, we believe that certain strong U.S. actions are required in Southeast Asia, that we must take them regardless of opinion in various other quarters.

About the same time, in commenting on plans for the air attacks, William P. Bundy, the Assistant Secretary of State responsible for Vietnam and vicinity, advised his fellow strategists that "Congress must be consulted before any major action, perhaps only by notification if we do a reprisal." He then indicated his preference for talking matters over with the Congressional leaders. This consultation, he thought, might be combined "with other topics [budget?] to lessen the heat." This does not accord an impressive role to the Congress in launching a war. A few weeks later, in informing its Far Eastern missions that military operations against North Vietnam would continue, the State Department announced that "focus of public attention will be kept as far as possible on DRV [North Vietnam] aggression; not on joint GVN [South Vietnam]–U.S. military operations. There will be no comment of any sort on future actions except that all such actions will be adequate and measured and fitting to aggression." It added, "You will have noted President's statement of yesterday, which we will probably allow to stand."

This suggests a will and an ability to manage public opinion that might impress Messrs. Brezhnev and Kosygin and a less than plenary power for the President.

Such are the bureaucratic origins of the Sub-Imperial Style. They meant, to summarize, that foreign affairs were managed by organization men, some of whom did a very decent job in a very decent way and some of whom got the majesty of the nation confused with themselves. There was further inability of organization to change course even when that course was palpably dangerous or damaging and there was indifference and resistance to outside and superior influence. That this caused us trouble in the years following World War II is hardly surprising. But there was another and much more alarming development. That was the discovery of what association with the new power of the United States, provided only that one could get hold of a piece of it at the right moment, could do for an aspiring citizen. The offenders here were less the bureaucrats and generals than more enterprising operators from outside the government who were attracted as moths to a candle by the new potency of our foreign policy.

It began in World War II. Anyone surveying that scene with a thoughtful eye to self-advancement could see how many men—Edward R. Stettinius, John Winant, Harry Hopkins, Sumner Welles, Robert Murphy, Charles Bohlen —were translated into world statesmen by their association with wartime foreign policy and, even more specifically, with Stalin, Churchill, and F.D.R. To have been at Argentia, Quebec, Teheran, or Yalta was to have had it made. Before he became involved with foreign policy Harry Hopkins was condemned by right-thinking people as a displaced social worker who had adopted F.D.R. in

order to further his own ambitions and do willful damage
to the moral fabric of the Republic. After he had served as
emissary to Churchill and Stalin he commanded universal
respect. Edward R. Stettinius has been described by the
late Dean Acheson, in one of his more charitable writs, as
an underachiever who was qualified for serious tasks
more or less exclusively by his good looks and good
humor. But these, in association with the power of the
United States, were entirely sufficient to make and sustain Stettinius as a world statesman.

But it was after the war in the occupation of Germany
and Japan, the administration of the Marshall Plan, and
the prosecution of the Cold War that it became fully evident what association with the foreign policy of the United
States could do for a man—almost any man. Lucius Clay,
John J. McCloy, Paul Hoffman, Robert Lovett, Christian
Herter, John Foster Dulles, Allen Dulles, Arthur Dean,
Henry Cabot Lodge all owed their eminence to the eminence of American foreign policy in these years. Several
score younger men—lawyers or college professors in the
main—acquired a less cosmic but, in their own circles,
not less impressive reputation for their service in Berlin,
Paris, or Washington where, in fact, they had done much
of the hard work. Thereafter they were revered figures on
their campuses, at Rand, in their law firms, or among their
clients. It was a time, notably in the case of the Marshall
Plan, when things worked. Association with success
makes men a success.

Of the great names it would be invidious to say which
not only owed their distinction not to themselves but
which owed it to foreign policy and to this source alone.
But a word may be said about the two who are most
famous—the Dulles brothers. Both were esteemed lawyers, John Foster in particular. Both, and especially John
Foster, had the confident manner that is essential to senior standing in the Establishment. Both had a simplistic,

conspiratorial view of history, the conspirators being the Communists. Neither, it seems certain, had any knowledge of the social forces shaping nations that went much beyond the revelation that Communism was wicked and free enterprise not only good but righteous. More than anyone else John Foster Dulles was responsible for making these beliefs the basis for policy—for the decision that we must everywhere stand guard against Communism or anything so designated and for the doctrine that so disciplined and comprehensive was the Communist conspiracy that it could only be contained by the threat of massive retaliation against Moscow, with the corollary that any disorder anywhere invited that retaliation. It was he who denounced neutrality in the Cold War as immoral and bound the poor countries of the world to the United States in a complex of military alliances which burdened them with costly and useless armies and us with the catastrophic commitment that, in the ensuing decade, brought us disaster in the jungles and rice paddies of Vietnam. Allen Dulles, proceeding in accordance with the same doctrine, authored in quick succession two of the greatest foul-ups in our national history—the shooting down of the U-2 and the Paris Summit in May of 1960 and the incredible comic-tragedy at the Bay of Pigs a year later. If foreign policy could make statesmen of such material—of men who were so error-prone, and even get an airport named for one of them—it could obviously do something for anybody.

Realization of the rewards of association with foreign policy came early. Joseph Jones in his book (*The Fifteen Weeks*) on the origin of the Truman Doctrine tells of the joy in Washington when word came in 1947 that the British were giving up responsibility for Greece and that the United States would have to take over. Now the United States would have "world leadership with all its burdens and its glory." The department felt called to a high mission. "Tenseness and controlled excitement" filled the room when Dean Acheson expounded the emerging policy at staff meetings. All felt that "a new chapter in world history had opened, and they were the most privileged of men." As the 1950's passed, more and more men saw foreign policy as an avenue to instant fame. One needed the position; one needed also a crisis that put the job in the public eye. That handled, a man could go back to a New York or Washington law practice in the rewarding knowledge that he was no longer a routine lobbyist, a fixer of corporate misdeeds or a silent partner in the higher cupidity. He was a statesman, a minor sage, a respected voice at the Council on Foreign Relations and with a better class of clients into the bargain. Nor should anyone suppose that liberal professors were immune. A successful tour in foreign policy and we were what Theodore White in an inspired phrase called "action intellectuals," no less. By 1960 the interest in getting a piece of the power of the United States was intense. To the bureaucratic tendencies of the Sub-Imperial Style was added a leadership which frequently (I do not suggest universally) saw in each new crisis the opportunity for display of that fortitude, imagination, insouciant spirit and firm but deft footwork that only the possessor had previously suspected.

Once in the mid-1960's I was having lunch at Averell Harriman's in Washington; a clutch of higher State Department officials was on hand. Conversation centered on a new crisis on the autobahn to Berlin; the East Germans, with the automatically assumed connivance of the Soviets, were holding up traffic. Everyone was excited; the most sanguinary measures were proposed. (In Washington, in those years, as I've previously observed, the man of least courage always proposed the most reckless measures. Nothing so ensured applause as to propose sending in the tanks. Real courage was required to argue for restraint—to suggest finding out if, as in this case, they were only filling up potholes.) Then as we were breaking up someone called to say that the traffic was moving again. It was quite a letdown and seemed very inconvenient of the Germans or Soviets or the construction company, whichever was responsible.

The Sub-Imperial Style had one further requirement and that was for a court. Men congregating in Washington in search of power and with added thoughts of self-advancement needed association with some tangible manifestation of their grandeur. There was no need for a Versailles; but life in Washington would obviously be incomplete were there not a place that men of importance could meet men of importance and by their presence be assured of their own importance. Their wives were also interested.

It proved easier to arrange this than it should have in a republic. The prestige and influence of the United States from World War II on attracted a steady flow of high-level visitors to Washington for purposes of business or for the official sight-seeing and freeloading which is imaginatively described by diplomats as business but which is really a perquisite of high public office. Even a republic could be expected to greet its guests with appropriate pomp and the visitors promptly came to expect it. (Angier Biddle Duke when Chief of Protocol told me that Sukarno, before coming to Washington, took the precaution of ascertaining how many motorcycles he would have in his escort.) This coming and going and the associated entertainments and levees provided, even if at an inferior level, some of the opportunity for exhibitionism that the men of importance required.

The Sub-Imperial Style also nurtured the notion that the White House had a social mystique that was related to larger public service. It was more than the residence and

the place of business of the President; in some undefined
sense (it was said), "it was the symbol of the nation." This
piece of nonsense became a truth in the quarter century
following World War II. It was assiduously propagated by
the Washington newspapers and press corps, both of
which were bribed by a judicious measure of participation. The notion of the levitated White House was, of
course, enthusiastically embraced by those who had
come to Washington to have a piece of the foreign policy
action. It provided yet further occasions when, along with
the Washington fixers, lobbyists, politicians, heavy contributors, diplomats and their determinedly glittering
wives, they could meet, reflect on their role and from
which their wives could return to confide in less favored
friends on "how well they *really* do things. One is *really*
proud!" It is a mark of the excessively compliant tendency
of Americans and their congressional representatives
that the emergence of the White House as a place of minor
courtly glitter attracted no serious criticism. It should
have produced a deafening denunciation from the Senators and Representatives from Iowa.

It was in keeping with this trend that the President, as
George Reedy has so well told, should himself become an
increasingly monarchical figure, increasingly sheltered
by subordinates and (as was sadly evident with Lyndon
Johnson) increasingly confined in his information to what
Walt Rostow believed he wanted to hear. It was in keeping, also, that from Harry Truman on, communications
from the White House to the people had an increasingly
imperial tone. Roosevelt talked to his audience and
seemed to be taking them into his confidence. He was the
last to do so. His successors, with the aid of their ghost-
writers, prepared Jovian bolts detailing the sins of the
Soviets (and the Chinese, North Koreans, Cubans, and
North Vietnamese), the burdens which the American people would be called upon to bear to enforce righteous-

ness on these wicked people, the fortitude with which good Americans would bear these burdens and the certainty, given the requisite fortitude, that freedom would triumph and without any damaging reduction in the American standard of living. When the democratic style gave way to the Sub-Imperial Style, it gave way everywhere.

I saw quite a few of these changes at firsthand—and, I may add, with a good deal less clarity than is now vouchsafed by hindsight. In 1946 I did a brief tour with the State Department where, in a highly nominal way, I was responsible for economic affairs in Germany and Japan and even more theoretically in Austria and Korea. In those days my colleagues were intelligent, unassuming civil servants who found the government a more than ordinarily interesting way of making a living and which, for the more devout, appealed to the natural preference for doing good. Our communications with other countries were polite and even deferential, as was also our business with their representatives in Washington. We weren't very busy but we did not try to make work for ourselves. The White House was still comparatively simple and accessible and just across the street, and Jim Byrnes, the Secretary, could walk in on Harry Truman at any time although, in his heart, he believed that Truman should call on him. This was how it still was after a very large war; it was only with the peace that things got complicated.

One could see then, however, the beginning of the new style. As might be expected it began in the occupied countries. In Germany, General Lucius Clay was in charge. As one of the most skillful politicians ever to wear the uniform of the United States Army, he was not a man to let power force him into foolish behavior. But in Japan, as most people in Washington recognized, General MacArthur was behaving like a pompous ass. His headquarters was organized along the lines of an Oriental satrapy; a mixed bag of military sycophants paid him homage on all occasions of public and private ceremony and applauded everything he said or did. Journalists and others who should have known better had devised the interesting rationalization that the Japanese were intrinsically authoritarian and thus submissive by preference. Now that the Emperor was a trifle tarnished, they greatly appreciated MacArthur as a surrogate. The rest of us were impressed by the fact that the occupation seemed to work, not realizing that the Japanese were so tired of war that they were in a mood to make anything work and (as subsequent history has shown) have a marked ability to make a go of things anyway. For the rest we made jokes about the new best seller in Tokyo—it was called *MacArthur Is My Copilot* and was by God. We should have wept, for it was the beginning of the Sub-Imperial Style. It was only that MacArthur was ahead of his time and more than ordinarily susceptible.

On returning to the State Department in 1961 one immediately sensed the difference. Official conversation reflected the new style. Before, one asked the Canadian, Turkish, or Uruguayan Ambassador to come in to discuss an issue. Now he was summoned "to be told the facts of life." The facts of life were what we wanted his government to believe and do. The communications I received in India had a peremptory tone unknown in the earlier time. They regularly began "You should leave the GOI [Government of India] in no doubt. . . ." The ensuing truth dealt invariably with the need to deal firmly with the Communists in some troubled theatre and in contrast with the compromising tendencies of Jawaharlal Nehru.

The number of people involved in any policy decision had also grown phenomenally in the fifteen years. This reflected partly the multiplication of agencies and sub-agencies—CIA, USIA, AID, new arms of State and the Pentagon—needed to express our new power. (In his recent book on the State Department—*The Foreign Affairs Fudge Factory*—the late John Franklin Campbell tells of the State desk officer working on behalf of a smallish African state who discovered in these years or a little later that he shared authority with sixteen other officials in sixteen other offices or agencies.) But a more important reason for the eager overcrowding of every meeting was the obvious desire to be in on the action and thus to share credit for the resulting accomplishment. The number seeking to make policy had increased more rapidly than the amount of policy to be made which led, naturally, to a very competitive situation. This was eased by an effort to increase the amount of policy to be made. There was, as Campbell says, a tendency "to glamourize even the most mundane international occurrences by calling them crises."

To have the reputation of being skilled in "crisis management" was the greatest goal to which one could aspire. It was not something I fully understood until the Chinese-Indian border conflict in 1962. (Then I also learned how much I rejoiced in crisis management myself.) That was a secondary crisis which coincided with the Cuban missile crisis, a truly big-league affair. Cuba being the big crisis, that was where the reputations were to be made and so completely did it preempt Washington ambition that Carl Kaysen (now head of the Institute for Advanced Study but then in the White House) was moved to cable me that I could not expect attention for my small crisis from anyone much above the level of elevator operator. The Cuban crisis was over before the Chinese withdrew. Immediately, as I have often told, I was engulfed by helpful crisis managers. My crisis was then the one to be managed. In a mere fifteen years the new style had taken hold and flourished. I do not suggest that the new style diminished under Kennedy. But it is a great mistake, as one school of historians now holds, to suppose that it began

with him or with Lyndon Johnson. It was already big by
1960.

The Sub-Imperial Style is now, I think, definitely in retreat. The Vietnam war deserves a good deal of the credit.
A new and more skeptical view of foreign policy and of
those who make it has greatly helped. Some credit, as I
have said, belongs to Richard Nixon.

The Vietnam war has shown in one of the most expensive but conclusive lessons of all time how limited is our
power to influence the inner life of other countries and,
additionally, how slight is our need to do so. When we
leave Vietnam, as one day we will, the development which
we sought to arrest will continue. We have merely ef-
fected a small postponement. What could only be fore-
stalled by half a million American troops won't be prevented without them. And, as most would now agree, the
effect on the United States will be largely invisible. The
threat of an imminent follow-up attack by Hanoi or Peking
on the beaches of Hawaii, once endorsed by President
Johnson himself, has now receded. The power that sustained the Sub-Imperial Style in the Third World, where it
was principally manifested, turns out not to have existed.
Nor does the need to exercise it. A most useful discovery.

The Vietnam war has also shown that foreign policy is
no formula for personal glory. On the contrary it is a first-
rate formula for political disaster. It retired Lyndon Johnson to the Pedernales. It sent Dean Rusk to Athens, Geor-
gia. For numerous others, involvement with the war ranks
as a tarnish with such past political aberrations as ado-
lescent membership in the Communist Party or support of
the Munich settlement. It would be civilized if, reflecting
on earlier cruelties, we did not allow it to become a basis
for persecution. (However, support for the war is not necessarily a qualification for high office.) One has difficulty
in believing that the men Mr. Nixon has brought to the

State Department or the Pentagon expect to emerge in enduring glory. Most must think they will be lucky to come out equal. I think Henry Kissinger has thought long and hard about simply making it back to Harvard.

The Vietnam war has also persuaded the American people that there is no longer a club of informed insiders who can be trusted on foreign policy to know what is needed and right. When informed insiders can bring off a disaster of this magnitude and duration, skepticism of their wisdom is not surprising. One could hardly envisage a better design for cultivating it.

A strong if inadvertently amusing confirmation of these doubts became available last year in *America the Dutiful* by Philip Quigg. A former managing editor of *Foreign Affairs,* he was well situated to view them as a recipient. He is deeply furious at the way people have turned against the men who are qualified by position and influence to have charge of foreign policy. He thinks the young have been outrageous in their criticism of what he does not hesitate to call the foreign policy establishment. Rarely did past dissenters "receive in a lifetime as much attention as a seventeen-year-old now can attain in a week." (The young are also further blamed for thinking the government is not listening, when, in fact, it is listening to them, but not following their advice, which is how it must be.) He blames congressmen for releasing information that fuels criticism of the Establishment—and being more concerned to reform foreign policy than to reform themselves. Vietnam, for Mr. Quigg, a subject that "cannot be avoided, but [which] will be treated with the greatest brevity," has been the source of an especially unfair attack. "For the most part they [the Establishment] did not favor U.S. policies in Southeast Asia, but until too late they felt constrained to remain silent." It was their patriotism. They did not wish to give comfort to Hanoi. Mr. Quigg concludes by asking people "to cease the assignment of

blame" and put their trust in the old leaders once more. I
think the skepticism will continue.

But Mr. Nixon is President and if the Sub-Imperial Style
is in decline some of the credit must go to him. Partly this
is a matter of personality. The world, except perhaps for Canada and China, has at the moment, to its
benefit, a remarkably pedestrian set of leaders—
Brezhnev, Kosygin, Pompidou, Heath, and Sato are all men
who administer but do not inspire and who, in consequence, cannot inspire their people to dangerous adventure. But Mr. Nixon has the advantage of being the least
charismatic of all. He was a loser who happened to win—
a man whose normal fate was to be rejected but who
made the presidency in the wake of the greater need to reject Lyndon Johnson. His occasional efforts since taking
office to galvanize the country, as at the time of the Cambodian invasion, have been a crashing failure. The ratings
indicate that his television style involves a built-in protection against any call to misadventure. People turn him off.
That, like his predecessors, he has Sub-Imperial
thoughts none can deny. He functions behind an even
more deeply layered palace guard. Ceremony makes him
smug. A couple of years ago he set out to dress the White
House policemen in uniforms copied from the late King
Carol's household troops. One reads of formal dress and
weddings. But such again is Mr. Nixon's personality that
people are more inclined to laugh than be impressed. And
he has made positive contributions to disintegrating the
Sub-Imperial Style at the White House. Sunday morning
religious services in the East Room are repugnant to men
of sound agnostic temper even when led by an old hoofer
like Billy Graham. But as Mr. Nixon's principal innovation
in White House ceremony they are certainly far superior
to soirees where sleek men (and their wives) pursue their
particular form of self-aggrandizement.

Much of Mr. Nixon's foreign policy is a puzzle, although that is better than a more crystalline error. Even granted the enormous power of the bureaucratic momentum which I have mentioned, the slow pace of the withdrawal from Vietnam coupled with the Cambodian enlargement and the Laotian episode are inexplicable and especially in the way they have allowed potential Democratic antagonists to inherit the peace issue. His support to the Pakistan government on East Bengal was foolish and uncivilized and the later condemnation of India was unfair and, for what it may be worth, strategically insane. There is no case for the aid to Greece. The Vice-President's visit last autumn to the Greek junta was especially reprehensible to the extent that it could not be interpreted as a rebuke.

But elsewhere Mr. Nixon and his people have shown a visible tendency to avoid the crisis and abate the tension which so rejoiced the practitioners of the Sub-Imperial Style. They have so far refused to become excessively aroused over the Communist in Chile. Foolish statements on this have come mostly from John Connally, a fugitive Democrat. To cancel a visit of a warship was better than to send several in—which would certainly have been suggested ten years earlier. Evidently the Administration negotiated some settlement with the Soviets on the matter of nuclear submarines in Cuba. It has been cautious in the Middle East and (by not sending troops to help Hussein in 1970) avoided the opportunity of doing something very dangerous. It ignored the call of the Democratic "elders and by-goners" (as Tom Wicker denoted them) for a crackdown on Chancellor Brandt's *Ostpolitik*—an action which would have kept him out of the clutches of the Nobel peace crowd. It appears, as this is written, to have made some modest progress in making life more tolerable in Berlin. Perhaps something will happen as the result of SALT although negotiating a treaty on arms reduction under the eye of the Pentagon is not different from putting

a heroin pusher in charge of an anti-narcotics drive. The
Cold War denunciation of Communist wickedness, which
was in decline under Kennedy and Johnson, has disappeared. The old China policy has been decisively reversed—and China in consequence of a brilliantly mis-
managed defeat is now in the United Nations. The suspicion that the China policy might be an anti-Soviet ploy has
been dissipated by the announcement of the President's
springtime visit to Moscow.

In aggregate this amounts to an important change in
policy. There is some reason to hope that it will force an
even more substantial change on the Democrats. It will be
the instinct of some Democrats, as they come up to the
election, to criticize the President on the details of his
China and Moscow performance and pretend that otherwise nothing much has happened. This accords with
party tradition. Until they left office the Democrats on
China had all of the mobility of a man who was up to his
armpits in prestressed concrete. Secretary Rusk was still
denying the Communist interlopers even the dignity of a
national capital—Peking was still Peiping, damn it. Elsewhere the Cold War, the domino theory, and Castro were
much as they had always been—and as they still remain
in L.B.J.'s memoirs. Mr. Nixon's ability to inspire dislike
among the poor, young and black is still unimpaired. This,
and the terrible fact that the bombers still fly in Indochina,
will, it will be hoped, be enough to do him in. People will
have forgotten the earlier Democratic complicity in disaster and perhaps even the role of some of the architects
who are still around.

Alternatively the Democrats can recognize that they
have been rather badly outflanked by Mr. Nixon—as has
also been true on economic policy. They can then make
clear their intention to reform ranks on the sensible side
of the Nixon policy. This means an even more positive
commitment to coexistence with the Communist coun-

tries. It means a much more determined effort to get the military competition with the Soviets under control, which means also a far firmer grip on our own military establishment and its spending. It means abandoning the effort to isolate Castro. It means abandoning the Sub-Imperial ambitions in the Third World and recognizing instead that there is little we can do to influence political development in this part of the world and less that we need to do. The principal need here is for a decent and generous concern for people who are poorer than ourselves. And it means, most of all, eliminating the intelligence and military bureaucracy, both in Washington and in the field, that these changes make redundant. Also it means making Washington a center of straightforward administration and making the White House not a symbol of anything fancy but a place where a sensible man lives and does business with the least possible ostentation and the greatest possible accessibility.

It is still uncertain as to how the Democrats will react. As I have just said, the party has a strong sense of tradition and this extends to the men and policies that have been its undoing. Mr. Nixon has made things very difficult. We should all be grateful.

March, 1972

THE END OF U.S. HEGEMONY

Nixon's New Economic Policy (NEP) marks the end of one phase of postwar global capitalist history and the beginning of another. This, rather than the specific actions it initiates or envisages, is its real significance.

The first post-war phase was that of U.S. hegemony, symbolized and to a considerable extent implemented by the Bretton Woods monetary system, according to which the dollar was established along with gold as the monetary reserves of all member countries. Nixon's formal abandonment of dollar convertibility ends that phase once and for all.

Partly by design and partly by chance, the Bretton Woods system became the financial framework of U.S. hegemony over the imperialist world in the period since the Second World War—the mechanism for financing wars of counterrevolution, foreign alliances, globe-straddling military bases, and the penetration of U.S. industry and banking throughout the capitalist world. Foreign exchange rates, some of which were set more or less arbitrarily by U.S. commissions or under U.S. influence, were designed with a view to propping up and strengthening allies in the Cold War. Political and military alliances were closely interrelated with financial alliances. While the United States carried the main military and financial burdens of the postwar imperialist system, the leading capitalist nations cooperated with greater or less enthusiasm, because the network of alliance, together with U.S. military strength, helped to stabilize capitalism and to initiate a new burst of prosperity. At the same time, from the point of view of these countries, such cooperation was essential in keeping the newly independent colonial and semi-colonial countries integrated into the imperialist trade and financing system.

But such an arrangement generated inevitable strains, which in recent years have been reaching critical proportions. These strains, in the final analysis, arose from two sources: (1) the very nature of capitalist states, each one must necessarily do its utmost to protect the interests of its own capitalist class; and (2) the restraints on U.S. financial freedom, since this freedom could ultimately only be bought at the expense of other capitalist nations. Thus, while we believe that Nixon's speech marks a turning point, it should be recognized that the turbulence of the international financial system has been intensifying over a period of years, approaching closer and closer to what the physicists call a critical mass, the point at which the chain reaction starts.

Once the cohesion of the post-war financial system is torn apart, it is reasonable to expect that the cohesion of political and miliary alliances will also be shaken. This does not mean that the essential nature of the imperialist system changes, but what it probably does mean is that important features of its structure are much more subject to change than in the past. During the entire post-war period, centripetal and centrifugal forces have been at work: those pulling the leading capitalist countries together under U.S. hegemony, and competitive strains working to break up the system. Hitherto, the centripetal forces have been the more powerful. From now on, and increasingly as time goes by, the centrifugal forces seem likely to assume the dominant position.

It is too early to characterize the new phase which is now opening in a definitive way, but it seems reasonably certain that no country or group of countries will be able to establish a clear hegemonic position, and that an intense struggle among the major capitalist powers is opening, in the course of which various alliances and alignments will be sought, sometimes succesfully and sometimes not, sometimes as a temporary expedient and sometimes for longer periods.

Domestically, too, the NEP marks a turning point—the

end of the era of illusions about the possibility of stabilizing capitalism by means of monetary and/or fiscal policies and the beginning of a new approach through which the United States will seek to "solve" its internal problems at the expense of foreigners and U.S. workers. The international and internal aspects of the NEP are of course intricately interrelated.

One of the clearest indications that we are dealing with a real turning point in capitalist history is the way Nixon's August 15 speech marks a clear break with the strategy and rhetoric of the U.S. ruling class during the preceding quarter century. Throughout that period, the United States was all for cooperation, internationalism, freer trade, mutual aid, etc. But Nixon now talks the language of hard-nosed national self-interest. Competitiveness takes the place of cooperativeness as the great virtue. And the NEP itself is a blunt rejection of negotiation in favor of a unilateral declaration of a *fait accompli*—the repudiation without prior warning, or even notice, of the whole system of money and trade created by the United States itself in the period of its maximum relative power. This procedure is a sure symptom that the United States has lost its hegemonic position, since there is no doubt that if Nixon had felt powerful enough he would have preferred to impose the new system at which Washington is aiming through a process of negotiation similar to that which established the International Monetary Fund (IMF), the General Agreement on Trade and Tariffs (GATT), etc. At the same time, and in a sense paradoxically, the U.S. ruling class seems to feel relieved to be able to throw overboard all that internationalist, liberal claptrap which its spokesmen have been mouthing so long, and to plunge into a good old orgy of national chauvinism. An article by Pierre Rinfret, head of a well known firm of financial consultants, in *The New York Times* of August 30 typifies a reaction to Nixon's speech which seems to be widespread in the upper levels of the economic and political establishments:

> I praise the program. I support the program. I applaud
> the program. I breathe a sigh of relief. I have a sense of joy
> and elation. I am proud of a President who had the cour-
> age, stamina, and strength to move forward vigorously. . . .

> This is the end of Marshall Plan liberalism and the begin-
> ning of Nixon-Connally pragmatism. For the past twenty-five
> years the United States has pursued a policy of excessive
> liberalism in international trade and international negotia-
> tions. Whatever we offered, they took and took. They took
> so much and we offered so much that there was a hemor-
> rhage in our balance of payments. That is over. We have fi-
> nally recognized and acted in the belief that the United
> States is the most powerful economic entity in the world
> and that we have economic muscle. . . .

> The real target of our international trade and monetary
> moves was Japan—not the Europeans. U.S. patience has
> worn thin with the onesided, lopsided, inequitable, unfair
> economic and monetary treatment we have received from
> the Japanese. The day of bowing and scraping to them is
> over. From now on the Japanese will have to give more
> than they get or suffer more counterattacks.

The fact that the New York stock market zoomed up by an unprecedented amount the day after Nixon's speech also seems to reflect a sort of national euphoria. The President was at last doing something, the eager buyers of stock seemed to be saying, but above all he was doing it to foreigners who in the folklore of the United States—as perhaps in that of all national societies—are regarded as the real source of the country's woes.

It might appear that the immediate aftermath of Nixon's initiative belies the thesis of the end of U.S. hegemony over the global capitalist system. Didn't his strong-arm measures achieve their intended purpose? Even the Japanese had to bow to the pressure and float the yen. And doesn't the 10 percent surcharge on imports give Washington an enormous reserve of bargaining power in whatever negotiations are to come? Certainly the idea of predominant U.S. power is far from dead in official circles in this country. In a news analysis entitled "Bitterness Abroad," datelined Washington and appearing in *The New York Times* of August 23, Edwin L. Dale, Jr., reported as follows:

What is entirely clear is that the United States in a single dramatic stroke has shown the world how powerful it still is, despite all the talk about a "weak" dollar. In breaking the link between the dollar and gold and imposing a 10 percent import tax, the United States has shown who is Gulliver and who the Lilliputians.

The Lilliputians obviously do not like it. But it is not at all evident that they can do anything about it that will hurt the United States in any significant way.

By "Lilliputians"—originally the little people found in Swift's *Gulliver's Travels*—are meant not the Nicaraguas or the Gabons but West Germany, Japan, Britain, and the other leading industrial nations.

If, as seems likely, this assessment of the situation reflects the views of Washington policy-makers, we can conclude that the Nixon administration is operating on the theory that U.S. hegemony is very far from a thing of the past. According to this way of thinking, the problem has been not loss of U.S. hegemony but a reluctance on the part of the United States to throw its weight around. Or to use the analogy introduced by Nixon in his August 15 speech: "There is no longer any need for the United States to compete with one hand tied behind her back." The implication seems clear that with both hands out in front, we'll soon see who is boss. The same idea was expressed by Pierre Rinfret in the article already cited (*The New York Times,* August 30). "The night of the President's speech," Rinfret reports, "one of the most powerful men in this country told me, 'We're smart and we're competitive and we're the biggest. We're in the driver's seat and, dammit, that's where we ought to be.' "

Before accepting this simplistic position, however, we should have a closer look at the realities. It has already become a cliché in the short time since the announcement of the NEP that the dollar is overvalued, the clear implication being that this is the root of the trouble and that it can be put right by a suitable devaluation of the dollar vis-à-vis the currencies of the other advanced countries. The cheaper dollar will supposedly stimulate exports and discourage imports, and the resulting improved balance of trade will lead to a progressive elimination of the balance-of-payments deficit. When this process has gone far enough, it should be possible to negotiate a new international monetary arrangement, with all currencies at new (and now "correct") parities and the dollar once again stabilized and able to resume its role as a reserve currency, possibly sharing this role now with marks, yen, Special Drawing Rights (SDR's), etc. Where gold would fit into the new picture has perhaps not yet been thought out, but the fact that Nixon terminated the convertibility of the dollar while the U.S. gold stock was still approximately $10,000,000,000 certainly suggests that he and his advisers have by no means written off gold's monetary future. In this analysis, the heart of the matter is trade imbalances, and the key remedy is readjustment of exchange rates.

But is this really so? Is the weakness of the dollar which precipitated the crisis the result of a *trade* deficit? No. The trade deficit is a very recent phenomenon, and in any case it would be quite normal for a creditor country like the United States (i.e., a country with substantial net earnings from foreign investment) to have a long-run unfavorable balance of trade, as Britain did in the half century preceding the First World War (how else are the debtor countries supposed to be able to make the required payments?). The *balance-of-payments* deficit, on the other hand, goes back more than two decades, and it is this which has been responsible for the trouble. The truth, in other words, is that the balance-of-payments deficit has not been caused in the field of trade at all, and even now only a small part of it is attributable to the trade deficit. Somewhat oversimplifying but still not falsifying the essentials of the problem, we can say that the balance-of-payments deficit has been caused by U.S. politico-military activities abroad (propping up client governments, maintaining U.S. bases and troops, subsidizing puppet armies, waging hot wars, etc.). These activities have poured out tens of billions of dollars which have gravitated into the hands of governments and financial institutions which have no intention—and by the nature of their functions could have no intention—of spending them for goods and services produced in the United States.

The question is what these foreign recipients of surplus dollars do with them. A detailed answer would involve matters of extreme complexity, some of which are understood only by a relatively few financial experts and operators. From our present point of view, however, the problem is not to try to explain these technicalities but rather to avoid getting bogged down in them while at the same time illuminating the underlying forces and relationships.

The Bretton Woods monetary system was set up in such a way as to provide a use for these surplus dollars—at least reasonable amounts of them. In dealing with each other, countries are constantly buying and selling and engaging in a great variety of other international transactions (for freight, insurance, borrowings, repayment of past debts, etc.). If each country's outlays always exactly matched its receipts, there would never be any need for money to change hands: bookkeeping entries would suffice. But of course this is not the case. For every country in any given period, outlays exceed receipts or vice-versa, and it is only over a succession of periods that a rough balance can be expected to be achieved. In the meantime, mutually acceptable means of payment must change hands to keep the system operating smoothly. For this purpose all countries need to maintain a reserve of such means of payment, and it is obvious that the total amount of needed reserves will increase as the volume of international trade and financial transactions grows. There are thus two basic requirements that a satisfactory international monetary system has to fulfill: it must define mutually acceptable means of payment that can be held as reserves, and it must provide a way that the overall amount of reserves needed by all countries combined can be expanded as the need grows.

How did the Bretton Woods system meet these requirements? First, by establishing gold and dollars, interchangeable at $35 an ounce, as acceptable means of payment for reserve purposes. As for the second requirement, Bretton Woods did not make any specific provision, and it seemed to many critics at the time that the whole system was irrationally dependent on what might happen to the world's monetary gold stock. It turned out in practice, however, that this was not the case. By running a continuing deficit in its balance of payments, the United States could feed out dollars (equally acceptable with gold as reserve money) to the rest of the world. And for a long time this device—always implicit in the Bretton Woods system but probably understood by very few of those who took part in the founding conference— seemed to work quite satisfactorily. Thus during the 1960's the world's monetary reserves increased by an average of $2,000,000,000 a year, only 10 percent of which was gold and most of the rest dollars generated by an uninterrupted U.S. balance-of-payments deficit. This increase in reserves proved to be sufficient to underpin an enormous expansion of international trade.

But this use for surplus dollars is obviously not unlimited, and beginning in 1970 the rate of outflow far exceeded the world's need for dollars as monetary reserves. During the single year 1970 the world's total monetary reserves increased by no less than $14,100,000,000, nearly all of which was accounted for by a flood of dollars originating in a huge U.S. balance-of-payments deficit. (It is important to understand that once the outflow rises above a certain critical level, it opens valves which increase the rate of outflow still further. This is where Nixon's *bêtes noires,* the international monetary speculators, come into the picture. But far more significant than speculation is the prudence of the treasurers of the giant multinational corporations who are charged with managing billions of dollars: their motives are not those of speculators, but the consequences are much the same.)

In the theory of the Bretton Woods system, there was a braking mechanism which was supposed to prevent an excessive outflow of dollars. This was based on the convertibility of the dollar into gold at the official price of $35 an ounce. Foreign central banks receiving more dollars than they wanted were supposed to be able to present them to the United States in exchange for gold, and the loss of gold would sooner or later induce the United States to adopt deflationary policies which would stem the outflow of gold. In practice, however, this mechanism was completely unworkable. The number of dollars held by foreigners long ago added up to more than the U.S. gold reserve, and it was clear to everyone that a scramble to convert dollars into gold would simply result in the suspension of convertibility. Moreover there was never any chance that U.S. economic policies would be dominated by considerations of the gold reserve. And finally, as long as U.S. global military policy remained what it was, the outflow of dollars would continue anyway. As time went by, therefore, the Bretton Woods system came increasingly to resemble a house of cards which remains standing only because no one tries to live in it.

So we return to the question of what to do with the growing pool of surplus dollars. For quite a while the usual answer was to lend them out at interest. This was the origin of the so-called Eurodollar market which in recent years has grown to enormous proportions. One of the ironies (and complexities) of the international financial system is that when central banks follow this course the result is to build up, via credit creation, still more dollar balances and thus to exacerbate the underlying problem. Finally, as the pool continues to grow, it becomes increasingly clear that the only sensible thing to do with surplus dollars is to get rid of them; i.e., to exchange them for currencies which don't have the same troubles as the dollar. When this stage is reached, the supply-and-demand relationships between the dollar and the currencies of the other industrialized countries is transformed, and the whole concept of fixed parities provided for in the Bretton Woods system becomes untenable. With more and more dollars being offered for marks, yen, etc., it is inevitable either that the price of these currencies should go up (and hence the dollar down) or that the central banks in question should create enough additional marks, yen, etc., to match the increasing supply of dollars coming on the foreign exchange markets. The latter course can be, and indeed has been, followed for a while, but not forever. Sooner or later the old parities have to be abandoned and the various currencies allowed to float on the sea of supply and demand. The approach of this situation has been signaled for several years now by increasingly frequent monetary "crises" which, following that of last May, were in the process of becoming the norm rather than the exception. What Nixon's speech of August 15 did was simply to acknowledge publicly that the jig was up. After twenty-three years the Bretton Woods system was dead.

What next? Nixon is said to be aiming at a devaluation of the dollar averaging something like 15 percent, apparently in the belief that if this could be attained the problem would be solved. We have not, however, seen any attempt at an analysis to back this up; and on the face of it, it seems highly implausible. As noted above, the favorable effect of devaluation comes through its impact on the trade balance: with dollars cheaper, exports are stimulated and imports inhibited. This cannot be an overnight process, however, and even the most optimistic projections seem to fall far short of what would be needed to produce the desired results. In the second quarter of this year, the trade deficit was running at an annual rate of $4,200,000,000 compared to a total balance-of-payments deficit at an annual rate of no less than $23,000,000,000. If we assume, what seems unlikely, that the trade deficit can be eliminated by the end of the year, there would still remain a probable huge gap in the balance of payments. (In this connection we must remember that devaluation of the dollar will *increase* the number of dollars needed to finance the overseas military establishment and in this way will at least partially offset the gains that may be achieved in the field of trade.) And even if we make what seems to us the totally unrealistic assumption that the trade deficit turns fairly soon into a surplus and that the latter expands to, say, the $5,000,000,000 level which existed in 1965 before the decline associated with the Vietnam war began, even then there is no assurance that the balance of payments would be brought under control.

Here we must digress briefly to stress a point which seems to have been largely overlooked in the discussions and debates of the past few weeks. The prevalence of multinational corporations in the U.S. economy has introduced a relatively new factor into the determination of the balance of trade which may make it considerably less sensitive than it has been in the past to changes in the rate of exchange between dollars and other currencies. Many companies which used to be large exporters now produce abroad much or all of what they sell abroad; and many have even taken to producing abroad (in their foreign subsidiaries) products or components of products which they import into the United States for sale in the domestic market. While no reliable quantitative estimates exist, there is no reason to doubt that relationships of this kind can have a serious adverse effect on the balance of trade and at the same time put roadblocks in the way of attempts to improve the balance of trade through manipulation of exchange rates.

We conclude that the outlook for the U.S. balance of payments, despite all the fanfare accompanying Nixon's supposedly decisive moves, is at best very uncertain and at worst very dark. Under these circumstances it is hardly surprising that Treasury Secretary Connally, reputed to be the main architect of Nixon's NEP, has been voicing demands on the United States' "free world" allies which go far beyond mere currency realignments. In a May 28 speech to the Munich conference of the American Bankers Association—which, with the benefit of hindsight, we can now see to have been a good deal moe important than it seemed at the time—Connally spoke as follows:

Inflation has contributed to the prolongation of our balance-of-payments deficit. But it is far from the only factor.

Specifically, we today spend nearly 9 percent of our gross national product on defense—nearly $5,000,000,000 of that overseas, much of it in Western Europe and Japan. Financing a military shield is part of the burden of leadership; the responsibilities cannot and should not be cast off. But twenty-five years after World War II legitimate questions arise over how the cost of these responsibilities should be allocated among the Free World allies who benefit from that shield. The nations of Western Europe and Japan are again strong and vigorous, and their capacities to contribute have vastly increased.

I find it an impressive fact, and a depressing fact, that the persistent underlying balance-of-payments deficit which causes such concern is more than covered, year in and year out, by our net military expenditures abroad, over and above amounts received from foreign military purchases in the United States.

A second area where action is plainly overdue lies in trading arrangements. The comfortable assumption that the United States should—in the broader political interests of the free world—be willing to bear disproportionate economic costs does not fit the facts of today.

I do not for a moment call into question the worth of a self-confident, cohesive Common Market, a strong Japan, and a progressing Canada to the peace and prosperity of the Free World community.

The question is only—but the "only" is important— whether these nations, now more than amply supplied with reserves as well as with productive power, should not now be called upon for fresh initiative in opening their markets to the products of others.

What Connally seems to be saying is that the United States expects the countries of Western Europe, Japan, and Canada not only to revalue their currencies upward but also to relieve the United States of a large part of its self-imposed burden of policing the world and to change their trade and investment policies in a way to favor not their own capitalists but on the contrary their most dangerous rivals, the capitalists of the United States.

Such demands might have been realistic twenty-five years ago, when the other countries needed U.S. help as a matter of sheer survival. But why should they knuckle under now when the shoe is on the other foot and it is the United States that needs *their* help? Isn't the Nixon administration talking the language of hegemony at a time when the objective basis of hegemony has disappeared?

And if it turns out that U.S. hegemony cannot be restored, what is the alternative? In as complicated a situation as this, specific prophecies are of course impossible. But there is no mystery about the general direction events may take. *Business Week,* for example, after noting what it called "widespread anger at the U.S. for letting the dollar get so overvalued," proceeded as follows:

Indeed, tempers are running high throughout the international monetary system. The spirit of cooperation that pulled the system through crisis after crisis in the late 1960's is badly frayed today. [This "spirit of cooperation" is essentially a euphemism for "acceptance of U.S. hegemony."] And the longer the present turmoil lasts, the greater the peril that nations will simply take off on their own—erecting more capital controls and more trade barriers. "What worries me most," says a Swiss economist "Is that there will be no action of any kind. We would then move into a generalized float—and that will be chaos."

Ironically, the most hopeful element in the whole picture is the memory that central bankers still have of the 1930's, when monetary cooperation disintegrated, the world moved into a generalized float, and there was chaos. No government official anywhere wants that to happen again.

It may well be true that no government official wants such a situation. But what government officials want is one thing, and what is possible in the global anarchy of capitalist production and finance is something entirely different. "If," warned the London *Financial Times* on August 23, "there were to be prolonged deadlock on the monetary front, the danger of a trade war would grow with every day that passed." Now almost a month later, with the deadlock on the monetary front showing no signs of easing, the warning takes on ever greater relevance.

Turning now to the domestic aspect of Nixon's NEP, we can be much briefer. To begin with, we may take note of the completion of Richard Nixon's economic odyssey. He started out as a great champion of free markets and swallowed whole the Friedmanite monetary nonsense which was supposed to provide a painless method of dealing with the twin problems of stagnation and inflation. When this showed no signs of working, Nixon suddenly proclaimed himself a Keynesian and plumped for salvation through fiscal policy. And when this too—or rather this in conjunction with continuing monetary expansionism—produced a disagreeable combination of supposedly incompatible phenomena, more inflation and more unemployment, he suddenly emerges as a protagonist of what he once considered anathema, direct controls over wages and prices. As a display of unprincipled opportunism, it would be hard to cite a more virtuoso performance. (At the same time it must be admitted that in this field unprincipled opportunism is a considerably less unattractive quality than stubborn adherence to worn-out dogmas. The discredited economists, whether Friedmanite or Keynesian, have absolutely no reason to adopt a holier-than-thou attitude: they have no more understanding than Nixon of the way monopoly capitalism really works, and a greater vested interest in defending their ignorance.)

Will the ninety-day freeze on prices and wages succeed? In the strictly limited sense of slowing down the rise during the freeze period, it doubtless will. But this is of no great importance since the troubles of the U.S. economy are in no sense ninety-day problems. The question is what comes after the freeze.

Even a month after the announcement of the freeze it is

clear that the Nixon administration still has no definite
plans. But obviously it has a tiger by the tail and can't simply let go. It must attempt to devise and operate some sort
of continuing incomes policy. But here past experience,
in other countries no less than in the United States, is anything but encouraging. Writing from Washington in the *Financial Times* of September 1, Paul Lewis reported that:

It is frequently argued here that as the administration could
not enforce an effective price and wages freeze during the
Second World War when it had an army of bureaucrats for
the job and patriotism was high, it has little chance of doing
so in the divided and embittered climate of present-day America and when it is pledged to reduce, not to increase, the
civil service.

There is of course no answer to this argument; and, so
far as we know, no one has even tried to concoct one. Nixon's dilemma is typical of the "damned if you do and
damned if you don't" variety. Without a new version of the
wartime Office of Price Administration (OPA), whatever
incomes policy he may adopt will certainly turn into a
fiasco. And with a new OPA it will turn into a bureaucratic nightmare and a bottomless pit of cheating and
corrpution, ending in a fiasco as well.

In practice what is likely to happen is that the whole
thing will be more or less rapidly transformed into some
sort of machinery for compulsory regulation of wages
(much easier to monitor and enforce than price controls)
based on alleged productivity criteria. This is what the
U.S. bourgeoisie has really been hankering after for a
long time, and the crisis atmosphere which will be generated by the end of the freeze can be expected to provide a
golden opportunity to turn wishes into reality.

There should be no mistaking the fact, however, that
this would be a perilous course for U.S. capitalism to em-
bark upon. The reason is that it would unavoidably put the

whole question of income distribution, now presumably determined by eternal and ineluctable laws of economics, into the very center of the political stage. It is hard to see how this could fail to initiate a process of politicizing the U.S. working class to a far greater degree than ever before, increasingly transferring the class struggle from the strictly economic sphere (bargaining table and picket line) to the political sphere where weapons and tactics, and in the long run strategy and goals as well, are necessarily very different.

The rest of Nixon's domestic package—providing tax incentives for more investment (at a time when 25 percent or more of existing capacity is idle), relying on increased production of automobiles as the mainstay of recovery (at a time when every high-school student knows that what the country needs is fewer, not more, automobiles), reducing government spending and employment (at a time when all sorts of needed public services are starved of resources)—all of this is a typical potpourri of reactionary, antisocial measures which rely for whatever efficacy they may have on short-run responses and trickle-down effects. In reality, however, there is not much reason to expect any great stimulus to the economy as a whole.

We are forced to conclude that the whole new economic policy—foreign and domestic—is essentially irrelevant to what is really wrong with U.S. society today: the mad expansionism of monopoly capitalism on a global scale and its growing inability to satisfy the essential needs of its own people for peace, work, food and shelter, and human dignity, at home. What Nixon's NEP presages, therefore, is not a period of peace and prosperity such as he likes to prate about, but rather a period of unprecedentedly intense imperialist and class struggles and more and deeper crisis.

September 15, 1971

ABOUT THE AUTHOR

A native of Delaware, Ohio, Lloyd Gardner received the B.A. degree from Ohio Wesleyan University, and the M.S. and Ph.D. degrees from the University of Wisconsin. He has taught at Rutgers University since 1963, and is currently chairman of the Rutgers College History Department. He lives with his wife and three children in East Brunswick, New Jersey.

His books include, *Economic Aspects of New Deal Diplomacy* (1964); *Architects of Illusion* (1970); and a joint effort with Thomas McCormick and Walter LaFeber, *The Creation of the American Empire,* to be published in 1973.